MY CALL TO THE RING

A Memoir of a Girl Who Yearns to Box

BY
DEIRDRE GOGARTY
WITH DARRELYN SALOOM

GLASNEVIN
PUBLISHING

First published in 2012 by

Glasnevin Publishing, 2nd Floor,
13 Upper Baggot Street, Dublin 4, Ireland
www.glasnevinpublishing.com

based in Dublin, UNESCO City of Literature

A CIP catalogue record for this book is available from the British
Library

Papers used by Glasnevin Publishing are from well managed forests
and other responsible sources.

ISBN: 978-1-9086890-4-7

For more information on the authors please visit:
Deirdre Gogarty: http://www.deirdregogarty.com/
Darrelyn Saloom: http://darrelynsaloom.com/

TABLE OF CONTENTS

DEDICATION:

To my boxing coaches:
Pat McCormack, Jimmy Halpin, and Beau Williford

PROLOGUE
SISTERS OF NO MERCY

Her eyes meet mine from where she hangs on the peeling grey wall, and I wonder if it's scorn or pity I see in the Virgin Mary's stare. Crucifixes hang like X-marks showing me the way to my classroom inside the Loreto Convent in Balbriggan, Ireland. I'm quiet at my school desk where I listen to children's shoes slap shiny floors and echo down the long halls. In the dim light, my classroom is colorless and smells like floor wax, chalk, and musty old books. Every surface is cold and hard, especially under my bottom. Smoked glass windows eclipse the slightest glimpse of birds or trees.

A vivid painting of Jesus hangs above the blackboard. He's impaled on a cross with a wound weeping down his chest, his skin blue, his head hanging from murder. The nuns say he died for us and we're all sinners, and I think that must be the reason the sisters seem always annoyed with me. But I'm only three, so I don't tell them I didn't mean for Jesus to die.

Mother Imelda scrawls on the blackboard with chalk as stiff and white as her fingers. I have no choice but to endure long, mind-numbing hours while she drones on and on. So I daydream until the lunch bell rings. Herded to the canteen room, I slurp oxtail cubes in warm water.

The clear brown soup does nothing to fill my tummy, but inflates my bladder beyond capacity. Back in the classroom I'm afraid to raise my hand to be excused. Mother Imelda is still writing on the blackboard and will be bothered if I interrupt her. I hold and hold. It can't be much longer until the bell. Suddenly, despite resisting with all my might, my seat grows warm and my face burns hot.

Seconds later, the bell rings. I sit in my pool of urine and wait for everyone to leave. But one of the girls spots the dark stain around my skirt. A gaggle of classmates points and snickers at my humiliating predicament. The nun marches over to investigate and plucks me off the molded plastic chair. My puddle of pee swims in the concave seat, a bubble floats on top, and the girls burst into laughter. The nun hisses at them and they scurry away like rats.

"Lord blesses! Look at the state of you, acting like butter wouldn't melt in your mouth. An animal has better manners," she snarls. "Follow me. You're going to take those clothes off at once."

Half naked, I watch Mother Imelda grab a kitchen cloth, swoosh my urine off the chair, and then hurl it into a sink. When she hands me a sour towel to dry myself, I thank the Lord above I wore bottle-green underwear as per uniform code.

"I'll give you a hockey skirt to wear home. You'll have to pay for it, and your mother will be very vexed with you," she says, shaking her bony finger at me. She then hands me a plastic bag containing my wet underwear and skirt.

"Thank you, Sister. Sorry, Sister," I mumble as I slink out the door and dash for the bus home, where no one takes pity on me. And I decide that neither does the Virgin Mary.

All through school the numbers and letters dance in my head, so my homework is never complete. Mother Imelda marks red X's through my conjured answers, makes certain other pupils know about my failings, and scolds me for not listening. Her efforts do not reach me, for my mind wanders beyond the banks of the River Boyne, far away from nuns and books and the eyes of the Virgin Mary. The only lesson that settles on me is that I don't belong here. What I yearn for won't be delivered with sympathy or pity—I'll have to fight for it.

CHAPTER 1
JACK THE GIANT KILLER

At night, lights from fishing trawlers and cargo ships glide across my bedroom walls. Sounds of foghorns float in from the Irish Sea as I climb into the bunk bed above my brother Brian, who is home for the weekend from an institution for the mentally handicapped. I ask him if he ever feels lonely like the ships far out to sea, but he does not answer. Mum says Brian could talk when he was four. But then he stopped. He has not spoken since. Not for twelve years. And during the decade I've shared a room with him, my own need to communicate has grown until it must be true that my desire for conversation is as strong as Brian's silence.

With no one to answer me back, I stop talking and listen to distant chattering, laughing, and clinking wine glasses. A loud whoop of laughter means Dad's telling one of his jokes. He always has a crowd around him. Mum and Dad are great entertainers and have lots of wine-drinking friends. Cigar smoke swirls its way to my room and I breathe in the scent as I drift off to sleep.

Weeks pass with no parties, and something's wrong with my mother.

I find Dad in his workshop, but he won't leave his hammer and saws and drills. He says Mum will be fine. But I'm eleven— and I am terrified by her blankness. I tell him that she's screeching and acting insane. He says again that she will be fine. But I don't think so. For days she has seemed an empty shell, a ghost. I feel I could pass my hand right through her body. Earlier today, as she drove me home from the train station on my last day of school at the Loreto Convent, she forced my friend Peter Harmon into a ditch on his bike. Now she's collapsed on the kitchen floor and wailing that my dad never loved her.

She's inconsolable. So I brown thick slices of bread and slather on her favorite marmalade. I place the snack on a dish and set it on the floor beside her. I cannot think of a word to say, so I also feed my dog Shoobee and escape to my bedroom.

Shoobee follows and studies me as I munch toast and stare at her long, black-and-white coat. Black fur circles her eyes and down her long ears. Her white muzzle makes her moist black nose stand out like a dollop of chocolate on top of vanilla ice cream. She is my constant companion and the best friend I've ever had. I look at Shoobee and I've got Mum to thank. She fought for me to have a dog because Dad doesn't like pets. I feel guilty for not sympathizing with Mum more now that she's down and needs a hand, but her dramatics just make it so hard.

A loud crash brings me running to the kitchen. The dish I offered Mum is shattered across the floor, and the sticky marmalade has glued the toast to the wall. My mother jerks open the dishwasher, pulls out a ceramic bowl, and throws it through the kitchen window. I scream at her to stop as shards of glass crash into the sink. She picks up another bowl—"Stop that bloody nonsense!" Dad yells as he bursts through the doorway.

She hurls the bowl through another window as Dad grabs her arms. Moaning and sobbing, Mum wrestles with him. As if his touch has sapped her strength, she buckles and drops back to the floor. I am unable to bear her hysterics, and I run to my room.

Even as the commotion fades, through the wall I can hear my mother muttering obscenities and Dad sweeping the avalanche of broken glass and ceramics. As tears soak my pillow, I begin to understand why my brothers, David and Shane, and my sisters, Katherine, Sheena, and Adrienne, have all moved away.

Noise from Dad's workshop jars me awake in the morning and I head to the kitchen. My parents' bedroom door is closed. The absence of light underneath tells me Mum's still in bed. I creep past to find boarded-up windows darkening the kitchen— a conformation last night's drama was not a bad dream.

Inspecting the dustbin, I notice the kitchenware my mother chose to destroy were the chipped mixing bowls, long worn and faded. The good dishes at the front of the dishwasher remain untouched. Mum had her wits about her all right, and I'm angry she put us through such a nightmare.

Frustrated, I search for my father and find him in his workshop. Unlike the heavy stillness of the house, my father's workshop is abuzz with activity. The stench of resin forces me to breathe through my mouth as I watch Dad and his eight employees labor on his latest project to build a forty-five foot yacht. The massive fiberglass hull is already constructed and sits upside down in the boatyard. Fishermen nicknamed the hull "Titanic," and I don't know if that's good or bad.

Two of the boat builders whisper to each other. One removes his cap and scratches his forehead as he stares at the yacht's blueprints. But Dad seems to know exactly what needs to be done as he explains the next steps to them. He cheers the men with descriptions of beams and bulkheads, and then he cranks up his wood saw. Baffled by my father's enthusiasm after last night's drama, I return to the house.

Mum's still sleeping as I make a bowl of Ready Brek and turn on the television, keeping the volume on low. Switching through our four stations, I hear a name that grabs my attention: *Dempsey*. A man with cropped, black hair punches a heavy bag in a black-and-white film clip. The bag swings with ease after each strike of his leather-mitted fists. His sinewy muscles flex across his chest and ripple down his arms. He turns to the crowd of onlookers and flashes a warm smile. Men and women in old-fashioned hats and clothes smile and applaud. This handsome yet rugged man the narrator describes as an "American icon" captivates me.

The commentator claims Jack Dempsey has changed boxing from a stiff, defensive competition to a wild almost sensual assault. I'm not even sure what the word "sensual" means, but it's the most exciting description of a person I've ever heard. The announcer goes on to say that in 1919 Dempsey challenged "The Pottawatomie Giant," Jess Willard, for the World Heavyweight Championship. Willard towered over Dempsey by six inches and outweighed him by sixty pounds, but Dempsey floored Willard seven times in the first round. The battered "Pottawatomie Giant" failed to answer the fourth-round bell, and Dempsey was christened "Jack the Giant Killer." The clip ends and I'm hungry to see more of the man who fights giants.

I finish my cereal and return to the workshop, where Dad asks if Mum has stirred. I tell him no while looking around the shop. I ask my father if he has an old bag I can have.

"I'm sure I do. What kind of bag?"

"The kind you hit." I show him, throwing a punch.

"Young ladies don't *hit* things."

I don't know if it's my pleading expression that moves my dad, or if it's the circumstances with Mum that he wants to atone for, but after a few minutes he concedes.

"All right, I'll see what I can find."

Delighted, I skip back to my room and write a letter to my best school friend, Jill Dempsey. I wonder if she knows she might be related to the former heavyweight champion of the world!

Mum's fourth day in bed, I bring her a hot cup of tea and warm toast. I take away the previous tea and toast, stone cold and untouched. I look back at her underneath the sheets. From the dim light falling across the floor from the corridor, her frame looks more skeletal than yesterday. My mother is wasting away, yet our lives continue around her. Her friends keep ringing, so I tell them she has the flu. How can I explain that she accuses Dad for making her ill?

My mother's fifth day in bed, I can hear Dad talking to her. I have a feeling he's the only one who can make her better, maybe convince her that life is worth living. My feeling proves right when she slowly follows him out of her room. A day in the garden helps her emerge from a cocoon of despair, and at supper I'm happy to see Mum eating again.

On the weekend my siblings trickle home from college for the summer, and I'm delighted by the life and sanity they breathe into the house. I tell my brothers and sisters that Mum broke dishes and windows. But they change the subject as though I hadn't said anything, and, no matter how I try they won't talk to me about our mother's problems. I suppose it's because they are older and I'm just a kid. They do step in to give Mum some company, and I am relieved of the burden of caring for her. I begin to believe that I can salvage my sacred summer.

Adrienne has invited a fair-haired boy to come over and play. I'm rolling on the ground with Shoobee when he cycles to the front door. Ignoring him, I continue to wrestle my dog on the sweet-scented lawn.

My sister steps outside to introduce us.

"This is Jonathan," she tells me. "He lives down the road at the Grammar School. His father's the headmaster. Now you'll already know somebody before you start secondary school."

I've been set up. But I know Adrienne means well. She wants me to have a friend in my new school.

"Wanna play Frisbee?" Jonathan asks, not missing a beat.

He flings the disc at me, and I scramble to catch it while trying to look cool. Jonathan is tall with bigger muscles than most boys his age. He is outgoing and talkative, and he makes me nervous. I'm glad when Peter shows up to relieve the pressure I'm feeling. Our friends, Joanna and her brother James follow Peter. I introduce Jonathan to the gang and invite him to cycle with us to the beach.

We hop on our bikes and Jonathan talks about tits, pricks, and farts. He makes us laugh until our faces hurt, especially James, who nearly crashes every time the new boy tells a dirty joke. When we get to the beach, Jonathan leans way back on his bike's seat to pop wheelies on the dunes. He is funny and fearless. And I think I like him.

Homeward bound we stop at Moran's pub to buy sweets. We gorge ourselves while chatting with Agnes, one of the shop's owners. On the way out Jonathan tosses a stink bomb over his shoulder. To my horror, it discharges in a splattering of liquid, so we jump on our bikes and take off. The headmaster's son is the only one laughing. I won't be able to come back to the pub, and I'm aghast that he has sabotaged my chance to shop for sweets at Moran's.

We ride in silence. Except for Jonathan, of course, who brags about forcing the drunks to sprint from the pub as they coughed, spit, and threw up their pints. When we split up to go home, the jokester is the only one to offer a goodbye.

"See you tomorrow," he shouts.

Jonathan becomes a regular visitor, and Mum acts more and more suspicious of him. When we go outside, she always tends nearby flowerbeds. But her spying only makes my new friend seem more dangerous and fascinating.

While playing in the boatyard, Jonathan tells me he wants to show me something. I know he's not talking about his mickey because he pees outside and doesn't mind if I watch. So I follow him to my father's Titanic, and we climb onto the crossbeams of her upside-down hull.

The sun tries to penetrate the enormous fiberglass shell but is muted into an orangey glow. Jonathan reaches under his shirt and pulls out a packet of cigarettes, then lights one with a match. The aroma of tobacco smoke is much more pleasant than the hull's stink of industrial solvents. My hand shakes as he shows me how to hold the cigarette to my mouth and light it. I pretend to inhale as he watches with approval. Smoking a cigarette feels sensationally wrong.

We crawl out from under my father's boat and walk Shoobee through the golden wheat field behind my house. Ripe kernels of grain slap against our thighs. I nibble the tasty, moist seeds and believe I could live off the land and never return to school.

Jonathan suddenly grabs my hand and pulls me to the ground. The wheat stalks crackle and crunch, but my landing is soft. He drops beside me, and chuckles at my startled expression. We lie still for a moment and my breathing slows to normal. Jonathan's chest heaves. I'm wondering why he is gasping so hard when his wet lips press onto mine. Did he just kiss me? He flashes a proud grin, and I don't know what to do. Does this mean I'm pregnant? What will I tell Mum?

I can hear Shoobee hopping like a jackrabbit as she searches for me through the tall stalks. She crashes into our crop circle and wags her tail. I'm relieved when my good dog steals Jonathan's attention, so I can wipe off his wet kiss with the back of my hand. We then stretch our legs and amble toward home as though nothing happened.

Jonathan saunters away in the direction of the school where he lives, and I wonder what it's like to live in a school where your dad is headmaster. I've heard his father is a terrible man, a dictator, always yelling and walloping the back of students' heads. Maybe that's why Jonathan does bold things when he gets away. I don't know if I should be annoyed with him or flattered. But one thing I do know—I've been given my first kiss. And I liked it.

When I arrive home, Dad hands me a dark blue bag.

"It's a sailor's kit. You can stuff it with rags and hang it with the drawstring."

"It's perfect!" I shriek.

I'm so delighted Dad remembered, I regret misbehaving behind his back. Ashamed of smoking a cigarette and kissing a boy, I swear to never smoke again. But I can't make the same promise about kissing.

Scavenging the house and workshop for rags to fill the sailor's bag, I take every scrap of cloth, foam, old clothes, and knickers—anything soft for stuffing, and I hope no one will miss what I've taken. With nothing left to rummage, I decide newspaper is what I need to finish filling the duffel.

I want to have the bag just right before I ask Dad to hang it, and I collect the *Irish Times* for two weeks, until I'm one fat *Sunday Tribune* away from a full punch bag. I hover as each family member finishes the paper, passed from Shane to Katherine to Sheena, ending up in the hands of Sheena's twenty-one-year-old boyfriend Liam. He torments me by reading every word as slowly as possible. It's not until Dad walks in that he hands over the armful of papers, and I run away with my treasure to finish filling my punching bag. It's heavier than I imagined, but my father lends me a hand to hang it from a pipe under the eaves of the house.

I stand before my makeshift bag and my breathing speeds up. I think of Jonathan and know better how excited he must have been with me in the wheat field with all his huffing and puffing. My heart races, too, as images of "Jack the Giant Killer" appear vivid in my mind. I cut a quick look at Dad. Then I thrust my bony fist into the center of my homemade punching bag. But even hanging in the air the bag is still heavy and doesn't swing when I smack it—it barely moves. I punch harder. And then harder. Finally, the bag starts to sway.

"My goodness! Is that my little girl with such ferocious punches?" Dad's voice is clearly full of surprise.

The canvas cover is sandpaper rough and stiff from salty sailing journeys. My knuckles redden and tingle when I hit the cloudy rings of sea-salt stains. But I love the feel and excitement of my fists crashing against the bag. Dad watches and again says, "My goodness!" And then he shakes his head and strides to his workshop to sculpt and fire pottery in his kiln.

"Look at the little boy." A brash voice startles me, taunting. "You couldn't punch your way out of a wet paper bag."

It's Liam, who no doubt lay in wait for Dad to leave. "Do you piss standing up as well?"

"I'm not a boy."

He comes close and taps the side of my face.

"C'mon little boy," he says. "Show me how tough you are." Liam always waits until no one is about to tease me. I look toward Dad's shop and hear a potter's wheel kick on. It's just me and Liam and I hate him and wish I were big enough to drop him where he stands. He uses his open hand and taps my face harder. I reach up and throw a wild swing, but he leans back and my fist misses his big nose. He grins and exposes his inward-slanting teeth, but I can tell he is shocked that I tried to hit him. He then slaps my face in retaliation, which jars my head and burns my cheek. I want to cry, but he shoves me down on the grass. He says, "Little bitch, wait till I tell your parents you tried to hit me." Then he stomps back to the house in a blur of tousled dark hair.

I run to the top of a hill in the field behind our bungalow and burst into tears. I am humiliated and angry with myself for wanting a heavy bag. I should have known someone would see me, someone other than my dad, and it would spark ridicule. And now I'm certain I'm in trouble. Liam is a guest and I took a swing at him. I know he will say I did it for no reason, and I believe his word will be taken over mine. Sheena's in love with him and will rally Mum to launch into me with one of her torturous lectures. I stop crying and start home but stop and sit in the weeds. I won't go home as long as Liam is there.

As I sit, I become a bit sleepy and a memory almost like a dream surrounds me. Children at the public bus stop stare down at me on the cold concrete. Their faces spin in a blur.

"Are you all right?" an older girl asked me.

"Yeah, grand," I told her. Struggling up on rickety legs, I used my sleeve to wipe the spit out of my eye. My shin throbbed. But mostly, I was in shock. A dirty-faced boy had been watching me. He darted closer and spit in my eye. A swift kick to my shin bent me over, and a roundhouse swing of his schoolbag bowled me to the pavement.

10

Then he just laughed and strutted away.

When the local CIÉ bus finally arrived that afternoon, I found refuge behind the driver in one of the seats where old ladies sat and clutched their shopping bags. None of the women seemed to notice the bluish knot on my shin.

The reverie swimming before my eyes is the memory of my first horrible day at the Loreto Convent in Balbriggan. The nuns were as bad as the ruffian at the bus stop because I could not put up a fight with them. They were the bosses of everything and everyone. And now the crushing helplessness I felt that day has returned to me. I hated it then and I still hate it.

I am pulled back from my dreamy spell by the sound of bats hunting insects above me as Liam's van pulls out of the driveway at dusk. I imagine if I go home, even with Liam gone, it will be a good scolding for me. No one will believe that he slapped my face. So I'm determined to stay in hiding, until everyone is panic-stricken, and the guards arrive flashing their torches in my direction.

I don't know how long I've been gone, or what time it is, but it's been dark for hours and my thin T-shirt is no match for the cold and damp air that followed the setting sun. I'm shivering and hungry, but it will be worth it when my family arrives in a frantic search party. They'll be so delighted I'm all right, they won't care that I tried to hit Liam. In relief they will listen and believe how cruel he was to me.

I wait and watch. And wait and watch some more. From my high vantage point, the only stirring I see outside is Shane leaving with Brian, followed by Katherine and Sheena driving off to Dublin.

Still, I wait.

It must be really late now. I'm guessing eleven o'clock. I decide the minute anyone starts looking for me, I'll reveal my whereabouts. But when Adrienne departs, I lose hope. I've been a runaway for what must be nearly seven or eight hours and can't bear the cold, hunger, and boredom any longer. I surrender and make for home, buoyed by my confidence that I shall receive a joyful welcome from Mum and Dad.

"There you are," Mum says, crocheting by the fire.

Dad looks up from his *National Geographic*. "You should run along to bed, Deedums," he says. "It's very late."

Did no one notice how *long* I was gone? Suppose robbers had taken me!

I look at my parents, who are not looking back at me. Not even a glance, and I ache to be comforted for my hours of misery while hiding in shame. But my parents are oblivious to my torment and by my shivering. So I dash off to bed and climb under the covers already warmed by Shoobee. I can tell by the way her warm eyes stare at me that she, at least, is glad to see me and wonders where I have been and why I am crying.

But how can I explain to Shoobee that, unlike Jack Dempsey, the giant has beaten me.

CHAPTER 2
BAD GRAMMAR

My new school offers a choice: day pupil or boarder? No need to flip a coin on that one. I choose day pupil so I won't suffer a second longer in school than absolutely necessary. As it is, classes are in session six days a week with a half-day on Thursdays and Saturdays. I'm glad for the short day during the week, but don't like at all going to school on Saturday even for a half day.

Even worse, the school is walking distance from my house on the Mornington Road. I worry about teachers spying on me as I tackle oak trees and sycamores instead of homework. Or perhaps they will send someone to bang on my window if I sleep too late.

As I amble up the wooded driveway to Drogheda Grammar School on my first day, a graceful regency house emerges with a fist-shaped brass knocker jutting from its enormous black door. Bordered by landscaped paving and modern dormitories, the twenty-two acre grounds sport an outdoor swimming pool, grass rugby fields, an all-weather hockey pitch, and a gymnasium that puts the Loreto in the dark ages.

A puny male teacher with hands like a porcelain doll directs us to line up for morning assembly. My class stretches across the front row, so I have to look up at the mock stage constructed of lunchroom tables shoved together. Jonathan's father, Headmaster Siberry, thunders across the platform followed by a flock of teachers. They open their hymnals while the headmaster seizes command of the students with a resounding "BE QUIET!" The foreboding headmaster recites a passage from the Bible, and I wonder if this will really be better than the Loreto. What would the moralizing headmaster do if he knew his son and I have kissed?

Unlike the Loreto, Drogheda Grammar School is open to boys and girls of all faiths. Walking to my first-year classroom, I try to find differences between Catholics and Protestants, but there appear to be none, though I notice plenty of differences between boys and girls. I'm eleven, so the girls are a year or two older. They're not interested in climbing trees or kicking a ball.

13

On breaks, they share nail-polish tips and rave about Adam Ant and Duran Duran.

I sit close to the gossiping girls, trying to decipher the secret code to break into their group. But the harder I try, the more they resist me. I do manage to acquire bullies, however, both boys and girls. They call me "Lion Head" because of my unruly straw mane and "Rust Face" on account of an undiagnosed rash on my cheeks and chin. Even my runners with the Incredible Hulk pictured on them arouse locker-room teasing. I can only imagine what they'd say if they knew I followed newspaper articles about another hulk—the British heavyweight prospect, Frank Bruno.

After several weeks, as I fail to discover my scholastic prowess, I realize Sister Imelda at the Loreto was right when she'd ridicule and nag: *Gogarty will dream her life away. Gogarty is away with the fairies again.* It seems I am bound to daydream my life away. But they'd be surprised to know it's Jack Dempsey I dream of, and the punch bag now tossed into a corner of Dad's workshop after Liam sent me hiding in disgrace. I decide to hang the bag in a secret place, too ashamed to ask Dad to help me. At least this time Liam won't be able to snoop about and humiliate me.

A specialist comes to school to test my IQ. She reports I just need to apply myself to studies, that I'm highly intelligent. She says I'm pleasant and approachable. She also claims I have excellent mechanical reasoning and dimensional skills. I'm delighted the teachers will now realize I'm not stupid. But they're not impressed.

At least the boarding school girls have warmed to me since they discovered I live down the road. I've been informed that after Sunday mass my house will be their welcome escape for tea and biscuits. I'm glad for their interest, and hopeful they will befriend me. But Brian is home on weekends, and I'm worried he'll embarrass me with his bizarre behavior.

The first Sunday I shuffle the girls straight into the sitting room and manage to keep my brother away. Brian is in a sultry mood and shying from the strangers. I ply the girls with pots of tea and coffee and Kimberly Mikado biscuits. We have a laugh and I begin to feel I'm making some good friends. Boarders generally don't hang around with day pupils, so I will tally some "cool points" at school.

The next Sunday, though, I'm nervous. Brian is active and in a boisterous mood. Mum says it's because he's sixteen and his hormones are raging. He's been listening to Shakin' Stevens all morning and bounding through the house. The beat spurs his unique dance, a sort of frenzied Nazi march. He has already kicked two huge dents in the freezer with his big swinging feet—not out of willful destruction, but the way a puppy knocks over a toddler with clumsy enthusiasm. Brian has also refused to change out of his pajama bottoms. His large manhood makes frequent alarming appearances through the hopelessly ineffectual front fly. Dad, who is normally the one to convince Brian to change his attire, is passed out at the dinner table from too much wine.

Three girls arrive, and before they even sit down, Brian springs into the sitting room and slaps his hands against the back wall, then leaps out again. The girls look at each other in disbelief and burst into laughter.

"That's my brother Brian," I explain. "He's autistic."

"Artistic? You mean, he's weird?" one girl asks and the others chuckle.

"No, *aw*-tistic—he's handicapped."

"You mean like he's mental?" the same girl asks, and the others elbow her while trying to smother another fit of giggles.

Escaping to the kitchen to make tea, I can hear Brian marching in and out of the sitting room and the girls' growing titter. I place a pot of tea and cups on a tray along with the last of Mum's favorite almond slices. My mother will be furious, but I need all the points I can score today.

I try to steady my return to the sitting room with a tray full of rattling cups and hot tea. Brian swipes an almond slice off the tray.

"Brian, stop!" I snap as he crams the slice into his mouth.

The girls laugh and Brian starts to jump up and down, rubbing his hands between his legs. I shuffle faster to put down the tray. But it's too late. Brian pulls down the front of his pajamas and exposes his huge penis to the girls and they run screaming to the door.

I would have tossed the scalding tea at him, but Brian is off and running. Slamming down the tray, I tear after him. I corner him in my parents' bedroom and draw back my fist to crack his arm. But he throws up his hands in defense and shoves me backwards. I crash against the footboard of the bed, and my breath vanishes as Brian bolts from the room.

Mum and Dad have spent years teaching my brother good manners, yet he remains barely manageable. In public, he takes whatever he wants out of shops and snatches food off strangers' plates in restaurants. Anything new we bring into the house he randomly throws in the fire. The slightest change in his routine provokes blood-curdling tantrums. My parents have been working to raise money to build a school for autistic children. In the meantime Brian remains at a school for the mentally handicapped that is more like a sitting service. The workers there have little knowledge of how to teach someone like my brother.

I stomp about seething over the ridicule I'm bound to receive. I want to kick or hit something, to rail with the freedom that Brian claims. Suddenly I think of my punch bag. I run to Dad's shop and exhume it from a drift of sawdust. I cannot hang it up, but I stand the bag and flood it with punches of anger and frustration. Tiny bits of wood fly into my mouth and stick to the tears on my cheeks. My knuckles break open and splinters of sawdust work into the cuts. But I don't care. I'm beyond the world where the sting of pain can find me.

When my punches become weak and exhaustion takes hold, I flop against the bag. Satisfaction replaces anger as my lungs gasp for breath. Blood runs through my arteries and bubbles on my knuckles like raspberry jam and I feel like no prayer has ever made me feel, like not one minute of the absurd tea parties. I feel as good as I do leaving school, kissing a boy, better and more relieved than I can remember. I don't need a nun's blessing because I know my salvation is buried in a punch bag stuffed with newspapers and rags.

CHAPTER 3
THE FISHMEAL FACTORY

Fire! Ring the fire brigade! Dad yells and then disappears. Mum leaps to the phone. I fly to the window and see flames shoot from Dad's workshop and stretch across the roof of my bedroom. And then I see Dad's silhouette dash into the inferno. I watch horrified as he rolls out four giant cylinders of butane gas, one by one. Burning embers cascade upon him. Mum and I rush to the fishpond to fill buckets with water.

The fire brigade arrives in a rush of reflective armor and it seems to take forever to extinguish the blaze. Afterwards, the charred firemen slog inside for refreshments. I scramble to brew tea and serve snacks while the tall, smoky heroes explain the fire was caused by Dad's pottery kiln's butane flames. They boast that Dad has saved the house and probably our lives by removing the explosive fuel. I'm so proud of my father. But Mum doesn't seem to share my pride as she stares into her tea. And Dad appears lost in blame, for he designed and built the kiln. My father escorts the firemen outside while Mum drops her face into her hands and sobs.

The next morning I stare into the black skeleton of Dad's workshop, and the smell of smoky ruin stings my nostrils as I push through cold, damp mush and pieces of busted pottery. One of the slippers Dad wore while retrieving the gas cylinders lies twisted and burnt in a pile of ashes. For me, it's a heart-stopping reminder that my father could have been killed.

Towards the back of the workshop I search for the punch bag that has now ministered me through nearly three years of teasing and failed exams at Drogheda Grammar School. But it's buried under a mass of debris and huge chunks of collapsed roof. I've been told girls aren't supposed to hit things, but the bag's possible loss freezes me mid-step.

I search, but cannot find my bag and I have to wait until Dad clears the ashy corpse of his workshop. When he finally uncovers my punch bag, it's in surprisingly good shape. Even after a day in the sun and fresh newspaper stuffing, the duffel still carries a smoky scent when I hang it from the clothes bar in my walk-in bedroom closet. Now I can pummel the bag as often as I want without anyone knowing how obsessed I am with my punching.

After rearranging my cupboard, I stroll back to the workshop to lend Dad a hand. Mum arrives from Dublin with a surprise: a brand new electric kiln for my father. He humphs and plods off with a handcart to unload the gift in a back room filled with salvaged bits of pottery. Mum says, "He may not bloody well like the new kiln, but at least he can't blow us all to smithereens."

When my father returns, he goes straight to work erecting a cinder-block wall. "So, Des," my mother says, "where's the electric kiln going in your new workshop?"

"This isn't a workshop," he says, lifting another block into place. "This is my new dental practice."

After my father cleans the mortar from his trowel, he relocates his practice, and our lives begin to change. I try to settle into a routine during my fourth year at Drogheda Grammar School, but our driveway is cluttered with awkwardly parked cars, and patient's children run loose in the garden. Dad's patients knock on our door all hours of the night. But it's worth losing privacy and sleep to have my father nearby. And it's especially nice that Dad's young nurse works here full time.

Jean was friendly from the first day I met her. After my first day at the Loreto Convent, just three years old, I rode the bus home, and then walked to Dad's surgery beside the twin towers of Saint Laurence Gate. Unable to reach the bell, I rapped on the thick, royal blue door, though my knock barely made a sound. When the door finally opened and someone stepped out, I slipped inside.

The wide hallway smelled like minty mouth rinse. Dental drills shrieked from the corridors. A young lady in a white coat sat at a desk in a small reception room. I thought she was pretty and looked like my oldest sister Katherine with brown eyes and dark hair worn in a shoulder-length flip. She turned—got a fright when she noticed me—and then looked puzzled.

"Bejanie! I didn't see you there with the size of you. Are you looking for your mammy?" she asked.

"No, my daddy. He works here."

"Oh! You must be Deirdre. My name's Jean. Would you like some crisps?"

"No, thank you," I said, though I was hungry and wanted to eat the snack.

Another lady in a white coat stepped into the reception room. She was shorter than Jean and not as pretty. The women lit cigarettes and chatted about me as if I couldn't hear them.

"Who's yer one?" the shorter lady asked.

"That's Deirdre, Doctor Gogarty's daughter," said Jean. "She's a dote, isn't she? Today was her first day at the Loreto, poor thing."

"Ah, God love her, she's very small. Them nuns will eat the arse off her. Load of cows. What age is she?"

"I don't know. She must be only four or five. What age are you, love?"

I awkwardly clasped my thumb over my little finger and raised my hand.

"Golly, she's only three. And it's such a long walk from the bus stop for her, tut-tut."

The women stubbed out their cigarettes and vanished into the rooms with eerie noises. I sat a long time and listened to the screams of dental drills. People left holding their swollen cheeks. Bloodied cotton jutted from their mouths, and I wondered why they came here in the first place. Across from me a towering grandfather clock ticked loudly. Its long gold pendulum swung so slowly I thought it must have been counting minutes instead of seconds.

Daylight spilled through the letterbox and faded to black when the women returned. They peeled off their white coats, slipped on their anoraks, and snapped up their handbags.

"Your father has one more patient. Will you be all right waiting?" Jean asked.

"Yes, fine thanks," I replied and gulped down my tears.

I've never forgotten Jean's kindness that first day I met her and I am thrilled to have her nearby. She listens to my accumulated fourteen years of heartache and loves to share a laugh with me now and again after classes.

How I wish to communicate with my brother Brian the way I do with Jean, but those prayers remain unanswered. My parents' dream, however, to have their youngest son housed in a facility for autistics has finally come true. Their tireless efforts with The Irish Society for Autistic Children has helped raise enough money to build a special housing community in Dunfirth, County Kildare. Brian no longer shares a dorm room. He gets full-time attention, endless cups of tea, and now he smiles often and with ease.

Even with Brian doing well, Mum seems still rattled and uneasy. She continues to terrify me with her death-wish driving. At dark, after dropping off Brian in Dunfirth, she often hugs blind bends on the wrong side of the road and refuses to turn on her headlights. If I don't show fear, she pretends to fall asleep by slouching over and jerking the steering wheel, which forces me to take control to keep us from crashing. Her fights with Dad, too, have increased and are much more disturbing.

As usual, my father seems unaffected by Mum's hysteria. The forty-five-foot yacht he'd been building has been abandoned and sits in his boatyard with a thick carpet of green algae. But the avid yachtsman nonetheless keeps to his sailing and has purchased a dazzling thirty-five-foot replacement. And he keeps to his bottle. Dad drinks every day.

After a particularly heavy night of spirits, he crashes his car. The next morning Mum begs him to stop drinking. Unsuccessful, she turns to me.

"Go and tell your father he must stop drinking."

But I can't confront my father.

"He could've been killed last night," she pleads. "He'll listen if you tell him to stop."

"No, Mum," I say, refusing to let her pull me into this in a way that tarnishes my relationship with Dad.

"If you don't tell your father to stop drinking," she says, "you'll ruin Christmas for everyone. You hear me? Christmas will be ruined, and it will be your fault."

Guilt-ridden, I relent. I walk away from Mum, ease down the hall, and tap lightly on Dad's bathroom door. I whisper for him to stop drinking.

"What did you say?" he asks.

"Mummy wants you to stop drinking," I mutter a bit louder.

Dad roars with laughter, and I rush off to school. The drama at home makes me late to school. Again. And, as usual, the headmaster publicly humiliates me in assembly.

And, again I am reminded how much I hate school and long to practice my punches or spend time with my two best friends, Peter and James. But even in the company of boys, when I feel the best, I'm afraid to voice that my favorite pastime is practicing lefts, rights, and jabs on my hidden punch bag.

Even during Easter break, when we cycle to the abandoned fishmeal factory at the end of Crook Road. James and Peter talk about movies like *Rambo* and *Rocky*, but I don't take the opportunity to mention my pugilistic fantasies.

The warehouse sits empty, strewn with broken glass from smashed windows. The smell of rotten fish permeates the salty air, and their dehydrated carcasses stick to the floor. Behind a cobweb-encrusted crate, James finds a rat's nest. As he and Peter scramble to gather ammo to pelt the babies, I wander outside to where fishing trawlers once unloaded their catch. I drop a broken piece of cinder block into the murky depths and watch it disappear. Sitting among dry-rotting ropes and rusty chains, utter despair pours over me.

Sitting at the edge of the pier, I imagine two cinder blocks chained around my ankles. If I shoved them over the edge, I'd plummet into the frigid depths to inescapable darkness. Even if I panicked and gasped for life, it would be too late. No one would ever know what happened. I'd simply vanish.

My plan has left me flooded by an unfamiliar inner peace. I know that if my despair becomes too much for me—I have a way out.

CHAPTER 4
THE CLONES CYCLONE

Tea is served in Beatrice Potter cups at Aunt Claire and Aunt Catherine's childhood home in an upper-class suburb across the street from Carysfort College in Blackrock, County Dublin. Mum grew up in this three-story Georgian with her five sisters. Their only brother died of tuberculosis at the age of six. Nothing masculine resides here.

A gold-framed, convex mirror captures the room in a distorted snapshot. A chandelier sparkles in the mirror's reflection and nestles in plasterwork of Prince of Wales feathers. Shimmering Waterford crystals cast a gentle glow on the white, Indian rug. Dresden and Meissen porcelain adorn the marble mantelpiece. To the right of the hearth, a white, enameled bell pull gleams, though it's been a generation since it signaled the maid.

My skirt is stiff and uncomfortable. I'm nervous about spilling the tiniest spot of tea on the pale Chintz-upholstered chair. My back is sore from sitting up straight, trying to look like a lady. Mum and Aunt Catherine watch ballet on the television. The choreographed prancing bores me, provokes me to consider survival in the wild—an undomesticated life, free of society's expectations.

"She's not a bit interested in the ballet," Aunt Catherine whispers to Mum. My aunt crosses her slim legs and adjusts her tailored skirt to drape over her knees. She then pats the back of her short, tight, ash-blonde curls that look fresh from styling. She smells of hairspray and Chanel No. 5 perfume. I pretend not to have heard her soft voice and turn to stare at the purple Dublin Mountains through eight panels of rippled glass.

"I can't make heads nor tails of what Deirdre likes," Mum replies, as if I've already set forth to discover my wilderness sanctuary.

"Deirdre love, would you not have a look at the ballet?" Mum urges. "You should take it up. It's great for your posture."

At the age of fifteen, my underdeveloped body and unfeminine interests are under the microscope. My elders feel the urgency to sculpt me into a marriage-worthy lady before it's too late. But I don't think I'll ever fit their criteria—my hands are too dry and rough for a gentleman to hold.

Aunt Claire arrives from University College Dublin, where she teaches social science and is the university's first female dean. She is brilliant and practical with a sharp mind for business. I love her because she always makes me feel at ease and unafraid to be myself. Unlike Aunt Catherine, whose countenance is regal, Aunt Claire's face is soft and a bit droopy. She would be as tall as her sisters, but her shoulders are narrow and slightly hunched due to a curve in her spine. Wearing slacks and a wool top, she waltzes into the room and announces, "Let's put it on BBC. The Irish fellow, Barry McGuigan, is boxing for the world title!"

As soon as the channel switches, a burst of mayhem replaces the gentle tweeting of ballet. The fever-pitch boxing crowd swamps the Irishman as he tussles his way towards the ring. The red-and-white-striped ring canopy serves as his only beacon in a sea of blinding fans. I'm surprised at McGuigan's tiny size because I've imagined all boxers to be hulking bricks of men like Jack Dempsey. Only McGuigan's bobbing head is visible as he trots to his destination.

"Such a big fuss over a slip of a thing," says Mum. But I'm fascinated by the adoration poured on him, especially since the fight is in London. I never thought with "The Troubles" I'd ever witness Englishmen cheering an Irishman.

A blue flag with a gold dove is jostled over the heads of McGuigan's team. The commentator explains that the flag represents peace between the North and the South of Ireland. McGuigan, a Catholic, is married to a Protestant and always wears neutral colors with the *dove of peace* on his trunks. He grew up in the South, in a small town close to the border of Northern Ireland called Clones (pronounced clone-us) so his nickname is "The Clones Cyclone."

The crowd lets out a mighty roar as McGuigan climbs through the ropes. I've only seen snippets of boxing since the Jack Dempsey clip four years ago that inspired me to hang up a punch bag and study everything I could find on the sport. I'm delighted with Aunt Claire's viewing choice and settle in to watch my first boxing match. The Irishman's task sounds daunting. The champion, Eusebio Pedrosa from Panama, has been king of his division for seven years with nineteen— nineteen!—successful title defenses.

The atmosphere sizzles as the fight begins. The champion is described as a legend. He is tall, dark, and graceful. The Irishman is short, pale, and solid. And McGuigan appears to be fearless as he pushes forward and attacks the larger man. Mum asks me if I want to change the station back to ballet, but I don't have to answer because Aunt Claire says, "Ah sure don't bother her, Edie. She's practically leaning into the television. Let her enjoy the match."

As I watch the fight, it occurs to me the human body is designed to box. Fingers curl into fists that are perfect punching weapons, a pair of lethal hammers that are projected by arms that can also shield the warrior. There is a defense and counter to every move and strike. But even the best of men are vulnerable—their guard can be penetrated. An assault can be terminated in the blink of a counter knockout punch. I detect only one design flaw: our brains are located in a primary target area.

In the seventh round, Pedrosa is not able to circle the ring as quickly and is forced to stand and fight McGuigan. My bum lifts off the chair when suddenly, *Bam!* McGuigan's right hand drops the Panamanian. The excitement of the crowd pours from the screen. Pedrosa rises and wobbles, but he boxes his way back into the fight. Relentlessly, the Irishman moves forward. He bobs and weaves to slip inside Pedrosa's longer reach. Once inside, McGuigan punishes his opponent with left hooks to the body. Pedrosa's hurt again in the thirteenth round as he teeters about on wobbly legs, but defies his body's wish to crumple.

The gallant Panamanian survives the fifteen rounds. But our man Barry McGuigan, "The Clones Cyclone," is crowned the new WBA Featherweight Champion of the World. Bursting with pride I clap and cheer along with Aunt Claire. Mum and Aunt Catherine are aghast at my joy. But I don't care, for tonight I've witnessed the dance of magicians.

Back home, knuckles wrapped in bed-sheet strips, I pummel my homemade punch bag in the secrecy of my cupboard. One minute I am McGuigan throwing a barrage, the next I am

Pedrosa, rising from the floor to battle back. It's long after midnight when I notice my hand cloths are soaked with blood.

As weeks pass, the McGuigan fight persists in my head. I try to simulate the movements in front of my bedroom mirror and invent my own battles. To enhance the scene in my mirror, I pop an orange peel into my mouth for the feel of a gum shield. But it just looks silly. Instead, I melt and roll white candle wax, scorch my palms, then mold the hot wax around my teeth. It tastes awful and breaks easily, but I'm pleased with its realism. I huff and puff about the room while I swing fists left and right. My head snaps back when my imaginary opponent fires damaging blows. I get dropped—but climb off the floor to win by knockout. My dog Shoobee sits on the bed and looks worried I've gone mad.

Two months later I'm standing a few feet from Ireland's sporting hero. Barry McGuigan dines above Weavers pub in Drogheda before a scheduled appearance at a local festival. When the champion rises from his table, my heart kicks my breastbone. A cold sweat dampens my light-blue pantsuit. As we pose for a photo, I am speechless. He seems to perceive my nervousness and firmly wraps his arm around me. His lower back feels tiny yet solid as I slip my trembling arm around his waist. Beaming into the camera I can't believe the famous Barry McGuigan is holding me. The camera flashes and I skip away. Meeting him has been the most thrilling moment of my life.

My friend Jonathan sneers at the photo of Barry and me. "You look like you could be going together if you didn't have that big goofy smile on your face," he says. We sit in the garage behind an apartment Dad built onto the backside of our house. I chalk on the side of the garage: *Barry rules OK* and *McGuigan is the Greatest!* This prompts more teasing and an abrupt change of subject.

Jonathan says we need to have sex before my period starts so I won't get pregnant. (I'm almost sixteen but I've not yet menstruated. Boobs still haven't sprouted either. Apparently, I'm behind other girls in everything.) Reluctantly, I listen to his gory details of periods, tampons, intercourse, and ejaculation. His matter-of-fact approach signals to me our childhoods have slipped away. Still, I'm not sold, and though I'm curious about sex I'm too scared to try more than kissing. Mercifully, Jonathan lets it go.

As we walk along the side of the garage apartment, Jonathan cups his hands against the window and peers in. "Who lives in there?" he asks, his voice muffled by glass.

"Nobody," I reply. "I guess Dad's planning to rent it out or something."

"No, somebody's living in there. Look."

I cup my eyes against the glass and my heart sinks. Dad's clothes are in piles on the bed. A sundry of his day-to-day belongings are placed about the room. The mystery of Dad building an apartment attached to the house is solved with a sickening sensation in my stomach. All this time he was building a way out of our lives.

Sure enough, Dad starts sleeping in the apartment every night. Mum and I are left behind. Adjusting to my father living in separate quarters wears hard on my mother. She fixes herself up after crying. She slaves over ambitious new recipes. By the time my father arrives for dinner, she has transformed into a stage actress desperately trying to resurrect a doomed play. But the curtain always closes and Dad never even spends the night.

Mum's irritable mood switches to upbeat and friendly. But the small talk between my parents quickly runs dry. The tension mounts and leaves me screaming inside for escape. I'd give anything for my brothers and sisters to be home. Dad seems unaffected by Mum's efforts and retires to his apartment. My mother retreats to bed to recharge for tomorrow's sad encore.

This evening Mum springs from the dinner table to fetch a special sauce she's spent hours perfecting. While her back is turned, Dad pushes his tongue out and thrusts his middle finger at her. Pure hatred is in his eyes. I'm shocked. Not only has my father left my mother's bed—he loathes her.

I jump at an invitation to a Christmas party by a fifth-year classmate. Anything to skip even one night's performance. At the party I'm once again dressed in my light-blue pantsuit and try to act cool. I manage to chitchat with friends but think it's going to be a long night. Then things look up when a good-looking guy introduces himself as Nick Ennis, the party-giver's cousin.

Nick is well groomed in dark jeans and a navy sweater. He's taller than the other guys and is slender but not skinny. His dark brown hair and eyes compliment his flawless complexion and a face so handsome I wonder why he's talking to me. The pretty and promiscuous Tara circles him like a wild dog. I don't stand a chance against her. As Tara moves in on her prey, I disappear into the crowd.

Sampling the self-serve buffet, I meander from room to room. If only I hadn't come to this party. I'm bored and uncomfortable. "There you are," Nick says. "I was looking everywhere for you." *Why?* I wonder. He continues to talk and I begin to relax. We dance together, first a few fast numbers, and then a slow dance. His arms feel strong around me as I rest my cheek against his chest. I like the smell of laundry detergent in his sweater and the hint of aftershave. May as well enjoy the moment, I decide, however briefly it may last.

Nick takes my hand and leads me to a quiet spot at the bottom of the staircase. He circles his arms around me and pulls me into a kiss. His lips pressed against mine feel nice, but then his tongue breaks through and touches mine. The sensation is a shock. Jonathan and I kissed but never like this.

The kissing goes on too long, and my neck begins to cramp. I don't know when we're supposed to stop. Is he waiting for me to stop first? I hear constant shuffling and excited whispers lurking round the corner. I am relieved to know it's the parent in charge of driving me home who has arrived. Nick scratches down my phone number and then gives me another kiss goodbye. I don't expect to hear from him.

But he calls the next day.

Throughout Christmas break Nick sends messages through his cousin that he'd like to take me to a nightclub. He also phones often and becomes my first official boyfriend. But dating him makes me uncomfortable, that if I'm to keep him, I've got to show him I'm his girl. He's too good looking. Some prettier girl who is willing to have sex will steal him away. And it doesn't help that everyone says what a "catch" he is. It only makes me nervous. When the rash on my face flares up again, I stop returning his calls without explanation.

CHAPTER 5
PILGRIMAGE TO BARRY TOWN

My sulking over the loss of Nick hangs on until spring when I become more worried about Mum. Her mental state continues to deteriorate. Fighting a losing battle for her husband has left her despondent. She's given up the gourmet meals and rarely even bothers to cook. She dresses and leaves for work so lost in thought she forgets to wear lipstick. Even her normally well-groomed hair is askew and flat in the back.

On Easter weekend Mum surprises me with a bit more spring in her step. She asks me if I'd like to visit Barry McGuigan's hometown. Normally, she escapes our lonely house by dressing up, putting a fashionable face on her sad state, and going out to visit the great homes and gardens of Ireland. So her offer to visit the working-class town of Clones is an unlikely choice. She's doing this just for me.

She seems happier driving away from the house. Her voice is livelier. But her eyes are hidden behind large, brown-tinted sunglasses with lenses that fade to clear toward the bottom. Her eyes, if I could see them, would tell me truly. We travel with the windows down, breathing in the day's warmer temperature. I watch hedgerows and farmyards zip by and wonder if my hero will be in town. McGuigan has made two successful world title defenses and is so popular it seems all of Ireland has united in admiration.

We arrive in the center of Clones called "The Diamond." The town is ablaze with banners claiming their famous son. Our first stop is to the McGuigan's family grocery shop. Mum chats up the cashier who is Barry's mother. She tells us her son is away in London. But I'm undeterred by this news. In fact, I'm thrilled to be in "Barry Town" and to meet his mother.

We stroll across "The Diamond" to the champ's father-in-law's hotel for lunch. Mum giggles when the owner pronounces á la carte.

"He said *car-tee*," she explains. But the humor escapes me.

Everything about Clones and its people seems to amuse her.

"I can't believe we're here," I say.

"Neither can *I*," my mother says and giggles again.

While Mum waits for lunch, I stroll past the hotel's bar and find a McGuigan fight on TV. I slip inside to watch, and a group of curious, pint-drinking men strike up a conversation.

"You like boxing, young one?" a shiny-nosed man asks.

"Yes, I love boxing. I came all the way from Drogheda just to see Barry's hometown."

"Really?" another man chimes in. "Well then, can you name the heavyweight champions of history?"

I've been studying the history of boxing. If this were on a test at school, I'd get top marks. My memory is fresh as the names pour out: "John L. Sullivan, James J. Corbett, Bob Fitzsimmons, James J. Jeffries, Marvin Hart . . ."

The men sit in stunned silence.

I am answering a Joe Louis question when Mum finds me.

"There you are, love. You were gone so long, I was getting worried."

The men explain I've been answering boxing trivia questions without a single mistake.

"I'm amazed," Mum declares on the drive home. She looks stylish in her pantsuit and sunglasses, the wind whipping her light-brown hair. "You're usually so shy. I don't know what to do with you. And there you were, answering boxing questions in front of all those strange men. You certainly are full of surprises."

Then a big surprise comes to me when on June 23rd, 1986, Barry McGuigan loses his title in the desert heat of Las Vegas to Stevie Cruz. Ireland is stunned. But I am devastated and cannot bear to read newspapers that headline his defeat. On the verge of tears I refuse to believe my hero is no longer world champion. I feel depressed and irritable as I reluctantly push the shopping trolley behind Mum in Quinnsworth market. She is also in a bitter mood. When I dare to inspect a pineapple, she screeches, "Too expensive!" And then she scolds me about money in front of strangers, but I know it's about Dad, and not about money.

In the checkout line my mother tells me to stop moping. I'm angry that she thinks she is alone in her right to disappointment. Though I agree I'm taking the McGuigan loss a bit too hard, I can't seem to swallow the sadness lodged in my throat. I have to fight the urge to burst out crying, but finally give in to the tears on the drive home. Mum's not seen me cry since I was a child, and the shock sends her into her own fit of tears. "I'm sorry, Mum. It's okay," I say, "I don't know what's wrong with me."

But the next day my answer arrives in a bloody mess. I've been lucky to reach my sixteenth year without tampons and pads and embarrassing accidents. The blood on my bed sheets could arouse suspicion of a murder scene. I'm not used to bleeding without injury, so I'm alarmed. But then I look through Mum's 'feminine products' and fumble through the procedure to stop the mess. I use Mum's bulky maxi pads, and I'm no longer able to walk normally, so I shuffle and fear someone will, heaven forbid, spot the bulge in my jeans.

My weepy emotional state does not mix well with Mum's mood swings. She snaps at me for eating too many groceries, for wearing nothing but dirty T-shirts and jeans. But when I do the laundry, she screams that it's too expensive to run the washing machine. Just when I'm about to crack, my cousin John offers me the perfect summer job. He is supervisor at a plant nursery and mushroom farm in Kimmage, a working-class section of Dublin. He hires me to tend greenhouses at the nursery. I'll have to move to Dublin, an hour's drive from my family home in Mornington. It is exactly what I need.

I stay at my sister Katherine's house in Goatstown and cycle four miles to and from work five days a week. I leave for the nursery in darkness at five in the morning. The deserted streets give me a satisfying sense of being the first person to witness each day. A genesis of sorts seems to have come my way, and I wonder if maybe I'm just growing up.

Working in the warm compost and damp greenhouses suits me, and I find Mother Nature in her silence is nurturing and soothing and wise. Supervision is infrequent and casual, but I work hard anyway, as though my future depends on every drop of sweat that seeps into the soil.

My blue-collar coworkers have a dry quick wit, a Dublin sense of humor that is well known. The men are macho and attractive. They are loud, gregarious, and uninhibited. I admire their lack of self-consciousness and willingness to have fun. They read tabloids in the lunchroom and wink at me. They even nudge a friendly young man to approach me. With an audience, he asks me for a date. So as not to embarrass him, I agree to go out with him.

"Me name's Colin," he says sheepishly. "Colin Brown. I hate me surname. It's brutal."

He takes me to see *Cobra* starring Sylvester Stallone. Every few minutes a woman is viciously murdered. I can't imagine a worse first-date choice, for the movie reminds me I'll soon be out on the shadowy streets of Dublin with a guy I hardly know.

Colin gets up to go to the bathroom. "Watch me jacket," he warns. "It's got bleedin' legs. Me brudders are always nickin' it."

I study his grey blazer in the flickering light of gunfire. It looks cheap, outdated, and grubby.

For dinner we eat greasy fish and chips and watch a brawl across the street. My date apologizes for the behavior of his Dublin neighbors. I pretend to be unfazed by the raw display of violence, and in fact, I use the opportunity to ask Colin if he's ever boxed.

"Yeah, once," he tells me. "Got bleedin' murdered. When I got home, me mudder asked if I had any luck at me fight. Yeah, I says to her—bad luck."

We laugh and I begin to feel at ease.

The film and the meal must have emptied Colin's pockets, for the next night we just stroll along the River Liffey. We follow the cobblestone alleys of Temple Bar and kiss under the blue light of a lamppost. He holds my hand and proudly greets his friends on Eustace Street. Colin makes me feel special and wanted, and I'm glad I'm out of my house and away from all the drama.

My summer job and romance ends but I've earned enough money to enter the sports shop on West Street and buy the boxing gloves I've admired for so long. The dusty brown leather resembles the gloves Jack Dempsey wore to knock out his opponents.

The second-hand gloves leave a bright silhouette on the dingy display board. They smell musty and their frayed laces don't match, but something magical happens as my fingers slide into the cushiony hollows. My thumbs seem to know just where to go as they veer into each sheath, and my fingers curl into perfect punch conformity, the gloves a chrysalis for my fists, now defined as weapons and equipped to see me into battle.

Back home, gloved and confident, I'm uninhibited without fear of sprained wrists or bleeding knuckles. The punch bag slams violently into the cupboard walls; the clothes rail rips out of its sockets and plummets to the floor. So I haul my apparatus to the hallway of Dad's empty dental offices now that he has moved his practice from his former workshop. I create a way to hang the bag by removing the attic access panel and hoisting a thick iron bar into the loft. I place it across the opening. The bag hangs high and the hall is narrow, but my punching range is greatly improved. I have to be careful though—when the iron bar shifts too far, it crashes down and threatens to give me my first knockout.

My heavy bag and Shoobee are my only companions since Dad is never here anymore. I can't talk to Mum, and I miss chatting with my father's dental nurse, Jean. So I visit his new surgery, a few doors down from a magnificent shopping center on Wellington Quay in Drogheda. The center is bright and cheery. Gone are the dreary, old malls, and a new car park accommodates enthusiastic shoppers.

The only structure that remains of the old docklands stands defiant at the edge of the car park—a dilapidated, graffiti-riddled, three-story building on Dyer Street. The faded wooden sign reads: DROGHEDA AMATEUR BOXING CLUB; FOUNDED 1936. A sapling grows from a clogged gutter on the roof to seemingly flaunt the building's timeline of neglect. I am transported into a fantasy. For many, the building might be an ugly leftover, but for me, it holds a magical fascination of what could lie within its walls.

I study the building for weeks from Dad's waiting room window. In the evenings tough-looking, young men work out on the top floor. Below, the heavy wood doors remain closed. I wonder how to make an initial approach. I've never talked to boxers before. I imagine a dentist's daughter would not be welcomed into their world. I want to knock on the enormous dark-blue door, but I think they'll never hear me over the din upstairs.

Besides, I'm a girl.

Girls don't belong at such a rough establishment, and truthfully I'm scared even as I think about asking to be let inside.

I try to accept the reality that women don't box. But I cannot take my eyes off the building. Two older men regularly sit at a mesh-covered window during the day. As they watch the passersby, I imagine conversations of boxing legends and classic fights. I want so badly to join them my hands clinch into fists as I pace in front of the window.

At home, I search for a boxing match on television. And on Sunday there's a bout on delayed broadcast from America. The boxers are Marvelous Marvin Hagler and Sugar Ray Leonard. Leonard is thin but muscular with small ears and a cute face. Hagler is an ebony-skinned tank of a man. His back is a rippling V of perfect fitness, his wide shoulders and thick neck topped off by a clean-shaven head.

Leonard looks in danger of serious bodily injury as the brooding Hagler viciously hunts him down. But each time Hagler has him snared, Leonard throws a blinding flash of fists and slips away. And then Leonard pours out a dazzling flurry, and my heart soars with the beauty of boxing.

For nearly two years "The Clones Cyclone" has inspired me to throw and duck a million punches, to rise from the floor countless times in victory in the confines of my bedroom. By the time Leonard's hand is raised in victory, another decision has been made. I vow to defeat my fear. I will enter the boxing club on Dyer Street. I will see what happens when a girl tells the men she wants to fight.

CHAPTER 6
DYER STREET DREAMS

The sapling on the roof of the boxing club waves in the Boyne breeze and entices me to enter the building with its tattered, graffiti canvas of pale yellow plaster. I gaze through the window of Dad's waiting room and will myself to cross the car park when his dental nurse, Jean, bounds in and chirps, "Whatcha lookin' at?"

"The boxing club," I answer, as though it should be obvious. I've spent countless hours at this perch studying the old structure on Dyer Street.

"Is someone spraying durty words on it again?"

"No. I'm waiting for it to open."

"What the Jaysus for, Deirdre?"

"I'm going to talk to them."

"Ah, yar not serious?"

"I'm going over there, Jean. I have to see what they do."

"They bash yar bloody face in. That's what they do."

Jean stubs out a cigarette and heads back to Dad's surgery. She hasn't changed much from the teenager I met fourteen years ago. She is tall and slim, even glamorous in her white coat, which accentuates her dark brown hair and eyes. She still gorges on crisps and chocolates, and roars with laughter at the tiniest invitation. Jean has married, given birth to a daughter, and separated from her husband. Her explanation of the break up: *He got tired of me sneaking out to the pub every night.*

Mum pities Jean, a single mother, and somehow manages to give her extra money each week. I don't know how Mum does this with her own financial problems, brought on by Dad's irresponsible spending and complete lack of money management. I also don't know how my mother practices dentistry with wrists painful and rigid from rheumatoid arthritis. But she manages to hire Jean to work in the mornings with her at the public health clinic and then releases her to Dad's private practice in the afternoons.

With Jean gone, I continue to gaze at the gym and send up a wish to the rooftop sapling: *Please help me find a way to go inside.* As if in answer, a stocky figure dressed in a red tracksuit shows up at the club's front door. He leans against the wall as if waiting for someone. My unexpected chance catches me off guard. Paralyzed by fear, I draw courage from a fight I watched last night on a delayed broadcast from America—Marvelous Marvin Hagler verses Sugar Ray Leonard—and cross the street.

I have no idea what to say to the man, so I amble along the pavement. I almost lose my nerve, but I siphon fortitude from Leonard's daring victory. I picture his whirling combinations and head straight to the club. The man sees me now, so I can't turn away. He shifts restlessly as I approach him. My pulse races and I think about running the other way.

"Excuse me," I croak, "My name's Deirdre Gogarty." I point to the window where I had been sitting. "I was wondering if I could find out some things about boxing."

The man's eyes dart to the window then land on me.

"Yeah? I'm Joe Leonard, the head trainer."

Leonard? But the irony of his name is lost as my tumbling query begins.

"How many boxers train here, and how often do they train, what ages are they, when do they fight, where do they fight, how do they get to their fight, if they don't have a car, somebody has to drive them, right?"

Joe Leonard keeps his answers short as he politely tolerates my barrage of questions. Finally, I am having a conversation with a real man of boxing. But I'm doing all the talking; I try to be quiet so he can answer. Joe resembles Harry Greb, a great champion who fought blind in one eye. Like Greb, the skin on Joe's brow is thick and creased. His nose is wide and flat. His hair is combed smooth against his skull, which is distinctively broad and angular as if designed to withstand punishment.

What must he be thinking of me? T-shirt and tattered jeans hang loose on my thin frame. Unlike my mother and schoolmates, I have no interest in fashion or makeup. Shadowing the lids of my blue eyes or taming my unruly blonde hair will do nothing to make me a fighter. My only interest is boxing. And I'm finally talking to a real man of the sport even though he keeps glancing from me to the club's entrance as if he's anxious to bolt.

When I ask about my hero, Barry McGuigan, he stops shifting his feet and perks up his head.

"Barry McGuigan practiced squad training with the Irish team at this very club. And he was a fanatical trainer. Always the first man in the gym—and the last to leave."

"Brilliant!" I say and flash Joe a huge smile.

I have his full attention now, so I ask about training routines, sparring sessions, even the layout of the gym. His eyes squint when he looks at me as if he's baffled by my interest and enthusiasm. But I do get the feeling he's curious about me.

"We'll be open tomorrow," he says. "You can watch the lads train if you want."

"Really?" I exclaim. "I will definitely be here."

Again, Joe shoots me a puzzled look and goes inside.

Tomorrow I will finally be allowed to enter the boxing club on Dyer Street. It's the only thing I can think about as I stand on my bike's pedals and pump my way home against a salty coastal wind.

The next day my hands shake as I push open the scarred wooden door I've stared at for several months. I step into the dingy hallway that stinks of beer and stale cigarette smoke from the downstairs bar. As I climb the steep stairs to the gym on the top floor, the stench of nightlife follows me. Turning onto the second-floor landing, I'm taken aback by the sight of three naked teenage boys in a dressing room with the door open. I slip past, hoping they haven't noticed me, not wanting to start things off as the girl who breached their privacy.

When I near the gym's entrance, I stand to the side of the door's large glass window, not ready to be spotted on the premises. I hear booming masculine voices that blend into a hum of skipping ropes, singing speedballs, grunts of sparring, shouts of instruction, and heavy bags pounding to the beat of my heart in my ears.

"Keep yer hands up or you'll be climmed!" Joe yells. I've never heard the word before, but I'm guessing no one wants to be climmed. It sounds painful. Almost as painful as the panic I feel walking into such a dizzying din of testosterone. I decide that I must be crazy. I stand frozen outside the door to the gym and consider sneaking away.

Then I hear footsteps on the stairs. The naked guys I spotted earlier must be coming up. I imagine they have their clothes on, but I don't want to see them again in such close quarters. I have only two options: stay or go. So I take a deep breath and open the gym's door. As I step inside, the bell sounds and training stops. All eyes turn toward me and blood rushes to my face. Joe turns to see what the distraction is. Even the two boxers in the ring have stopped to stare, and I'm sure I'm in big trouble for interrupting their rhythm.

Joe turns to see what the distraction is. When he spots me, he makes his way over. "So, you decided to come," he says, and I suddenly feel less like an intruder. But when the bell rings, he walks back toward the ring, and I feel as naked as the boys from the dressing room.

"Back to work, the lot of ya," Leonard admonishes the curious onlookers. "This isn't a holiday camp!"

I'm standing alone in the gym's center as the percussion slowly cranks up like the train that I used to ride to school. Not sure where to go, I follow Joe to the ring where leather slaps flesh. The smell of beer and cigarette smoke must be back on the stairs—up here it's all musk and sweat and a hint of the River Boyne, for the Drogheda Amateur Boxing Club sits smack on her banks.

The controlled sparring in the ring and the camaraderie in the gym surprises me. I always imagined flesh-betting old men circling the ring and shouting at their mean-spirited sons to knock each other's blocks off. Instead, the boxers chat between rounds like best friends. The fit young men who trade punches shake hands and say goodbye to each other. I'm so mesmerized by their actions, I stand ringside until the last bloody nose is wiped and the gym empties.

After haunting the gym now for two weeks, I fear I've become a nuisance. Club members nudge each other and ask, "Who's she anyway? What's a girl doing here?" I've told Joe I pound a punching bag at home and have hinted I'd love to train, but he only responds with a low hum. So I keep watching the men work out until they look back at me. Then I study the fight posters on the wall.

As I prepare to leave one day, Joe takes me aside for a chat. I'm sure he's going to tell me to stop coming. "Look," Joe says, "since you like boxing this much, you can train if you want." I beam at Joe and nod so vigorously I must resemble one of those bobble-head toys. Then I dash off without saying a word. I cross the car park toward Dad's surgery and wonder how my feet manage to touch the ground.

At home I run straight to my room. No time to waste. I must prepare to train. I bob and weave and pelt my gloves into my makeshift bag. I know to keep my chin down, throw straight punches, and stand with my left hand forward because I'm right handed. What I don't know is what to wear to the gym.

The next day before training, I visit a tiny sport shop on Dyer Street. A tall, grey-haired man points to the tracksuits, and I see a plain grey one like Sylvester Stallone wears in *Rocky*. It's my twig of a size, so I don't need to try it on, and it's perfect because I don't want to draw attention to myself. Or get Joe in trouble for allowing a woman in the club.

But my new jumpsuit does nothing to calm my fears the first day of training. I'm as scared as the first time I climbed those pub-smelling stairs. The boxers watch suspiciously as Joe wraps my hands with bandages. As the white strips tighten on the flesh of my fingers and knuckles, I feel I could punch through a wall without my gloves.

Joe tells me to start by skipping rope. But the rope whips my legs and trips me. I pretend it doesn't hurt, just as I pretend no one is gawking at me. Then he tells me to sit on the wooden floor so he can stand on my toes while he counts my sit-ups. When is he going to stop—thirty-five? Forty? Fifty? My stomach muscles burn and my stupid bra clasp digs into my spine. I wear it only because I'm seventeen and I'm supposed to, not because I need to, and now I want it off.

Like a not-so-mean drill sergeant, Joe orders me on my feet, tells me to spar with a make-believe opponent. Shadowboxing for three rounds warms me up for the heavy bag. Joe ties my hands into a nice pair of blue and white gloves, and *pop-pop*, *pow!* I bask in the luxury of hitting a real bag that doesn't crash down on me like the one that hangs in my bedroom closet.

Awkward attempts at hitting the speedball are followed by grueling duck walks, weighted leg lifts, and squats with the medicine ball. The workouts at home have helped my arms, but the rest of my body is jelly. Finally, Joe signals the end of my first day of training. I lean against a grimy windowsill and stare at Dad's surgery and the four panes of sparkling glass where I used to dream of this moment. Sweaty, achy, exhausted, I am delighted—with myself, with where I am, with what I'm doing. I am learning something so important to me—I vow to myself that I will succeed here, as I never have in school.

I refuse to miss a night at the gym despite the fact that it's June, the dreaded month of Ireland's Leaving Certificate—my final exams. I have already failed the Inter Cert, and with this test I am about to fail the most important exams of my academic life. I've feared this ordeal since my first year of school at the Loreto Convent.

At home, hours tick by in my bedroom as I try to study. Perhaps I can scratch out a pass. But the task seems overwhelming, so I swap my *World History* book for *The History of Boxing*. I'm glued without effort to stories of Jack Dempsey knocking out bigger men, Sugar Ray Robinson's epic battles with Jake LaMotta, and Henry Cooper dropping Cassius Clay with his famous left hook.

Mum appears in the doorway of my bedroom. Her light brown hair is styled in teased but smooth, short waves that don't move as she glides in high-heeled, open-toed pumps toward my bed. I can't help but wonder if we are related.

"I want you to see a specialist," she says.

"Why?" I groan.

"I think you have a condition that's causing your trouble with spelling and mathematics. I'm taking you to Dublin tomorrow to be tested by a psychologist."

"Jeeze, Mum. What's the point of me even going to school if I'm so bad I need to see a psychologist? It's such a waste of time."

"You'll never get into college at the rate you're going," she snaps. "Do you want to end up on the dole? Honestly, Deirdre, I'm at my wits' end with you. You're taking the tests tomorrow and that's that!"

I nod and she storms off.

I'm glad I didn't put up a fuss. The tests are not so bad. And the psychologist is a friendly, young man with black hair and thick-rimmed glasses. After hours of puzzles and questions, reading and spelling, I am sent home, back to the dizzying schoolbooks. I'm sitting in my bedroom and trying to study when Mum pops in.

"It's dyslexia," she says. "As I suspected, you are dyslexic."

She tells me because of my diagnosis the spelling part of my Leaving Cert will not be graded as strictly as the other students. But that's the only compensation I'll be given, she says. She continues to talk to me, but my mind is stuck on the word *dyslexia*. I am dyslexic. There's a reason for those swimming numbers and letters: my brain's tossing them about. Maybe I'm not so dumb after all.

This revelation inspires me to sign up for the honors section of the Leaving Cert in my most competent subjects: art, English, and biology. I cram for two and a half weeks, finish my exams, and fourteen years of school misery are over.

My exam results won't arrive until September, but I know my higher education options will be limited. My father believes I should pursue an artistic career. But he no longer sits on my bed to chat about sculptures, frameworks, molds, and finishes. His long, graceful hands used to show me ways to enhance light and shade on my charcoal horses and pencil rock stars. His eyes would gleam above half-glasses as we'd discuss alternatives to medium, application, and subject. But our bedtime chats have stopped. Instead, what I hear from Dad are the familiar, late-night sounds of car tires grinding the pebbled driveway as he races from his apartment to tend to his patients. He's never been so busy. I suppose every townsperson and villager on the east coast of Ireland must have aching teeth.

I rush from class to celebrate my freedom at the gym, but I've only been here an hour when Joe delivers bad news. The club will close for summer. This is the last night of the season. I protest but Joe calmly explains that summer is ripe with sports and most boxing clubs close until autumn. I don't understand why anyone would agree to this. And I've certainly never heard of the great champions taking the summer off.

Joe suggests I play soccer to stay in shape. One of the boxers has a sister who plays and I can join her team. I want to please Joe, so I sign up for soccer. But I hate the game and feel ridiculous chasing a ball with a bunch of girls kicking my shins. Feebly pretending to know the rules but without love or passion, I am no good at this game. Half my Boyne River teammates play with hangovers and love bites the size of beer coasters, yet they run circles around me the way the posh girls did during field hockey at Drogheda Grammar School. At the end of practice a spiky-haired player sums up my problem: "You play like you don't know your arse from your elbow." I agree. And I know that team sports will never appeal to me.

At home I write punch combinations, pin them to the wall, and repeat the drills over and over. Deep in Dyer Street dreams, I beat my worn punching bag until I can't move my arms. Resting between bouts I think about the gym reopening and my hazy future.

CHAPTER 7
THE BETRAYAL

When the club reopens, I watch the men spar and long to be in the ring with them. After a lot of hinting, then outright begging, I get my chance.

But not with a guy.

Joe wants me to spar with Lynda, the soccer-playing sister who's been working out at the gym. I don't want to spar Lynda because she's not a real boxer. Regardless, it's my first chance to land a gloved fist on living flesh.

We're in the ring but can't stop giggling. We giggle our way through round one. But by round two, we've lost our nervous hysterics and begin to hit each other in earnest. The punches sting but are tolerable. I'm surprised how tiring and downright exhausting it is to hit and not get hit for a whole round.

While Lynda and I spar, a heavyweight watches me gasp for breath. He approaches me afterward and says I need to run to be fit for boxing. His nickname is Blackie—I assume it's because of his dark, shoulder-length hair. He resembles Patrick Swayze in the popular movie, *Dirty Dancing*. He not only looks like Swayze, he stands like him and moves with the same grace. My smile answers his offer to run with me.

The next day Blackie and I trot along the quays, the setting sun behind us, casting our bobbing shadows far ahead. The only sound is our feet pounding pavement and the river slapping ships along Merchant's Quay. I try to hide my strained breathing by soundlessly sucking the cold, fishy air deep into my lungs as we push hard against the steep pavement of Constitution Hill.

As looming stone warehouses enclose us in shadows, I imagine Mum's reaction if she saw me running these deserted backstreets of Drogheda with the tough-looking Blackie. A deep pain in my legs burns away the thought. Blackie glides with ease down Laurence Street as I struggle to shadow him and wonder if I'll make it back to the club.

But I do, and the workouts with Blackie motivate me in the ring. After a few more spars I'm serious and aggressive with Lynda. She doesn't reciprocate. I have no problem hitting another person; on the contrary, it is liberating. After a lifetime of being polite and considerate, I climb through the ropes and transform into a fighter.

Out on a run with Blackie I confess my wish to spar real boxers, the guys at the gym. "No problem," he says. "You can spar me."

"Why not?" I reply naïvely. "Jack Dempsey fought people bigger than him lots of times."

After the run I stare at Blackie's imposing mass in the opposite corner. Joe's thin-lipped silence while tying my gloves makes me nervous. Young boxers quietly gather around the ring.

The bell sounds and I press toward Blackie. I'm determined to show off my skills and toughness. I'm halfway across the ring when a heavy *thud* against my padded forehead snaps back my head. I don't understand how he hit me. I'm nowhere close enough to hit him. *Bop!* My heads snaps back again. How is he hitting me like this? *Bop!* Again! Blackie effortlessly sticks out his jab and can't miss. He pulls his punches but they feel like hammers. My neck hurts and it's only seconds into the round. I swing, he leans slightly, I miss him wildly and he hits me with ease. Over and over again. The more I charge him, the more I damage myself by running into his fists.

Racking my brain for a solution, I picture Rocky Marciano rolling under punches, getting inside, and landing bombs. Mimicking my vision, suddenly I'm inside. Blackie's hairy chest is in my face. I can't miss. As my right fist travels toward his bristly chin, he casually leans away and throws a halfhearted uppercut. My head rolls, almost touching my back, and prompts Joe to take a quick step closer. Blackie raises his palms as if to gesture *I'm sorry*. I'm fearful Joe is about to stop the spar, but the bell rings and saves me the humiliation.

Joe asks if I'm all right, so I must look bad. Strangely, I feel chilled even though I've thrown punches for three minutes. I'm weak, shaky, and nauseated. But worst of all, I'm disgraced in front of the guys who stare at me with sympathy. Joe implores me to keep my hands up and move my head to avoid getting "climmed" again. I can't believe Blackie is beating me so easily, and he's not even trying. After the years I've spent pounding my bag, the weeks I've trained at the gym, the handful of times I sparred Lynda, why can't I land one decent shot on a guy the size of a bulldozer?

The bell rings and I'm furious. With no more pretensions of showing off skills, I'm determined to prove I'm not afraid. I attack Blackie again with no form or defense. I rush forward and flail my shots like a buzz saw. Blackie steps back and taps his right hand into my stomach. My lungs deflate. My last bit of breath is snatched from my body. I don't think I can stay on my feet. I can't breathe. Am I *dying*?

Blackie is oblivious to my suffering as I try to recover my breath. I must have been hit in the breadbasket, the famous solar plexus punch Bob Fitzsimmons used to knock out James J. Corbett. No doubt, if Blackie even touches me there again, I will tumble.

My legs are rubber. I'm dizzy. My vision is blurry and I can barely hold up my hands. I'm a joke—nothing like Barry McGuigan. What made me think I could be bad at everything but good at boxing? I've reached the bottom of the pit. I found something that gives meaning to my life and I can't handle it.

I'm helpless on the ropes when a strange echo tolls in the distance. Through the ringing in my ears, I hear a muffled sort of chorus. Louder and louder, the rhythmic sound engulfs me. Male voices from ringside are singing. They are chanting. They can't be. They are! *Deir-dra! Deir-dra! Deir-dra!*

It's the most uplifting sound I've ever heard.

Teenage guys who have never made eye contact with me are chanting my name, cheering me to win. Their support inspires me to fight back with renewed energy. I fire a harmless flurry off the ropes to a roar of approval. I finish the round with one-two-three's, and more importantly, on my feet. Joe smiles and Blackie gives me a hug of respect. The boys continue to cheer and clap as I climb out the ring. As I remove my gear, our eyes meet and kinship is born. I am no longer an outsider. I am part of a team.

I am a fighter.

My new status prompts an invitation to join my gym mates to witness my first amateur boxing show at the National Stadium in Dublin. I enjoy the company of my down-to-earth friends, and I love everything about this night of fights—the crowds, the atmosphere, even the drama of a local favorite's terrible knockout as he struggles unsuccessfully to beat the count. Afterward, it's all I can talk about.

After the next day of training, Joe and I stand on St. Mary's Bridge near a part of town called the Bull Ring, my bike propped against my side. Engrossed in conversation about the fights, I don't notice the way the minutes stretch into hours. It's been dark a long time when a brown Renault zips up and slams to a stop. Mum rolls down the window and hisses, "Get. Home. This. Minute. People will think you're a prostitute!"

Joe slinks away.

"Prostitutes don't wear tracksuits and ride bicycles," I hiss back.

"Go!" she shrieks, pointing homeward.

I hop on my bike and push the pedals hard and fast, but I'm no match for my mother who follows me bumper-to-tire the whole way home. I think she's the one who needs a specialist to find her own psychological disorder.

At home Mum follows me to my bedroom and screams, "Why would you hang out on the street so late at night with a man? What will people think?"

I know better than to answer back, so I shrug my shoulders and slip out of my bedroom and into the bathroom to brush my teeth, but she stays on my heels and asks, "Why do you want to hang around a boxing gym and not play a civilized sport like golf or field hockey?"

I spit into the sink, and again she shrieks, "What will people think?"

I just turn on the faucet and let the water run down the drain.

In spite of Mum's efforts to discourage me from boxing, I refuse to quit the gym. Other areas of my life begin to improve. My Leaving Cert results arrive. I've passed with honors in art, biology, *and* English. Comparatively, the rest of my results are nothing special. In fact, I failed mathematics and Irish. But for me it's a great personal victory.

I've applied to a veterinary nursing school, with horticultural college as my backup plan. For the first time, I feel excited about my future. I'm even looking forward to Christmas and an opportunity to work for my cousin John at his florist shop in Swords, a forty-minute bus ride from Drogheda. I can bus back and forth and not miss a single night at the gym.

It's only four days before Christmas, and darkness comes early. Outside the crowded florist shop, the lights glow brightly. I don't like being stuck inside since the small store is crammed with customers, so I volunteer to sell Christmas trees in the car park. I enjoy assisting busy shoppers in their last days of gathering before the holiday. Everyone is cheerful and can't leave without saying *Have a lovely Christmas, young one. God bless you and your family.*

Customers bustle home across shimmering streets, and colored lights blur as the icy drizzle nests on my eyelashes. I can't help but smile at the possibility of a white Christmas. I warm myself with thoughts of going home to a roaring fire and a hot cup of tea.

A familiar figure marches toward me from the darkness of the car park. I'm surprised to see it's my brother Shane. He doesn't look like he's in the mood for a Christmas tree. He skips the greeting and barks he has come to take me home.

"But I still have an hour to work," I protest.

"I've already talked to John. It's all right for you to leave. Now!"

"What's the matter?" I ask, suddenly frightened. "Did Dad have another car crash?"

"No. Mum's discovered that Dad and Jean are having an affair."

Shane bolts for the car and I follow without question. I'm too shocked to think and need to absorb what he's just told me. As he slams into the driver's seat, he tells me Mum caught Dad at their dental assistant Jean's house in the early hours of morning. Again, I don't ask any questions because Bernie, Shane's pretty fiancée, is in the car. I'm ashamed she'll witness the awful events that are bound to unfold. The drive to Mornington is loudly silent.

At the house Mum is screeching "I'm going to throw myself in the river!" My brother pleads with her to pack her things so he can take her to Dublin. She ignores him and continues to wail. "How could he do this to me? Thirty-five years of marriage... seven children..."

Shane boils with frustration. He snaps at me to pack my things.

"What?" I protest. "*I'm* not going to Dublin." The thought of leaving the boxing club is too much for me.

"Jesus, don't be a pain. Pack your bloody stuff."

"I'm not going," I say defiantly.

Crack! Shane slaps my face. My cheek burns and my eyes water. Alarmed by his uncharacteristic physical attack, he stares at his hand, then at me.

I weep all the way to Dublin in the back seat, while Bernie attempts to comfort me. My mother hiccups and sobs as she pulls at her fat lip. Dad socked her during their confrontation. It must've been bad because Dad's never hit her before. My weeping combined with Mum's loud sobbing is getting to Shane, who grips the steering wheel so tightly his knuckles turn white.

Outside Dublin's city center, I try to memorize the streets to plot my escape. We offload Mum, a blubbering mess, at my aunts' house in Blackrock. She is weak and unable to walk without assistance. I am to stay at Shane's apartment.

After midnight I toss and turn on the couch. I'm torn by Jean's betrayal. Through all the years I poured out my heartaches to her, shared concerns about my mother, laughed about Mum's outbursts, she was sleeping with my father. I unknowingly betrayed my own mother. How could I not see the warning signs? Now it seems so clear. The after-work drinks in the surgeries, empty vodka bottles in the storage room, Jean's mysteriously affordable new house, Dad leaving his apartment in the middle of the night.

What will happen to my parents, my family? I'm not sure I want to stick around to find out. I want to be a boxer—to achieve something great as a fighter. So I struggle to stop my thoughts from returning to my watery grave off the pier of the fishmeal factory.

Our broken family collects in Mornington on Christmas Day. My brothers Shane and Brian are here; David is unable to travel from his home in Vienna. I'm grateful Sheena and Adrienne have flown in from London. But the day grinds past without any sign of Dad. Though he has done terrible harm, I'd give anything if he were here. I think my mother wants him home, too.

We endure fake smiles and forced cheer when visitors in a curiously high number stop by. Our family has been torn apart and humiliated in front of a community who tell us over tea and biscuits they knew about Dad and Jean the whole time.

Five days pass and Dad doesn't show up, so my siblings and I visit him in a damp and dingy basement flat on Laurence Street. We don't know where he spent Christmas and we don't ask. Within the week, we learn he's moved in with Jean.

Mum threatens suicide on a daily basis. I often have to chase her down and drag her from the river. Today, as I snatch her from the Boyne, I notice she has lost weight. She is weak from not eating and easier for me to carry. It seems strange I've become my mother's keeper since I've considered ending my own life in the same river. I know how quickly a person can drown there, so I'm afraid to go to sleep. Eventually, for her safety, Mum is admitted into St. Edmundsbury Psychiatric Hospital in Lucan. But our relief is shrouded by guilt for locking her away. My only comfort is in knowing she will be guarded twenty-four hours a day.

My mum needs a miracle.

Our sprawling bungalow in Mornington is eerily empty. Like leaves on the empty trees outside my snow-covered window, everyone has gone. David lives in Vienna. Sheena and Adrienne live in London. Shane and Katherine live in Dublin. Brian lives in Dunfirth. My mother lives in a mental institution. My father lives with Jean.

And I live with my dog Shoobee in this deserted war zone.

CHAPTER 8
IS THIS LOVE?

The empty house creaks and groans, haunting me as I toss sleepless in my bed. Staring into darkness, I recount my nightly lockdown. Did I latch the back door? The kitchen window? Lights from passing ships flicker through the trees and project silhouettes on my thin curtains. Sea gusts whip the shadows into pugilistic rapists and robbers. Shoobee's burrowed beside me in the bed. Her stillness is the only reassurance of our safety.

Three months after our life-changing Christmas, Mum is still locked away.

She is an open wound struggling to heal in the cavernous echoes of a psychiatric hospital. I remind myself she has specialists tending to her broken heart. And those creepy noises in the house are better than smashing glass and screaming insults—right?

As sunlight fills my bedroom, fear slips away. But I have no reason to spring out of bed. At eighteen, I've just lost my first job in the art world. A Drogheda print shop owner allowed me to work for him to gain experience as a favor to Dad. I was grateful and worked hard. But my zeal could not overcome my fumbling, and I got sacked from a job I was doing for free.

I'm shocked and disappointed that my artistic prowess is not welcomed into the working world. Did I expect fanfare? Perhaps, but I must keep trying because my applications to veterinary nursing and horticultural college were flatly rejected. So I fill long days compiling my art portfolio and bi-weekly projects for Dad's artist friend, Liam O'Broin. O'Broin critiques my work with varying degrees of enthusiasm and assigns each new project. Our goal is to build a portfolio that's a strong presentation for entry into the National College of Art in Dublin.

When the stare-down with a blank page defeats me, I take Shoobee for a walk. We amble through the surrounding fields that isolate our property. My dog's darting motions incite the hormone-injected cattle to chase us. Laughing, I escape the stampede. Near the riverbank, I watch flocks of sandpipers flip from dark to light as they simultaneously swoop and sway in the sky.

My life without parents finds a rhythm of training at the boxing gym three nights a week where my need to belong is fulfilled, accompanied by grunts and groans and human breathing. Dodging punches to my face temporarily erases my loneliness.

I'm sparring regularly with guys now and I'm improving. I've bloodied several noses and even scored my first knockdown. My defence isn't good, though, and Joe's been stingy with instruction. He offers excuses not to hold up the hand pads for me. Perhaps he doesn't want to be seen wasting his time training a girl. I try to learn by watching others and studying books, but it hasn't stopped me from getting pummeled.

I'm not proud of my scrapes and contusions because a good boxer shouldn't be marked up all the time. Every fortnight when Dad takes me grocery shopping, I worry he'll notice my hard-to-hide facial bruises.

My sparring captures the interest of a *Drogheda Independent* sports reporter, Hubert Murphy. I'm afraid he'll blow my cover. Dad doesn't know I spar with guys, so I tell the dashing journalist I'm the first female Master of Ceremonies for boxing in Drogheda, a total contradiction to my shy nature but encouraged by the club's treasurer, Séamus McGuirk. The only thing Murphy wants to know, however, is why a young girl would get hit for a sport with no future. Don't I know girls aren't allowed to box? *Because I love it* is the only explanation I offer. I don't try to explain that boxing is as important to my life as breathing.

Thank goodness my face is unmarked when Dad picks me up for our grocery run. We head to Harry's Supermarket beside Mornington Beach, and Murphy's article is due in the newspaper. Sure enough, there's a write-up and big photo of me posing a staged left hook on the jaw of a young man. The caption reads: *"Take that!* Deirdre Gogarty with sparring partner Barry Leonard, Brookville."

Dad gasps at the photograph. "I hope you don't do anything silly like actually getting hit? You don't even have a gum shield!" This is true. I don't have a gum shield. Dad would be horrified to know I've had terrible pain in my front gums where a poorly padded knuckle slammed me. But I'm afraid to upstage the guys by showing my seriousness and buying a gum shield. "I don't need to be repairing my little girl's mandible," he warns, half-joking.

To escape Dad's further scrutiny, I roll a trolley down the food aisles and buy whatever is easiest to preserve and prepare: frozen stuffed pancakes, frozen peas, spuds, powdered milk, cereal, tea, Mr. Kipling's custard pies, and of course Pedigree Chum for Shoobee. Sandy-footed children in their bathing togs slurp Choc Ices and surround the checkout stand, where I find Dad waiting for me.

I look forward to these shopping trips. I can't carry much on my bicycle, and the bread man and milkman have stopped delivering since Mum's not home to pay them. Besides, shopping is the only time I see my father. It's too awkward to visit his office with Jean there. I don't know how to face her. I'm hurt and angry, yet I miss her company, and I feel guilty for it. She's my father's lover, my mother's enemy.

My sister Katherine is furious with Dad for abandoning me to live with his mistress. When I explain to her that Dad takes me shopping every other week and even lets me keep the change, her voice tightens. "It's a disgrace your father has left you in that house by yourself," she says. "Something terrible could happen." But Dad moved out a long time ago when he built the apartment. I know he's not coming back.

Shane and Katherine try to drop by every other weekend, but with their busy schedules it must be hard to visit this depressing house. Shane is married to Bernie now and works long hours as a pharmaceutical engineer. Katherine has a baby, a doctor husband who often relocates, and a demanding airline career. The only frequent visitor is my Indian friend, Seema, who is finishing her last year at the Grammar. Seema's dark, exotic looks make it difficult for her to fit in at school, but she and I bonded well as misfits.

On weekends I look forward to Seema's visits. Her deeply traditional and protective parents approve of me enough to allow their daughter to ride the bus from her home near the beach to spend the day. One day her parents will arrange her

51

marriage. This makes my house the ideal hideout to sneak a visit with her boyfriend, Willie.

Willie is always good for a laugh. "Why don't you just call me Penis," he jokes of his name. He and Seema hang out while I work on my portfolio in the dining room, which I've converted to an art room. I moved the silver candlesticks and spread paper and pencils over the mahogany hunting table, where my assigned art projects are often set aside because I prefer to illustrate the magnificent muscles of boxers in battle.

A talented artist, Willie sometimes draws alongside me. He insists his brother Paul would love to see my work. Seema also urges me to meet Willie's brother, and a few days later, Paul appears. He's tall and skinny with long, dark, curly hair like a heavy-metal band member. He admires my artwork without overdoing the praise. His confidence and quick wit appeals to me. As he leans on the hunting table to study my drawings, his brown eyes gaze into mine. I'm worrying what he would think if he knew of my boxing when Seema blurts out, "And she's a boxer, too. Her picture was in the paper."

But Paul surprises me by saying, "You're too pretty to be a boxer."

A short while later, the four of us are zipping through the countryside in Paul's gleaming red Ford sedan. We're off to experience one of Paul's favorite sports, stock car racing. While Paul and Willie discuss throttles and spoilers, Seema gives me the details: Paul is twenty-four, a drummer in a heavy metal band (no surprise there), and a chef at a retirement home (a total surprise).

My new friends bring life and noise to my empty house. The next time they come over, Willie sets the stereo speakers outside to blare music as loud as we want. Depeche Mode and Howard Jones for Willie. Guns 'N' Roses and Queen for Seema and me. Megadeth and Metallica for Paul. We have water fights, Frisbee games, and we wrestle on the lawn. We eat rubbish and watch TV. Willie drinks beer and sunbathes on the roof in his underwear. Seema won't join him because she doesn't want her foreign skin any darker. I'm living a teenager's fantasy: a big house in the country with friends to share the fun of unsupervised living.

And nothing's more fun than speeding along country roads in Paul's sporty car, which he skids into patches of loose gravel. One day, while ripping snake marks into the earth, Paul builds up too much speed as he curves back to the road and smashes into a telephone pole. His prized possession is a steaming heap. But he's not distressed over the car—it's the blood oozing from my lip he cares about. Paul's concern is so sweet and amusing because I've taken much harder punches. Heavyweights hit me full force in the face, yet this cool, head-banging drummer is concerned about a simple bloody lip.

The night of the accident, long after I've gone home and cleaned myself up, Paul cycles miles to my house to offer another apology. Saying goodnight from his uncharacteristic bicycle seat, he leans forward and gently kisses my bruised lip. That little kiss weakens my knees more than three rounds of boxing.

Now I can't wait for the days Paul is home from his job in the nearby coastal town of Skerries. Some nights, we watch TV and snuggle on the couch with his arm around me. He wrestles me to the floor while Shoobee darts about barking. Can this be happening to me? I'm amazed by my good fortune to have Paul in my life that sometimes I wonder if he just isn't a dream.

To add to my good luck, I win a *Daily Mirror* newspaper competition by answering questions about Barry McGuigan, and the prize is an all-expense-paid trip for two to London to see the former champion's first comeback fight. It's been two years since the agonizing loss of his title. It's the event of a lifetime. But I don't choose Paul to accompany me, or even my best friend Seema. I'm afraid to jinx my own access to boxing by allowing non-boxing people into my sacred world. So I choose Joe Leonard, the man who invited me into the gym.

The slagging I endure over choosing Joe is long forgotten as I look around London's breath-taking Alexandra Palace, a spectacular venue in which to witness my first professional boxing show. I am awestruck as "The Dark Destroyer," Nigel Benn, wins the Commonwealth middleweight title with a snarling destruction of Abdul Sanda in less than two rounds.

When the main event finally starts, my longtime hero enters the arena to hysterical applause. I clap until my hands throb and cheer until my throat burns. I can hardly contain myself as I watch McGuigan bob and weave, slip and counter, jab and hook his way to a fourth-round knockout over a game Nicky Perez. The thrill of watching McGuigan in the ring confirms my desire to box in a real fight. I'm giddy as I confide my wishes to Joe.

"The Irish Amateur Boxing Association will never allow women to box," Joe says. "Not in a million years." I swallow my disappointment and swing my thoughts to something that I can have, and it makes me miss Paul like crazy.

The first night I'm home, Paul comes over and we cruise through the night in his repaired and polished car. The headlights jolt along the sudden dips and twists of the dune roads. He rumbles straight for the Maiden Tower and swerves from her base at the last second. We catapult onto Mornington Beach and carve deep circles into the smooth black sand. The crests of the Irish Sea blur in streaks as we twirl under the stars.

Paul stops the car and we get out. He takes me by the hand and we stroll a little way across the beach, then lie down on the ground. There on the cold sand against my boyfriend's warm body, I'm content and happy. I listen to waves crash on the shore as the lyrics to Whitesnake's new hit, "Is This Love," play over and over in my head.

The next week I pine for Paul while he works in Skerries. He is the rock on which my contentment is founded, and he has made living alone in this house more than just bearable. It is a treat. I make up my mind—no more playing it cool. The next time Paul is home, I'm telling him I want to go steady. I do not eat or drink or sleep or even box without thinking of him.

Love is exhausting.

At last it is Paul's day off, so I stay in earshot of the phone. But he doesn't call. So I watch the driveway. But he doesn't appear. Maybe he had to work an extra day. I call his house. Willie answers and says Paul is busy. I don't ask questions because I don't want to sound desperate—but I am desperate. The following day I can't stand it any longer. I ring until Paul answers the phone. He is friendly but does not mention coming over. It's as if nothing ever happened between us.

Days grind into weeks and my heart aches in turmoil. All I can do is cry and listen to love songs. Embarrassed that anyone might know I bought The *Greatest Love Collection II*, I pull it from its hiding place in a drawer under my knickers. The CD echoes my heartbreak. Terry Jacks makes me miss my childhood friends with "Season in the Sun." Sad Café lets me wallow in pain with "Every Day Hurts." But the most embarrassing is a song by Cliff Richard. What would my friends think if they knew I listened to Cliff Richard? But no one is here, so I turn up the sweet falsetto on my uncool CD and croon: *But these miss you nights are the longest.*

Two months of Paul's kisses have turned me into a heartbroken fool. Now, when I most need his comfort, he's nowhere to be found. It seems the pain of rejection cannot be soothed. Even my best friend Seema offers no solution, because she's got her own boy problems: she's busy spying on Willie, who's been avoiding her with cancelled dates and lame excuses.

I devise a scheme to run into Paul in a way that will seem completely casual. The love of my life and his family are regular patients at my father's dental practice. So I will swallow my pride and face Jean in order to gain access to Dad's appointment book.

When I break the ice and approach her, Jean, she seems excited at the prospect of facilitating an ambush—or perhaps she's just glad I'm speaking to her again. Either way, I get what I need and find out that, sure enough, Paul is due a checkup. I tell Jean I will happen by, and we will just see what takes place.

The day arrives and I lie in wait for my chance to pounce. When I show up at just the right moment to bump into him, Paul seems genuinely pleased to see me and is friendly and funny as always. But my optimism is dashed when he leaves without any suggestion of a date.

Meanwhile, Willie has met someone else and has ended his relationship with Seema.

Heartbroken, my best friend finishes her leaving exams and moves to Dublin with her family. Now only Willie comes to visit me, and he comes only to whine about problems with his new girlfriend. The summer I looked forward to sharing with Seema, Willie, and Paul has been dashed on the rocks. To make matters worse, the boxing club is preparing to close for the season.

Bored to tears, I'm lost in fantasies of Paul realizing his mistake and skidding back into my driveway. But my hope is like a slowly deflating balloon. Then all the air goes out of it when, on a warm and windy day on West Street, I spot Paul strolling hand in hand with a pretty girl with long dark hair. They are both smiling. When he sees me, he drops her hand and his grin vanishes. He offers a warm greeting, so I nod back and pretend to be unfazed.

But of course I'm hopelessly lost, and lonely days of summer grind by with nothing to do but brood. It seems I've even managed to bore Shoobee, who looks at me with concern before she circles down to the floor with a sigh. I waste time trying to figure out why I'm rejected by everyone, but I find no answers and only deepen my self-pity. I glimpse my image in the mirror and am struck by the resemblance to Mum the fateful day when Dad left her. My emotional state scares me, so I sign up for two education courses in Dublin: graphic design and journalism.

I travel to Dublin to visit Mum, who has been relocated to St. Patrick's Hospital near Kilmainham. It's a shock to see her light brown hair sprouting grey roots. Gone are her fashionable outfits, high-heeled shoes, and make-up. Still, she looks graceful in her long, creamy-white nightgown and matching robe.

My mother is allowed to leave her room but refuses. Her progress is slow. She wails and moans about thirty-five years of marriage and seven children. "How could he do this to me?" she asks, as if I have the answer. She interrogates me incessantly about Dad's activities and is irritated by my lack of knowledge. But patience with Mum comes much easier since Paul left me. Now I understand the pain of a broken heart.

Mum gives me her ATM card to travel to my classes, but I'm afraid to spend any of the few hundred pounds left in her account. Her insurance only covers six months in the hospital. With guidance from her psychiatrist, she has arranged for a tenant to live in Dad's vacated apartment. I tell Mum I'm horrified at the thought of a stranger living on the grounds of our family home. But she insists it's the only way to keep us going.

I leave Mum's hospital room and walk to the National College of Art to drop off my portfolio for review. I am buoyant and certain my masterpieces will quickly ensure a letter of acceptance. On my way to the train station, I pass a bookshop where the image of Barry McGuigan catches my eye. He's on the cover of a book in the window called *The Fighting Irish*, by Patrick Myler. Without hesitation I purchase the paperback with my mother's ATM card.

On the train ride home I study the book's cover. The main photo is in color, McGuigan throwing his famous left hook. Five small black-and-white photos are stacked down the right side: tough-looking boxers in their stance or throwing a punch. But one photo looks out of place. The image is of a fighter with long hair that juts out in wavy curls. Behind him, half the wall appears to be fake bricks with spray-painted graffiti. The other half is plastered by gaudy, bold-patterned wallpaper. The out-of-place boxer holds a shillelagh in his fist and sports a mean face like an angry leprechaun.

He's got to be off his head to pose like that. Wondering how this joker made the cover, I open the book and turn to his story first. He is Pat McCormack from Dublin, described as "a reincarnation of the bare-knuckle, fight-to-the-finish pugilists of old." His story is colorful. He smokes between rounds and is led about the ring in a chain and collar like a wild animal.

Excited by my new purchase, I pull out a sketchpad and draw all the boxers on the cover, excluding McCormack. He just seems out of place, a painful reminder of how I must look in the boxing gym

A rejection letter from the National College of Art arrives in early September. A year spent working on my portfolio has come to nothing. Once again, failure knocks down my plans. But the boxing club is now open, so my shame and anger are unleashed on the heavy bag, which I hit harder and harder.

Even Dad is concerned about my stalled prospects. In October, he helps to enroll me in the Fitzwilliam Institute in

Dublin for a six-month course in animation, finished art, and graphic design. It is an intense full-time program.

Five days a week, transportation to university includes a three-mile cycle to the station in Drogheda, an hour-long train ride to Dublin, and then a bus ride to my course in Milltown. And then I do it all in reverse in the evenings with an added trip to the gym every Monday, Tuesday, and Thursday. It's dark as I cycle home down Mornington Road. I push against wet, icy gusts rolling in from the sea while my dim headlamp searches for potholes. The only sign of life is a jagged line of smoke from the cement factory across the river. Chilled to the bone I enter my dark, frigid home.

The Irish winter ushers in rats and field mice. Their scratchy feet scurry across the ceilings and along the corridor as if they own the place. It seems I've become like the old people in *Alone*, a booklet I flipped through in Dad's waiting room. The elderly depicted had no families and lived with rats in their squalid flats. I lie awake terrified by the stories of long-tailed, beady-eyed creatures darting into inhabited beds. Surely I'm too young to be living with vermin and loneliness. But I am, in fact, alone.

The apartment tenant, a young woman named Jackie, bitterly complains about infestations and various appliances not working properly. I report her problems to Dad, but he has no interest in spending time or money on the house. He says Mum needs to pull herself together and check out of hospital to take care of her responsibilities. I explain the disrepair to Mum, who says to ask my father. The tenant is nothing but a nuisance and an extra worry. I have enough problems with my own clogged toilets, roof leaks, and a broken washing machine.

The morning of November tenth, I'm boiling water to wash clothes when the doorbell rings. I hurry to answer, excited that someone has remembered my nineteenth birthday. But instead of a friend, I come face-to-face with a scowling stranger. A man I previously spied from my bedroom window ringing the bell. He always looks annoyed, so the door is never answered. Besides, strangers don't need to know I live alone.

"Where's the owner?" he snaps.

"Eh—my Dad will be home later," I lie.

"Well tell 'im he better pay his oil bill," he barks, shaking an invoice. "I've been waitin' for friggin' ever. I'll be back this time tamarra for me muney." He marches off before I can answer.

I'm relieved to spot Willie rambling up the driveway. I pour out my woes about the oilman, but Willie offers no advice. Instead, he whines that his girlfriend might be cheating on him. *Serves you right for cheating on Seema*, I think. Willie leaves without remembering my birthday.

Later that night Katherine rings from Dublin. Her twenty-one-month-old daughter wails in the background. My sister delivers my first birthday wishes and apologizes for our parents forgetting. She repeats how disgraceful it is that Dad has abandoned me. Her consoling voice is a moment's comfort, but when she hangs up there's nothing to soothe my disgust at the world.

Despair engulfs me as I weigh my options. I aspire to be a professional boxer, but women are not allowed to fight. None of the universities I applied to want me. I've lost all hope for Paul's return. And my family has disappeared. Is life worth living when it's filled with nothing but rejection and sorrow?

At midnight, I decide to put an end to my worthless existence and punish those who don't take notice of me. I'll disappear into the deep water. It'll be a couple of weeks before anyone realizes I'm missing, and I am sure I won't be hard for them to forget. To assure Shoobee's survival, I rip a hole in a giant bag of dry dog food and position bowls of water to look like they're collecting roof leaks. My beloved dog licks my face and whines to tag along, which intensifies my grief as I hug her goodbye.

The east winds whip my hands and face as I pedal to the fishmeal factory under a moonless sky. With countless reasons to die, I question why it's taken me so long to decide. I could've saved myself tons of angst. I don't want anyone to recognize me, so I pull up the hood on my jacket. When distant headlights flicker toward me, I swerve into the hedges and shut off my bike's headlight.

It's been said the Boyne drowns seven people a year on average. Now I want to be one of them. Silently, with no one to pull me to safety.

As I cycle the last lonely stretch of coastal road, the decaying shell of the fishmeal factory moans in the winter winds. The salty air stings my nose and ears, and I speculate whether the freezing water will kill me instantly. I also wonder what it feels like to drown. Is it painless or painful? Peaceful or terrifying?

I push through a gale to the pier and ponder the mechanics of my suicide. I become uncertain of how it will go. Of course, I will have to send my bike down first. But what if other evidence is found? I imagine Dad and his friends dredging the choppy waters. And then I see Dad's face when he discovers my lifeless body. I can't stand the vision of his pain. I also fear Mum will join me if I'm not around to save her.

But I move on and wobble my bicycle around the fishmeal factory toward the pier. Nearby are piles of fishing nets, ropes, chains, crates, cinder blocks, buoys, and barrels. I cull though the debris and choose a thick, heavy chain to sink my bike. My hands burn raw with cold as I pick through ropes and cinder blocks to attach to my legs and feet.

An icy wind slaps my face, and I drop a crumbling cinder block. I stare at the river's waves, kindled by a nearby starboard light that glows green and shimmers beneath the gaps in the pier's weathered boards. Halyards clang against the mast of a small yacht moored to the wharf. Maybe it will be the last sound I hear.

Do I want eternal silence? I search my soul for an answer, for a glimpse of hope, for a reason to be in this world. Then over the clanging of the halyards, I begin to hear the young men cheering my name while I sparred with Blackie: *Deir-dra! Deir-dra! Dier-dra!* I yearn for the sound of their cheering again, and that desire is a little spark of hope, a glimmer of a question that beguiles me. What if I could find a way to box, to compete in the ring? What if there is even a remote chance? I'll never find out if I slip to the bottom of the river. I look at the cold black water and I know boxing is worth a shot.

I grab my bicycle and pedal home to Shoobee as fast as my legs can take me.

Chapter 9
Soul for Sale

The next night I head straight to the gym. Joe gloves me up to spar with my frequent partner, Pentony, a fifteen-year-old boy with light-brown hair and faded freckles. He circles the ring with his chin up and thumps together his poorly padded gloves—the same gloves he wore a few weeks ago when he damaged my front gums.

It's still early, and not many fighters have rolled in, so the gym is quiet. There will be no band of boys to cheer me on tonight. But that's okay. Their cheers and this sport have saved my life—from now on, I'll be nothing but serious about becoming a champion boxer.

Gloved and ready, I am fueled by a renewed energy that grows with every bounce on my toes. As soon as the bell rings, I double jab and snap back my partner's head, three times in a row. Pentony draws back his right hand, but I step back, out of range. The boy hesitates, and then loads another right. But I slip away again, and he fails to launch a bomb.

"Just throw it!" shouts Joe.

"I can't! She keeps stepping back," says Pentony, as he glances toward the coach.

Never take your eyes off your opponent is a golden rule of boxing, and my sparring partner has just broken it. So with a sharp twist of my hips, I strike his nose with a left hook. Blood splatters across the teenager's face, and a drop of his blood lands in my mouth. I batter his damaged nose with left hooks and right hands. Then I fire a right uppercut, which he falls into, his expression twisted.

Near the end of three rounds, Pentony bends at the waist, so I club his ribs with left and right roundhouses. At the sound of the bell, I am intoxicated with the new shift of power between us. My sparring partner storms out the ring. I lean on the ropes and watch him shove toilet paper up his nose.

I finish my workout by pounding the punching bag and speedball for an hour. My motions are in perfect rhythm. I am controlling the speedball the way I just took control of another human being, no longer the victim. If I can continue to repeat this scenario, I will have a future I can live in.

By December, I need every ounce of my new resolve. The oilman has not been paid and shuts off the central heat. He bangs on the front door. I have no money to pay him, so I hide until his blue van peels out the driveway. I try not to turn on any lights for fear of running up an electric bill. But mostly I sit in the dark to keep the tenant and her complaints away.

A family friend, Brendan Traynor, tends the grass without asking for payment. He even lugs over a scrawny Christmas tree, which I set up in the front window. My intention is to quell local gossip that the house is abandoned. Nothing feigns joy and togetherness better than a glittering tree in the window. Even if it's a sparkling reminder of the one-year anniversary of Dad's leaving.

I spend Christmas day at Katherine's with my siblings and Mum, who's out of hospital on a holiday pass. Some holiday. She is pale and bony, so thin her pants look like a long, straight skirt. She's wearing a smear of lipstick but forgot to comb her hair. She spends the afternoon sobbing, her face in her hands. She looks up only to pull tissues from her purse and dab at her tears. At the dinner table my sisters and I coax her to eat.

"C'mon, Mum, eat up, it's a lovely meal," my sister Sheena says. But Mum does not respond. So we exchange pleasantries among ourselves and eat turkey and stuffing, roast potatoes, and cranberry sauce. Mum stares with half-open eyes at the untouched fork beside her plate. Afterward, we steer our mother into the sitting room. We tear open our gifts, but Mum's colorful packages sit neatly at her feet while she stares blankly at the fire. We dare not mention Dad. It's as if he died and is buried under our inability to explain him. Relieved when the day finally ends, I wonder if tomorrow, Saint Stephen's Day, will be any better. The family gathers again but this time at Shane and Bernie's Georgian house in Sandyford. Mum brings along the same strange stare.

I spend New Year's Eve in Mornington and snuggle with Shoobee next to a sluggish electric radiator in front of the TV. We watch smiling people ring in the New Year as they kiss and hold hands and sing along to words that ask should old acquaintance be forgot. Perhaps Mum could move on with her life if she could just forget about Dad. She's given him all control. I wish she could take it back, the way I've learned to control the heavy bag and my sparring partners at the gym.

From winter to spring, I become more and more like one of the guys on Dyer Street. When I hold out my hands to be wrapped, no one seems to wonder why a girl is there anymore. And in the ring, they have no time to even think about the fact that I'm not a boy. They're too busy ducking or eating my punches.

The control I feel in the ring begins to follow me out of the gym. In March, the Fitzwilliam Institute delivers on its promise of a job placement opportunity. Japanese/American animator Jimmy Murakami visits our class to recruit employees for his new company, Murakami Wolf Dublin, Ltd. I am one of only five students selected to work on a new television series, *Teenage Mutant Ninja Turtles*.

I graduate from the Fitzwilliam Institute with a degree and strive at my new job painting animation cells. Weekdays, I cycle the long, potholed road to Drogheda, ride the train into Dublin, and then walk a half hour to work. Training at the gym is held only three evenings a week, so nights without boxing I spend working overtime.

As soon as I adjust to my new routine, Mum is released from hospital under the care of physiatrist Dr. John Cooney. Declaring the house is too painful a reminder, he refuses to allow her to move back home to Mornington. She rents an apartment in Dublin and sends a realtor out to sell the family home.

The realtor crawls through my house and complains of leaks in the roof and rotten window frames. I don't want the house sold, and I feel alternately angry and ashamed when potential buyers criticize it. Mum's garden is wild. Overgrown clematis and wisteria have smothered the sun-lounge windows, and Dutch elm disease has killed the trees that mark the front entrance.

A few months pass and the condition of my Mornington home dampens any buying interest, which suits me fine—it's not just a place to live, it's a big piece of my soul. But tonight, as

I cycle home from the gym, something about the house looks different. I jam down the brake pedal, and my bike wobbles underneath me. I step off and let it fall to the ground. As I stand, staring, the sign blurs through my tears. The FOR SALE sign has been tacked over. A brash SOLD sign looms out of the darkness.

CHAPTER 10
SAVIOURS

After eighteen months in and out of the hospital, Mum and I are together again. We live in her tiny apartment in Clontarf, an area on the north side of Dublin. The flat is comfortable, but my mother sips so much vodka, the drink rarely leaves her hand. Her cockeyed self-medication scares and angers me. On the list, too, I miss Shoobee, who's had to go and live with my sister Katherine.

But my top priority is to find a gym here in Dublin.

I dig though the five small boxes that hold my belongings and find a list of phone numbers for the Irish Amateur Boxing Association's board members. Breathing courage, I dial the number for IABA President Felix Jones. But there's no answer. Next on the list is Vice President, Breandán O'Conaire. After punching in the numbers, I double cross my fingers. When a man answers, I ask for Brendan O'Conner.

"This is Breandonn O'Conair-ra." He corrects my ignorant English pronunciation of his Gaelic name.

"My name is Deirdre Gogarty. I—I just moved here from Drogheda. And I'm looking for a gym—I want to train."

"I'm sorry. We only offer boxing."

"Yes! That's what I'm looking for. I've been training at the Drogheda Boxing Club for two years now and—"

"Women can *not* box," he interrupts. "Not according to the rules of the European Amateur Boxing Association."

"I just want to train," I lie.

"There are plenty of other sports for women. You would be much better off putting your efforts into one of those."

"But boxing is the only sport I'm interested in."

"Perhaps you could take a test to become a judge or a referee."

"Yes, sure but I love boxing—I just want to train. I don't need any special facilities. I'll come dressed in my tracksuit and won't interfere—"

"All right," he says, clearing his throat. "I'm the head trainer for Bay City Boxing Club. We'll be open tomorrow at seven. Up the road from Kilbarrack DART station. Do you know where that is?"

I want to tell him everyone knows it's one of the most dangerous parts of Dublin. I just say yes.

"And there is also a place called Saint Saviours," he adds. "It's in the old fire station on Dorset Street. Perhaps they will let you train."

While pouring out my appreciation for O'Conaire's offer, I suddenly realize he has hung up. My fingers are cramped as I put down the receiver.

After a sleepless night on Mum's couch, I cycle to work. Dublin Bay and the sleepy flowerbeds of Fairview Park awaken to the hum of city traffic. I maneuver my bike through crossroads with impatient drivers who have no tolerance for greenhorns. Double-decker buses bully past and leave me behind in dark plumes of stink.

Inside the lofty glass offices of Murakami Wolf, I paint endless animation cells of the teenage mutant ninja turtles. In the scene on my work table, Leonardo, Michelangelo, Donatello, and Raphael stuff themselves with pizza and ready their weapons to spring into action. But I can only imagine what happens in the scenes. Working art is drawn and painted by dozens of artists in an assembly-line environment without the benefit of storyboard or sound. We will not see the finished work until it airs on Saturday morning television after months, or possibly years, of production and negotiation. It looks like a pretty weird cartoon, and I wonder if it will even make it.

Many of my co-workers resemble two of the cartoon's characters, Rocksteady and Bebop. They wear their rebellion as mohawks, nose rings, and painful-looking piercings. I'm less afraid to be myself here than in school or with any other group. Yet, even among these nonconformists, I'm still on the outside. I've no interest in nightclubs or raves, alcohol or acid. I've read too many stories of nightlife ruining good boxers. My workmates say I'm too young to be slogging in a gym instead of going out on the town. I don't tell them I would never trade my boxing for forgotten small hours of dim lighting, cheap drinks, and sticky-fingered fumblings.

Besides, I need to keep my wits about me. Every day employees slip through the Murakami Wolf turnstile of hiring and firing. I've already been warned for my slow working pace. My mind too often drifts to boxing. I'm both excited and anxious, wondering if things are going to work out for me at the new boxing club. Like the cartoon scenes I paint, I just can't see the storyboard.

After work, in a bathroom cubical, I quickly change into my tracksuit. Another battle with Dublin traffic ends without mishap and I lock my bike to a railing at Connelly Station. It actually crosses my mind to jump on a train to Drogheda. I resist the temptation and board a northbound DART train. As the train pulls into my station, I'm reminded of a half-joke among train travelers: *Always duck while traveling through Kilbarrack.* Rocks often crash through train windows to shower passengers with glass in the jurisdiction of unruly teenagers. Maybe I should be afraid of getting off the train in a notoriously bad area of Dublin, but I'm not. My only worry is what will happen when I enter the new boxing club.

Stepping onto the platform of Kilbarrack station, alone, where weeds poke up between the cracks, I'm struck how my love for boxing sometimes overrules my better judgment. The train doors hiss closed behind me and I'm left to fend for myself. Scar-faced high-rise flats loom above me as I climb the pedestrian bridge steps. At the top I turn onto the crossover. Tall metal barriers ablaze with graffiti obscure the outlook. I don't want to risk the danger of getting trapped in this blind alley, so I push into a sprint. Broken bottles crunch under my feet as I rush to the far side, back into plain view. An incoming southbound train tempts me to board. But I've come this far, and I'm not turning back.

A group of teenage skinheads loiter nearby as I negotiate the stony slope of crumbling concrete that leads to the pedestrian walkway. The teens wear spiked neck collars, black bomber jackets, turned-up jeans, and Doc Martens boots. A boy mutters something about my "arse," and they laugh while I hurry past and pretend not to hear.

I cut through a housing facility where small children play unsupervised. A pretty girl, hardly more than five, hops on a colorful tricycle and pedals into the street. An older boy, perhaps her brother, calls after her, "Veronica!" I'm warmed by his concern for the girl until he yells, "Get back over here, ya fockin' slut!"

Approaching Bay City Boxing Club, I feel a familiar dread. But this time the boxers do not stop and stare when I walk in. They are deep in the rigors of circuit training. The gym is huge and bare, devoid of the posters and spirit that Drogheda boasted. There is no ring, and the two punching bags hanging from basketball goals look unused.

I introduce myself to a silver-haired man by the door. He is friendly but appears confused when I start wrapping my hands. He points out O'Conaire, who looks nothing like a boxing coach. He is a skinny, delicate-looking man with long, wispy side-hair, balding on top. But he has a powerful voice and instructs the circuit training with military precision. I give O'Conaire a friendly smile. He sends me a tiny, expressionless nod.

I wait for an invitation to join in as the silver-haired man tells me O'Conaire works as a Gaelic schoolteacher. This explains the strict régime. The only sounds are the squeaks of rubber soles twisting on the gym floor, heavy grunts, and the lone voice of O'Conaire barking orders. There is no chatting.

Finally, the schoolteacher motions for me to stand in a line for picking partners.

Big surprise, I'm not picked.

O'Conaire has to perform the exercises with me, which adds to my unease as we stand back to back and twist to pass the medicine ball back and forth to each other. Then we sit on the floor sole to sole, to do sit-ups while holding the medicine ball and passing it again. After an hour of awkward exercises with my new coach, I walk in darkness back to DART station and ponder the strict workout.

I'm grateful for a place to train, though it reminds me more of school than a boxing gym. I miss Drogheda Boxing Club so much I have to choke back tears. As much as I am reluctant to enter yet another strange gym, tomorrow I will try Saint Saviours.

Back at Connolly Station my bicycle is destroyed, its lights smashed and tires punctured. I carry it home and to the repair shop the next day. I'm on foot when I leave work to find Saint Saviours. I pass the tranquility of Saint Stephen's Green and the Grafton Street shops that are closing for the evening. Around the dignified curve at Trinity College, I cross the River Liffey and climb O'Connell Street.

As dusk falls, I leave the bright city center. The streets are quiet and gloomy. After I walk around Parnell Square, people fade into shadows. I lift my shoulders and quicken my pace in order to appear in control and unafraid. In truth, I feel vulnerable to the faceless thugs on the streets.

Around the corner on Dorset Street is an old fire station. I stop and take it in, the mood of my reverie romantic. Its ghostly bell tower has an old-world dignity amid the rundown council flats. Long gone are the shiny machines that thundered through the enormous doors to save Dublin's fair city. Now those doors are closed and bricked up. The station looks tired and beaten, jaded and dirty, its breath shallow as it struggles to breathe. But it's easy to imagine wisdom in her battered old eyes.

My urgency to escape the streets pushes me right into the gym called Saint Saviours. No hesitation this time. Only a couple of steps, and I'm surrounded by a blaze of yellow- and red-painted walls. I have to turn sideways to slink past wall-to-wall guys skipping rope; my hand is wet from scooting my way along, my palm flat to the sweating ceramic tiles. I am relieved to see that they have a ring, at least, and I approach two older men standing beside it puffing cigarettes, watching dispassionately as two boxers destroy each other. The smoke drifts into center stage, where quick fists shred it. Up close, I smell tobacco and fresh blood.

Catching the eye of the smaller man, I tell him I'm looking for the trainer.

"I'm Pat," he replies, poking his thumb into his chest. "That's me bruder, John." He thumbs toward the taller man.

I introduce myself and tell him I want to train at this gym.

Pat furrows his scarred brow and tilts his head. "Now why would a pretty girl like yourself want to train with these bums?"

I laugh nervously and stare at the bloodstained canvas.

"And what about breast cancer?" he continues, cigarette hanging from his lips.

"Well, the chest area is not really a good target anyway," I try to explain.

"Does it hurt?"

"Not really," I lie, remembering a blow to my breast around period time. I divert the conversation. "So, were you a boxer?" Pat's silvery-blue eyes light up with familiarity.

"That's me winning the British light-welterweight title." He points to a fluorescent-faded photograph on the wall. A man with rippling chest muscles, hands stretched upward, his face beaming toward the heavens, and the Lonsdale belt strapped proudly around the tiny waist of a rugged youth.

"You look very frail," he says. "Can you take a punch?"

"Oh, yes. I've been sparring a lot, even with heavyweights."

"And do those fellas hit you?"

"After I give them a good pop on the nose."

Pat gives me a broad smile of neatly fitted dentures. As if I've passed his code of ethics, he asks, "So how'r'ya gonna be gettin' here?"

"On my bike," I chirp.

"All right then," he says, and then pauses to light another cigarette. "I'll train you the best I can. You can park your bike over there. It'll get nicked outside. You can change in the loo, so you don't have to go in the men's room. See you Monday."

Back at the flat, I search through boxing books for any mention of my new trainer. After I locate The Fighting Irish, the book I bought with Mum's ATM card, it dawns on me why Pat's mischievous eyes are so familiar. He's one of the five boxers to the right of McGuigan's larger photo on the book's cover. In fact, he's the corner-smoking, chain-wearing, shillelagh-yielding "bare-knuckle reincarnation." My new coach is Pat McCormack—the only boxer I didn't sketch because he seemed so out of place.

But I don't feel out of place on my first night at Saint Saviours. I'm in awe and eager to impress Pat McCormack. This man, after all, is hailed as a "modern-day Jack Dempsey." After critiquing my feverish shadowboxing, my new coach delivers his verdict. "No, no, no!" he scolds, grabbing my shoulders to hold me still. "Jaysus, you'll be bleedin' lifted out of it with footwork like that. Balance is the key. It will open all doors. Two weeks of *only* footwork. No punches!"

I want my new coach to show me how to knock people out, not put me through the tedium of where to put my feet. But for two weeks I step and slide, front to back, left to right, until Pat is satisfied with my balance enough to let me spar. At last, a chance to prove my fighting skills. But my opponent is tall with long arms and a lot of experience. The only thing I prove is that I have an appetite for raw leather.

"Well, yer balance is a lot better. But Jaysus, yer defense is bleedin' terrible. How were the club in Drawda lettin' you spar?"

In front of a mirror, I practice my punches and Pat strolls up to guide my hands forward and then back to my face. My reflection disappears behind his thick arms and wide shoulders. My coach smells of spicy cologne and tobacco.

"If I had a daughter boxing, I'd want someone to teach her how to defend herself," he says. "I got paid for this ugly mug. But you'll never get paid enough to end up with a face like mine."

He's still guiding my punches when a drunk stumbles into the gym. He takes one look at me and makes the shape of a woman with his hands, managing a long whistle.

"Piss off!" Pat yells, without diverting his eyes from coaching. The drunk ignores him and continues to whistle.

"Out!" Pat yells again and points a stiff-armed finger at the door. Then he marches up to the intruder, picks him up by his coat, and tosses him through the doorway and onto the street.

"Stupid bastard landed on his head," Pat says as he resumes coaching. "There's blood everywhere."

Minutes later, red lights flash outside to the howl of an ambulance siren.

"You see, you have to turn your fists over," Pat tells me, ignoring the drama beyond the windows. "It'll give you better snap on your punches."

The ambulance speeds away. Pat doesn't so much as look toward the door.

My weekly routine becomes to attend Saint Saviours on Monday, Thursday, and Sunday. Gyms are only open three days a week, but I can train an extra day since Bay City is open on Wednesday. Besides, I don't want Breandán O'Conaire to think I don't appreciate him letting me participate.

On Fridays after work, I take the long bike ride to Katherine's house in Goatstown to visit my beloved dog. Since the move, Shoobee's black patches of fur have turned grey and dull. Even her once-sparkling eyes are now cloudy. Her tail used to wag with a fierce samurai quickness when I'd enter a room, but now she just sniffs my feet, her tail hardly moving.

She has infuriated my brother-in-law by escaping the garden to scratch gouges in the neighbor's wooden gate. Katherine's more sympathetic, but her patience has thinned since Shoobee pooped on a handmade rug and the stain rotted the wool. I feel guilty that I can't rescue my best friend.

I can't rescue Mum, either.

She's stopped drinking, but I'm still unable to cope with her moods, so I spend most evenings away from the flat. The tiny apartment keeps me too close to her obsessive thoughts, complaints, and outbursts. And her constant warnings that I'm spending too much time in "those bad areas with strange men" only push me further away.

One night I visit one of my favorite hangouts, Moy Pub, on Dorset Street where Pat and his brother John are regulars. They tell me about the days of winning their British Crowns. Their connections to professional boxing in England are full of exciting possibilities. *And good thing*, I think, *since my hope of ever boxing in Ireland is rapidly fading.*

As if reading my mind, Pat says, "You can forget about boxing in Ireland. Those sexist fuckers will never give you a chance. There's no way they'll let a woman box in a man's world." He pauses to gulp his lager. "You've got to go abroad."

My chance to explore such possibilities comes along quickly. In February, Sheena invites me to visit her and Adrienne in London. I jump at the prospect. I hope for a change to find a fight through Pat's old acquaintances. After a couple nights with Sheena in her fashionable neighborhood on the outskirts of London, I convince her to let me stay with Pat's friend, Mickey Daniels, in Fulham on the east end of the city.

Mickey greets me warmly and sits me in his tiny kitchen. His wife serves a delicious fry-up of sausages and rashers and eggs while he reminisces about John and Pat's fighting days. I'm glued to his stories of Pat traveling the world in his thirst for blood, knocking people out—or getting knocked out.

We retire to the "good" room after dinner. A framed picture of Barry McGuigan hangs over the mantle. He's wearing his world title belt and standing against a gaudy backdrop of blue fading to mustard brown. I'm glad Mickey boasts this tacky picture of my idol. I muse over a collection of dramatic photos of Pat at war and can hear my coach's famous quote: *When the punches are going in and the blood is flowing, that's when you'll see me enjoying myself.*

The next morning, Mickey takes me down Old Kent Road to visit the Henry Cooper Club and the Upper Cut Club. I listen to hours of stories about "Enry's hammer" and his famous battles with Cassius Clay, a.k.a. Muhammad Ali. Mickey's elderly frame sags as the day continues, so I assure him I'll be fine researching London's legendary boxing scene on my own.

My first stop without Mickey is at Thomas á Becket Pub and Gym, where Pat trained for most of his professional career. I meet the proprietor, Gary Davidson, who is a friend of Pat's. He stops a solo game of snooker when I mention that Pat is my trainer and listens patiently while I explain my desire for a fight. "Sue Atkins is recognized as the British lightweight champ," he tells me. "Not officially, of course—it's all underground."

"Do you know how I can get a fight with her?"

"Not sure really, I don't know who's got her. Dean Powell might know. He's upstairs in the gym."

I go upstairs and find Coach Dean Powell lounging on a windowsill. I politely explain my quest to find Sue Atkins. But he only grunts a disdainful *dunno* in response. As if lifting his head would waste energy, Powell never takes his eyes off the magazine he's holding. I try again to get some information, but all my questions are met with a shoulder shrug and the back of his bald head. I leave empty-handed.

The next day I visit the famed Royal Oak gym in Canning Town, where heavyweight Frank Bruno trains. Trainer Terry Lawless flashes the familiar what's-a-woman-doing-here look, but Jamaican-born heavyweight Gary Mason is a friendly fellow. He allows me to stay and watch him spar. He asks me the one question everybody is so curious about: getting hit in the breasts. And what if I can't have children because of boxing? Great, I joke to myself. *No need for contraception.*

When I finally return to my sister's house, Sheena and Adrienne ask me about my future. They want to know why I've been wandering London, chatting up strangers, and what I'm planning to do with my life. So I tell them I have big ambitions to be a graphic designer. How could I explain that all of my ambitions are focused on the boxing ring?

CHAPTER 11
BLOOD, SWEAT, AND RAIN

I return home dejected over my inability to find a fight in London. Still, resolved not to let my determination waver, I attend an ex-boxer's dinner in Dublin with Pat and his brother John. I explain to anyone who will listen, my desire to find a match, hoping my quest falls on the ears of former British champions John Conteh, Howard Winstone, and John H. Stracey, who are the guests of honor. A man attending the event is struck by my story and offers a bit of hope. He tells me he's involved in an upcoming event and promises to help me find a fight in Ireland. I'm excited by the news, but Pat tells me the man's a bullshitter.

The following week at Saint Saviours, I'm excited to receive a letter from London. I rip the envelope open, praying for a fight offer. But no—it seems I've attracted a pervert who discovered me in a *Sunday World* newspaper article about my attempts to find an underground fight. The letter's author tells me he gets aroused sitting in bed with my photo on his wall. In my head I hear echoes of my mother's warnings about strange men.

When I arrive home at Mum's new townhouse—on the outskirts of Dublin, in Sandymount near the beach—I'm surprised to find the house cold and dark. A phone call reveals Mum is back in the hospital. She had stopped eating a while back and refused to get out of bed, but I had done my best to sustain her with a nutrition drink. I push back against my usual guilt for the relief I feel that Mum is under professional care.

Months pass as I continue to prepare for a possible fight. I do not go back to Bay City. Instead, I substitute by going to Mount Tallant to spar with eight-time national bantamweight champion Mick Dowling. Though Dowling hung up his gloves fifteen years ago, he infuriates me with his uncanny defence. He holds his left hand down and buries his chin behind his left shoulder. There should be no way he can lift his shoulder high enough to block a shot to his temple. But every time I fire my right hand, it slides harmlessly over the top of his headgear. I try to follow with a sharp left hook, but it only connects with his perfectly placed right glove. As he slips and slides, my hands hit nothing but arms, or air. I am baffled and exhausted. Dowling teaches patience, but also that I have to run extra miles to build my stamina.

Saint Saviours becomes my haven when it doesn't close for the summer, and I'm given the chance to spar with amateur champion middleweight Tommy Mullen. Tommy returned from England to box in the Irish National Championships. He emulates fellow southpaw and idol Marvelous Marvin Hagler, and even though I'm a Sugar Ray Leonard fan, it's amazing to watch Mullen's precise impression of Hagler. He throws a short right hook off his jab to turn foes' legs to jelly, and then he finishes opponents with a devastating straight left.

Preparations for my possible matchup at an upcoming boxing promotion in Ireland are clouded when Pat is told by the higher-ups of boxing not to train me anymore. Apparently, they don't want Pat to encourage me as a potential liability. On the verge of the event, someone wants to impound my trainer. But Pat ignores the order and our training continues.

Despite the gathering storm clouds, I wait for an opponent to step up. My hopes are dashed, though, in the days leading to a potential match. Acting as a go-between, former amateur great, Harry Perry, informs Pat and me that the IABA is adamantly opposed to a women's fight and will never allow it, not even as an exhibition. Hiding under the umbrella of the European Amateur Boxing Association, they claim women can't box for "medical reasons," namely the risk of breast cancer. There have been no studies that conclusively link breast cancer to contact sports. Regardless, my debut is off.

Pat tracks down an old friend in London who knows Sue Atkins: Mick Hussey, my new campaigner for a match with the British lightweight champion. But months pass with no word from Hussey. My chance to fight Sue Atkins looks slim. But my disappointment wanes when Katherine brings Shoobee for a weekend visit.

Monday morning I reach across the bed for the comfort of my dear friend, but Shoobee is gone. I can hear my mother in the kitchen. She's been home for a long stretch and has even gone back to work. I join her near the sink and ask if she's seen my dog. "She was scratching to go out," Mum says, as she fills a kettle for tea.

Not wanting to be late, I hurry to dress for work. The phone rings. I want to ignore it, but I'm curious who would call so early.

Over the line, Katherine's voice is low and gentle. "Someone spotted my number on Shoobee's collar and called me," she says. "She was hit by a car."

A punch to the stomach. I can't speak.

"I'm so sorry, Deirdre. She was killed."

Katherine's next words fade as I crumple to the floor.

At work I'm unable to focus. I've spent half my life with Shoobee. My thoughts drift to memories of stomping through fields of wheat. Her eyes gleaming with curiosity, delight, even compassion. She witnessed my first kiss, and I'd swear she felt my first heartbreak. Shoobee was my most devoted friend.

The phone rings and jolts me back to the office. My supervisor complains I'm taking too many calls. I explain they are sympathy calls. "Cheer up," she tells me. "It's just a dog."

Four weeks after Shoobee's death, I'm sacked from Murakami Wolf. I'm due a raise, but instead I'm dismissed without warning. I am furious and file a lawsuit.

As it always seems in my life's story, something comes along to balance the score. It's the break I've been waiting for—an invitation to fight, not in London but in Holland.

I need medical clearance, so Pat sends me to Doctor Purcell on Amiens Street. I wait outside for hours with coughing and spluttering vagrants. Doctor Purcell finally arrives in a muddy, cluttered van with a large mutt in the passenger seat.

Purcell has wild hair and an unkempt beard. He slams the door and hurries inside. He looks more prepared to treat cows than people. Surely he'll sign anything. His informality ends when he sees TO COMPETE IN BOXING on my medical release form. He gruffly tells me to go to a boxing doctor and shouts, "Next!"

I'm desperate to get medical clearance, but I can't go to a boxing doctor. They operate through the IABA, and there's no way they will approve me. I choose a female physician out of the phone book. But she refers me to a female coworker who says I have an irregular heartbeat and cannot approve the release.

I try another doctor on the far side of Dublin for fear those in a neighborhood talk to one another. After a ten-minute appointment, which I spend praying he doesn't detect my so-called irregular heartbeat, Doctor Casey approves my medical for a fee of forty pounds.

A week after I post the paperwork to Holland, someone from RTÉ Broadcasting phones to say chat show host, Pat Kenny, wants to interview me on his national radio program. I agree to the meeting and my host begins with a warm, to-the-point introduction, "Twenty-one years of age," says Kenny, "nine-and-a-half stone, lightweight division, in the prime of physical fitness, and yet cannot get a bout. What sort of boxer is that? I'll tell you what sort of boxer that is—it is a female boxer and her name is Deirdre Gogarty, and she is here with me now in the studio. Good afternoon, Deirdre."

"It's great to see you, Pat."

"It's great to see you, too. I read about you—you're intent on having a career in amateur boxing."

"That's right," I say. "I've been trying for four years and I'm still trying to get a contest. I haven't succeeded. And there seems no possibility of having a contest in this country because under IABA rules, it's not allowed that women box."

We discuss the details of IABA rules, and then Kenny surprises me with an arranged call-in from my boxing hero, Barry McGuigan. I am so excited that I fumble my words. However, McGuigan disappoints me by saying, "I believe women are things of beauty and shouldn't be gettin' hit." I am stunned, utterly speechless. But then Barry brings a lump to my throat when he says, "However, if you have a talent, Deirdre, go for it. Because without boxing, I'd'ave been nothin'."

Late that night, a man calls to say he heard the interview and can find me a fight. His name is Jimmy Finn. He claims to have witnessed several topless boxing shows in England.

"Sue Atkins boxed in one," he says. "She was not topless herself, but she fought a girl who was. Maybe you should think of fighting that way? Just to get some experience."

"This is a sport, not a freak show," I snap, surprised by my venom, and I hang up.

After the interview there is no response. Not even the people in Holland, who requested the medical release forms, bother to contact me.

Then Jimmy Finn calls again—this time with news of a three-round exhibition match in Limerick in one week. Not a real fight, he reminds me. That would be illegal. But he's scheduled a nine-stone fight - a 126-pound limit - against an experienced kick-boxer who wants to try boxing. "With clothes on, of course," he adds.

I finally have a chance to compete in the ring and prove that women can box.

On June 30, 1991, Pat and I travel an hour by train to Jimmy Finn's hometown of Portlaoise. Finn, a sandy-haired man with the slender build of a track runner, picks us up at the station. Before he drives us to Limerick, about a two-hour drive, we stop at Finn's upscale apartment to watch a tape of Sue Atkins versus Jane Johnson. I'm relieved it's a real fight, with both boxers properly dressed.

"Aren't they something? Mighty tough," boasts Finn. "You'll need a few fights before you get in with one of those gals."

"Bollox!" says Pat, then dismissively swipes the air. "Deirdra'd destroy both of 'em."

On the way to Limerick, I become suddenly suspicious that Finn may be the letter-writing pervert. I explain my suspicions to Pat while Finn pays for petrol. Pat rummages though his glove box, looking for Finn's handwriting to compare to the letter that I brought along on a hunch. We can't find anything that matches before Finn peers through the gas station window and sees Pat searching his car.

"I was lookin' for chewin' gum," my ally tells him.

We arrive at the Shannon Arms pub for the weigh-in. The outdoor ring, the centerpiece of the pub's colorful back garden, surprises me. P.J. Bennis, the show's promoter and my opponent's trainer, examines me and nods his approval without asking me to step on the scales.

My fight is the only boxing match scheduled on the day otherwise devoted to kickboxing. Early-comers order drinks and claim spots under giant patio umbrellas advertising Harp and Carlsberg. Fight fans are unfazed by the grey clouds that threaten rain.

Jimmy Finn is giddy as he searches the growing crowd for my opponent. I don't want to meet her—I'm glad just to know she's here and ready to box. But Finn comes back with a tall, slender redhead and introduces me to my challenger, Anne-Marie Griffin. She is a local girl and a seasoned kick-boxer. She seems as uncomfortable as me when we exchange nods and brief eye contact. I'm glad when she turns away—I don't want to see her again until it's time for our bout in the ring.

As the large crowd cheers the strikes of its local fighters, I realize they will not be rooting for me. With the rest of the day's visiting fighters, I'll be placed in the cheerless blue corner. But it's my fault I have no supporters here—not a single friend or family member—because I've kept my match a secret.

It begins to rain, and the fighter's shiny bodies spray on impact. I'm worried they'll stop the show, but the Limerick people huddle under thin summery hoods and patio umbrellas or simply hunch their shoulders against the downpour. They lean over their pints or cover them with coasters. This cocktail of beer and fights is too good to abandon.

Finally, it's my turn. As Pat tightens my gloves, a shiver crawls into my stomach for the first time today. Why am I suddenly afraid? My coach hangs a towel around my neck, and another fighter offers his robe. "So you won't get the chills," says Pat. He places the robe over my shoulders.

As I step across mud puddles, I imagine a hundred eyes on me. I study the ground on my way to the ring. As I climb through the ropes, a welcome sense of calm replaces the trembling in my stomach. Then a barefooted Anne-Marie springs into the ring. Her long, lean muscles seem to twitch with confidence.

Face to face, I try something I learned from my sparring partner, Tommy Mullen, and stare into Griffin's eyes. To my surprise, it works. Her eyes dart away, and I know I've already won the psychological battle.

Pat gives me his final instructions: "Jab to the head, right to the body. And careful, the ring's slippy."

At the bell I shoot toward Griffin and pop her face with left jabs. She retaliates with a one-two that grazes the side of my head. The crowd applauds their girl as I dip underneath my opponent's attack and throw left and right hooks to her stomach and penetrate her defence with a right hand to her head. Pat roars instructions while Griffin struggles to move out of my way. The referee breaks the action and cautions Pat against coaching from the corner.

I continue to breach Griffin's long reach and defence. Every time she knocks down my jab with her right hand, she fails to follow up with a jab or a punch. Pat's instructions echo in my mind, so I work up and down her tall frame: *body, head, body-body, head-head, body-body*. My momentum forces Griffin backward. She tries to grab onto my shoulders. But her efforts busy her arms, so I attack her exposed midsection.

In the second round I go over the top and land several rights to my opponent's nose, which gushes blood. I instinctively go after the injury. The referee breaks us apart just as Griffin shoves my forehead with her right hand in frustration. But I work my way right back inside and land two hard rights to her face.

The ref stops the action to wipe and pinch Griffin's nose to stem the flow of blood. I wait in the neutral corner, where a rush of adrenaline and a great idea invigorates me. As soon as the action resumes, I'll allow my opponent to back me into a corner and unleash another right to her injured nose. The force should increase the bleeding—or better yet, drop her to the mat.

After a long break I back toward the corner as planned. Griffin senses an advantage and rushes forward. But when she arrives, my feet are squared. *Thwack!* Griffin snaps my head back with a right of her own. My cheek stings as the crowd cheers. I quickly exit the foolishness of the corner and, as if sensing my embarrassment, Griffin cooperates by quickly backing away from my retaliation. I track her down and find her with a body shot and two snapping rights that drill past her guard. I pile on the pressure to erase her moment of victory.

In the final round, I rush in for the finish. Griffin's nose pours blood and the referee steps in and calls for the doctor. During the break my mind races with thoughts of ending the bout. I begin jumping in the air like the Cuban boxers I saw at the world championships—I thought it looked intimidating. Pat frantically waves his hands and motions for me to be still.

After the medical break, Griffin rushes me, but this time I have my back foot properly placed and she runs into my punches. I work her up and down, landing shots to score points and to confirm my control of the bout. The crowd applauds our efforts as the bell rings—the fight is over all too soon.

"You done brilliant!" Pat praises as he towels Griffin's blood off my arms.

"I felt so sloppy," I complain. "I could've done better."

"For the first time, your form was great. You done better than most of the fellas."

Jimmy Finn nods in agreement. Then he then raises and pumps his fists. "My goodness," he says. "I didn't know you were *that* good. We'll definitely have to get you a match against Atkins."

Griffin and I are motioned to the center of the ring for a decision. I realize I'd forgotten this was an exhibition, not a real fight with a winner and a loser. That is not allowed. Perhaps my opponent forgot as well; we fought like a championship was at stake. In fact, it looks like everyone forgot.

"A unanimous decision of the judges," the announcer begins.

I can't believe it. This was scored like a real fight after all.

"The winner," the announcer continues, "in the blue corner."

The referee raises my hand.

As I leave the ring, I notice the rain has stopped. An orange sun peeks from the clouds to dapple the crowd with luminous rosettes. Rain droplets sparkle on the trees and umbrellas, and the flower-scented breeze fills my lungs. Strangers smile and stop to praise my performance as we pack up to leave.

"They tried to pull a fast one," Pat says, "not tellin' they'd score it."

But I don't care. Four years of hard work has paid off, and being alive has never felt this good.

Chapter 12
London Underground

My sister Sheena moves back to Dublin from London. One afternoon, I sneak over to her apartment to visit Dad, unbeknownst to Mum. My father quietly flips through photos of my Limerick bout as I gnaw the inside of my cheeks. Surely my father, the inspired surgeon, artist, sculptor, inventor, titanic boat builder, and philanderer will understand my desire, my longing to pursue my dreams. He studies the last image, sinks into a chair, and says nothing about my victory.

"I'm emotionally exhausted," he jokes.

His bewildered expression pains me as he waves goodbye for his drive back to Jean and his home in Julianstown, near Drogheda.

A week after Dad's visit, the post delivers an English magazine called *Amazons in Action*. It features a full-length article and action shots from my fight with Griffin. Our piece is well written and photographed by an acquaintance of Jimmy Finn. But to my horror the magazine also features seedy mud-wrestling and topless boxing photos.

The videotape of my bout arrives a few days later, and it more than makes up for the magazine, for it captures my Limerick victory blow by blow, move by move, allowing me to critique the whole fight, to celebrate my best punches and defensive techniques. I yearn to share the tape with my family, but after Dad's reaction to the photos of my match, I'm careful to keep the tape and the magazine out of sight. I don't want an intervention.

On the bike ride into Dublin's city center, the tape plays in my mind and makes me feel like the victor of a championship fight, not a mere exhibition. My excitement wears away with another trudge into the unemployment office. Standing in a long queue with fellow ex-workers doses me with reality. They grumble about Ireland's chronic joblessness and share stories of their hardships as we wait for our dole money.

Back on the streets, I snake my way through hurrying workers, whom I feel are carrying the burden of supporting me.

At the Manpower office I press forward between people to read posted job advertisements. Once again, I find nothing.

At Whelan's pub on Wexford Street, I meet a group of animation friends. Former coworkers encourage my gutsy legal pursuit of Murakami Wolf for unfair dismissal. They remind me I'm the only one to take action. My friend Dave was also fired and craves justice. The others hang on to their jobs and tell me they hope my case will cease their employer's callous manipulations.

I don't like to talk to non-boxers about my sport, but I can't hold it in and tell them about my win in Limerick. Perhaps my friends will now understand why I often decline offers to join them in nightclubs and why I prefer to spend evenings in a gym.

"You finally got a fight?" says Grace. "And won? That's brilliant!"

"Fair play to you," chimes Tanya.

"It's about time," says MJ.

"How much did they pay you?" asks Dave.

"Nothing," I say defensively. "I'm not doing this for the money."

"You're feckin' mad," says MJ. "You spend all this time doing something you *don't* get paid for? And you might never fight again?"

"In the States, women boxers have been licensed since the seventies," I counter. "If I get enough money from the Murakami case, I can go there. I've written to tons of addresses in the States, New Zealand, Italy, France, and Denmark asking for a fight."

"Have you heard anything back yet?" asks Tanya.

"No," I tell her, not disclosing the offers of topless boxing. "Nothing yet."

"Don't go to the States. You'll get killed over there," says Dave. "They'll throw you in with those ghetto girls. You can't compete with them. They're natural athletes."

"What makes you think *I'm* not a natural athlete?" I retort.

"You're just so pale and skinny," says Dave. "Athletes are born, not made. Look at you. You're just not."

What does he know? Dave's a talented artist, but he looks like he's never thrown a punch or lifted a weight. He's cute but in a pudgy, balding thirty-something sort of way. I guess I shouldn't be surprised it's unfathomable to him I could ever be successful as a boxer.

I bid my friends goodbye and head to the tatty legal-aid offices of FLAC. My assigned solicitor and I go over tedious details of my life. Into the third hour of questions and negotiations, my enthusiasm for justice wanes. My premeditated judicial retaliation is painstaking and lacks the spontaneity and exhilaration I felt on the train my last day of school at the Loreto Convent, when I tossed the nuns' favorite weapon—a big wooden spoon—into the River Nanny.

When my court date arrives and I panic over what to wear. I only own T-shirts, sweaters, jeans, and sweatpants, so I search Mum's wardrobe for something appropriate to borrow. I find a matching tweed skirt and jacket and rig it to fit with concealed safety pins. I slip on Mum's tan high-heeled shoes and hobble onto the street. I figure I'm providing hysterical entertainment to corporation workers on my way to the DART station. Arriving in the city center, I stop and stuff tissue into the toes of the shoes to keep them from sliding off on my long totter to the courthouse.

Throughout the hearing I marvel at the formality of the courtroom—not just the architecture and furnishing, but its occupants, too. The three elderly gentlemen assigned to hear the case are suited up, and even my balding, heavyset former boss is stuffed into a crisp coat and tie. My solicitor, a young woman, glides about in heels with self-assurance and ease. Thank goodness I am sitting where I can hide my kicked-off heels and bleeding feet.

As my barrister shoots questions at my former boss, his rosy cheeks glisten with sweat. When the court demands answers about employment practices well beyond my case, his neck seems to expand and protrude as he sinks into his suit. Watching his ruthless interrogation—albeit well deserved—is painful. I'm relieved when his torture is postponed to a later date.

Luckily, before the court date, Murakami Wolf offers a settlement. My solicitor recommends I agree to one thousand pounds. They are getting rid of me for a bargain, but I've made my point and gladly end the ordeal. I never want to work in the animation industry again.

Meanwhile, outside the courtroom there's another fight on the horizon. The kind I want.

Pat's friend, Mick Hussey, snagged a four-round match for me in London with Jane Johnson, who was Sue Atkins' opponent on the tape Jimmy Finn showed me. I'd much rather be fighting Atkins, but I figure a win over Johnson could lead to a crack at Sue Atkins and her British lightweight title.

Unlike the short notice for my first bout, I have three weeks to train for this fight. And Mum's new townhouse near the coast in Sandymount offers the perfect environment for road work. Every morning I run on the nearby strand to strengthen my legs. Moving parallel to the landmark twin red-and-white smokestacks, I dig my heels into the sand and sprint to the Martello tower.

In the evenings I cycle to the gym and picture myself as Rocky Balboa in his training sequences. I skip rope until my heart and lungs threaten to burst. I tune my shoulders and hand velocity on the speedball until the metal swivel emanates heat. My stomach muscles burn as Pat urges me to increase my usual fifty sit-ups. He then bludgeons my tensed abdominals with a fifteen-pound medicine ball to prepare me for body shots.

Sparring four rounds with league champions and holding my own, I discover my defense improves if I relax and gaze at an opponent's chest and simultaneously use my peripheral vision to keep track of an opponent's arms and legs. The technique allows me to better react to unexpected movements or incoming punches and jabs.

"Get worms!" Pat yells as I spar. "Gotta have worms!" He wants me to pretend I'm full of wriggling worms in order to bob and weave unpredictably.

A new coach in the gym quietly observes my workouts. His name is Jimmy Halpin and he's a retired amateur boxing star.

"You've lovely balance," Halpin tells me after practice. He's not the first person to notice my balance, but Halpin's sincerity confirms Pat's decision to force me to practice nothing but footwork my first two weeks of training. It's become one of my best assets, increasing my punch power and improving my much-needed defensive abilities.

Halpin offers to hold the hand pads for me. I've only been lucky enough to work with hand pads twice: once with the Irish National Team coach, Nicholas Cruz Hernandez when he visited the gym a few months ago, and once with Pat's brother, John. Pat never holds hand pads—not with me, not with anyone. And he never explains why.

Dancing round the ring, Halpin instructs me on every shot and suggests a corresponding follow-up shot. I'm keyed up from his lesson and can't concentrate. I have to stop myself from grinning for fear he'll think I'm laughing at him. So I think about my departed Shoobee in order to quell the giggles bubbling inside me.

Then news arrives that my match is cancelled.

The boxing higher-ups refuse to allow women to fight, and they're doing all they can to get in the way. But my bout is quickly rescheduled for Saturday, April 11, 1992, at an undisclosed location. The day before my fight, Pat and I fly to London and take the Underground for Gayhurst, where we will stay with Pat's friend, Paddy Sower.

Our host, originally from Dublin, is a big man with dark, bushy eyebrows. He's a retired professional boxing referee with a strong London accent. He takes us to his corporation flat, a high-rise block of concrete with pointed railings, and entertains us for hours. The retired referee recalls his years in the boxing ring, and even Pat can't get a word in to tell his own stories.

The next morning we travel to Park Tavern pub in Streatham, a London suburb, for my afternoon fight. Leaving the sunshine, we descend into a small basement gym. Our underground fight is literally underground.

Fight organizers have gathered and include our friend Mick Hussey and the infamous Sue Atkins. I'm excited to finally meet the champion, who in my mind has risen to legend status. I thank them both for the fight opportunity, and am honored to find out that Atkins played a large role in arranging my fight with her former opponent.

"Are you boxing today?" I ask her.

"No," she replies. "I'm coaching Jane."

That's odd, I think. *Why is she coaching her adversary?*

"And I'm doing an exhibition with John, the referee," she adds, pointing to a beer-bellied, middle-aged man with a thick black moustache.

I wonder why she would waste her time with an exhibition match when she could have fought me. But I don't say anything. The arrangements are casual at best. Even the formality of a weigh-in is disregarded.

My dressing room is in a corner next to the ring and is only separated from spectators by a partition wall on one side and a flimsy curtain on the other. I change into my custom-ordered outfit—a gold robe with matching sleeveless top and shorts, complete with white tassels. Tommy Hearns' trademark Kronk Gym colors inspired the gold, Sugar Ray Leonard the flashy fringe. I've put more contemplation and effort into this outfit than anything I've ever worn before. My moment has arrived, and I shadowbox my way to the spotlight in a tassel-festooned, shiny-gold getup.

As I step into the tiny homemade ring, I shed every trace of self-consciousness. To intimidate my opponent, I demonstrate my speed by rolling my fists in a feverish warm-up. Johnson's sleeveless terrycloth robe accentuates her burly arms. She is slightly shorter than me but thickset, dressed in a red-and-black outfit. Word has spread about our illegal fight, and curious pint-drinkers shuffle in from the pub upstairs.

"In the red *cor-na*, we've got 'Rocky' Jane from Tunbridge Wells," announces the referee in a thick Cockney accent. "Com' on!" he encourages the small crowd, "show yer hands for 'Roc-keee'!

"And in the blue *cor-na*, we've got 'Dangerous' Deirdre from Dublin." I'm surprised by my new nickname and the friendly applause from the English patrons.

"And two better-lookin' fighters I've never seen," continues the referee. "No hittin' below the belt, by the way."

Round one begins with a weak ding of the bell. Johnson starts fast but, just as Pat taught me, I block her jab with my right palm and counter with my own jab. Keeping my opponent on the end of my longer reach, I'm able to make slight shifts away from her dangerous right and counter with snappy one-twos. Repeatedly, I break through the shorter Johnson's guard and enjoy the loud *thud* of my punches in this intimate setting. I can also hear the anxious voices of Jane Johnson's supporters.

"Jab her, Jane!" shouts Sue Atkins. "Jab her! Body, Jane! *Body!*"

As Johnson tries to rally to her coach's instruction, I fire sharp rights over her low left hand and snap her head sideways.

"Hands up, Jane!" Johnson's team cries. "Hands up!"

I'm still penetrating my opponent's guard when she retaliates and lands a stinging right to my cheekbone that jolts my head backward.

"That's a gurl!" a man shouts.

Johnson's power jars my brain as I turn up the pressure to show I'm in control of the fight. I land a sharp right and follow with a left hook. Glassy-eyed, my opponent dips downward to search for safety. I dig body shots into her open ribcage. She bends further, groaning and breathless. Excitement fuels my assault. I smell a stoppage.

"Hands up, Jane!" her supporters beg. "Hold her, Jane! Grab on!" they scream as I pummel her on the ropes and back her into her own corner.

"Ah ref, stop it," a man pleads. "Stop it!"

The referee moves in as I batter my rival's head with a combination. The bell dings and grants Johnson a reprieve. Atkins leaps in the ring, grabs my opponent, and guides her onto her stool.

Listening with half an ear to Pat's calm instructions, I watch Johnson's three-corner crew, two men and Sue Atkins, work in a frenzy. The referee hovers nearby to observe my opponent's condition while her team massages her limbs. Atkins pours water over Johnson's head, sponges her face, and gives her advice.

During the second round Johnson revives. She charges toward me and fires blistering right hands into the side of my face. Her strength drives me back to the ropes. I slide sideways to escape and pump my jab to prime my right-hand weapon. My fist spears over the top of her left hand and penetrates her gloved guard. I press my opponent to the ropes and work in close with short punches and uppercuts. Johnson gasps for air as I punish her with body shots.

"C'mon on, ref, give 'er a breather," a man begs.

I respond with a torrent of punches. A right hand jerks my opponent's head sideways and ignites a burst of sweat from her short, spiked hair. The referee steps in and peers into Johnson's watery eyes. He quietly asks her if she wants to continue. Without hesitation she says yes.

Johnson charges with a vicious attack. My energy evaporates as she drives me backward and pegs me with powerful rights.

"Stick it out, Jane!" The crowd senses an advantage. "That's a gurl! Go at her! That's a gurl!"

I struggle for control of the match by sticking my jab in her face and circling. My strategy works, so I continue to jab until my opponent's burst of energy fades. I manage to escape the round without further damage, but I'm perplexed by my lethargy.

"Box, Deirdre. Box!" implores Paddy Sower as I begin round three.

I keep Johnson under control again with my jab as my body slowly recharges. Even though my opponent manages to cut through my defense to land a few rights, within seconds my renewed strength allows me to throw crisp, sharp combinations. Johnson's best asset is a relentless right hand. I dodge it by turning to my left and twisting back to shoot a left hook into her body. I miss with a follow-up hook to the head, but she is visibly hurt by the body shot. I fire a straight right to the solar plexus and freeze her momentarily. Johnson drops her arms to protect her mid-section, and I'm able to land a searing left hook on her chin. I land another head shot that folds my opponent and prompts the referee to give her a standing eight count.

"Deirdre," Pat shouts while I wait in the neutral corner. "Nice and sharp. Gotta go to work." And then he emphasizes, "Go. To. Work!"

Back to full strength I unleash left hooks and straight rights to stagger my rival backward and pin "Rocky" Jane in her corner.

"Stop it, ref! Stop it!" the fans cry.

"That's it, that's it," the referee declares and steps between us as I freeze a punch over my cowering opponent as the anemic bell dings.

Johnson's coaches rush up to the ropes to console her brave effort.

"No! The bell went!" insists the timekeeper. "The bell went!"

Seconds pass before it dawns on everyone that if the timekeeper says the bell went off before the fight was called, the bout is not over. And I can't help but wonder if timekeeper rang the bell to save my opponent.

"Put a stool in and let her sit down," a man yells to rally Johnson's corner back into action.

In the fourth and final round, I go straight to work. I'm determined to score my first stoppage. The left hook hurts her, so I hook off my jab to land combinations with ease. No amount of encouragement can help my opponent now.

As I punish Johnson into the ropes and spin her around, I resist the urge to hit her while her back is to me. She acknowledges this with a nod of battered relief as the ref steps in to turn her around. Face-to-face, I stagger her with a jolting left hook and whip her head with a four-punch combination.

"That's it, that's it," the referee steps in and pushes me away. This time there is no *convenient* ring of the bell. The fight is over.

The referee puts his arm around me and waits for the applause to die down.

"You're a better fighter than Barry McGuigan," he proclaims to another round of claps and whistles.

"Listen," the ref continues, pointing to Sue Atkins, "no one wants to fight this lady over 'ere, the British lightweight champion." He then turns his attention to me and asks, "Does *she?*"

I raise my hand to make it clear Atkins is the next opponent on my list. I'm on a mission to beat the best.

As we pack up to leave, Sue Atkins offers me money from a collection at the door. Since we never discussed payment before the fight, I refuse her offer. Fortunately, my wise coach says, "Don't be bleedin' stupid, Deirdre. Take the money!"

Back at the flat, my coach, Paddy Sower, and I discuss my performance and my future. We agree my best opportunities are all in one place—America.

"You ever 'ear of a Yank called Beau Williford?" Paddy Sower asks as he grabs a copy of Nat Fleisher's *The Ring Record Book and Boxing Encyclopedia* from his collection. "Have a look in there," he says and hands me the book. "He was a professional fighter. But he's a manager and trainer now."

I open the hefty yellowed book right to Williford's record.

"There ya go, that's 'im. That's the fella I'm talkin' 'bout," says Paddy. He tells me Williford revitalized the careers of two English boxers, Glenn McCory and Dennis Andries, and led them both to world titles.

"Nice fella is Beau," Paddy continues. "Write 'im a letter, Deirdre. He'll know if there's any fights for you in the States. Believe me, anything Beau Williford don't know, ain't worth knowing."

On the train to Heathrow Airport, Pat and I rumble above London's mossy, pigeon-ridden rooftops. Pat helps me count the collection money, and I feel like we just committed a heist. Even though I'd have gladly fought for nothing, it's a thrill to count fight money.

"This doesn't even cover what you spent on our flights," Pat scolds me. "Deirdre, you gotta understand, this is a harsh sport. You need to earn what you can while you can. Atkins did the right thing, but there's plenty of wankers who'll take advantage of you. Never say no to what's rightfully yours."

CHAPTER 13
TRUTH AND CONSEQUENCES

Back in Dublin I write a letter to the American, Beau Williford, in Lafayette, Louisiana. I tell him that Paddy Sower suggested I contact him in my quest to find a fight in the States. I make it clear I will pay my own way and that I'm willing to box any opponent he can find for me. Absolutely anybody.

I hop on my bike and drop the letter in a post box on my way to a FÁS class in graphic design. I signed up for the course while training for the Johnson fight and have been enjoying eye-flirting with a fellow student from electronics class. But today in the lunchroom, I avoid his delicious green eyes and tilt my head to hide the yellow contusion on my left cheek. It's unlikely I'll ever befriend the guy, never mind actually date him, so it seems silly I should worry what he thinks of my battered face. Still, I can't fight the instinct to turn away.

Once my bruise fades, I flirt with Green Eyes again when I pass him in the halls. "Jesus, he's ancient," my classmate complains when she spots him winking at me. His greying hair must be premature, because his workingman's face is young. Still, he must be too old for me, so I can't pin my hopes on a date. I just can't help playing the game.

Another classmate, Adam, is the one I'm really pursuing. Aloof, he sits at the desk in front of mine. I admire the confident way he wears shabby, outmoded clothes even Saint Vincent de Paul would burn in a heap. Adam's a brilliant artist, and he pays no heed to our frustrated instructor. He's so absorbed in his surrealistic masterpieces, he seems to forget the whole point of the teacher's assigned projects. I'm in awe of his autonomy and intend to be just like him. I pledge to follow my instincts, impervious to everyone's expectations.

Outside the classroom, Adam is flirtatious and funny. Every day after class we cycle into the city center. At the end of O'Connell Street, I veer along the quays toward Sandymount while he veers toward his flat, wherever that might be. I fantasize that some day we will turn in the same direction on our way home together.

My classmates tease Adam and me about the spark between us. I don't discourage them. But our FÁS course is ending soon, and I worry he won't find the courage to ask me for a date. So I arrange to share the darkroom with Adam one afternoon.

We arrive at the darkroom at the same time, lock the door, and stand side by side in the glow of red light. Adam puts on a pair of gloves then hands me a pair. My heart pounds as I stand next to him and we burn bromides and watch images appear. But he never leans over to kiss me, and the rousing arrangement passes innocently.

I can't let a possible love story slip away for want of a little courage. So I decide to ask him out and hope that my valor will be justly rewarded.

The last day of FÁS, my classmates and I plan to meet at Fibber Magees on Parnell Street for a goodbye drink. Adam and I are the first to arrive and wait outside for our friends. I don't waste a minute of my chance.

"Em—I was wondering if, eh—you would like to go out sometime?" I croak.

"Deirdre! Are you making a proposal?"

"If—you're like, you know—interested," I murmur.

"Eh, sorry, but I'm already hooked up."

Christ! Mortification! I'm a feckin' eejit! My audacity has blown up in my face. What's worse, I'm sure he's lying about his relationship. How could I have misread all the signals? I swear to never ask a guy out again.

Two weeks later I cycle back to FÁS to pick up a certificate of completion. I rush inside to collect my exam results, praying I don't bump into Adam. My scores are not the top honors I'd hoped for. Even in adulthood, keen to do my best, I'm still not an impressive student. Distraught, I dash from the building and nearly crash into a man's chest. Thank heaven it's not Adam.

It's Green Eyes.

"Where's the fire?" he asks.

"Oh, I just don't want to run into my instructor," I say. "My results aren't the best."

"Mine either. Would you like a lift into town?"

In a flash, my bike is in the back of Green Eyes' car and I'm sitting right beside him.

"Where's your boyfriend?" he asks. "Did you dump him?"

"I don't have a boyfriend."

"What about the fella you always cycle with?"

"Oh, he's just a friend."

"In that case, my name's Gavin. Are you hungry?"

"Yes," I say, suppressing a nervous giggle.

Gavin takes me to lunch at Café Kylemore on O'Connell Street. I am so thrilled by his company I can barely swallow my soup.

The next day we have lunch again. But this time Gavin kisses me goodbye and asks me to go out on Friday evening. Our date seems ages away, so we talk on the phone every night. I rarely chat with anyone at length, so when I'm on the phone with Gavin Mum circles me, huffs, and darts in and out of the room. When she decides it's time for me to hang up, she actually presses the hook to disconnect us. I turn and look at her in silent shock as she marches back to the living room.

Friday evening arrives and I meet Gavin in the Oliver Saint John Gogarty Pub in Temple Bar. Gavin asks if I'm related to the great poet, Gogarty, and I tell him that Dad says he may be his great uncle, but no one really knows. Then he offers me a drink and I have to explain that I don't drink alcohol while training to fight. He doesn't insist.

I like that Gavin's not pushy like the guys my own age. He seems so mature and now I know why. He tells me he's thirty-five, thirteen years older than I am. My friends were right that he's too old for me; I wonder what they will think.

We leave the pub and stroll along the darkened streets. In the mild summer air my first worries about Gavin's age have slipped away. We sit on the steps of the old Ha'penny Bridge, a pedestrian walkway over the River Liffey. The cast-iron bridge has three lanterns supported by curved, rising arches. The lamps provide perfect lighting and seem to float above the river as Gavin wraps me in his arms and kisses me on the cheek.

And it's not just the night that brings romance.

Sunny afternoons are spent on Killiney Beach with Gavin, whose kisses ease the angst of my chronic unemployment, and I'm given over to the poetry in our setting: warm, smooth pebbles that allow us to stretch out and listen to the surf blanket the shore. The surrounding terrain soars to the quartzite mountainous tip of Bray Head and unfurls into a glorious expanse of lush greenery. Embraced in the vast alcove, we bask under a blue satin sky and admire the sail-dotted horizon.

Glacial cliffs and majestic rocks march out to sea in perfect stillness beyond the round Martello tower that looks like a stone nipple on Dalkey Island. It's as though I'm noticing the stunning beauty of Killiney Beach for the first time. It's no wonder the area is home to celebrities and pop stars like Bono, whose estates nestle in the woods behind me.

When not with Gavin, I spend hours at the gym training or writing letters to boxing contacts, begging for the slightest chance to advance my career in the ring. In every post I emphasize the ability to pay my own way and I make it clear I'll fight anyone. But my letters are rarely answered. Invariably, I'm thrilled to receive a letter from the United States, only to find it stuffed with topless boxing and mud-wrestling opportunities.

As I wait for Beau Williford in Louisiana, as well as numerous coaches, managers, promoters, and female fighters across America to respond to my letters, I fall in love with Gavin. He tells me he loves me, but the longer we date, the more he hates that I box. He'd be horrified to know I'm willing to leave him for a chance to fight in the United States. And he could never go with me. I'm having a hard enough time finding someone to take me on without a man attached to me.

Of course, I could avoid the heartbreak of leaving Gavin if I just gave up boxing and settled down with him. And why not? He loves me. And boxing is fraught with frustrations and pitfalls. But marriage, from what I've seen, is fraught with frustrations and pitfalls as well. Though it seems like a dilemma, I'm not really torn, because I know I can't live without boxing. And there's no time to spare. I'm twenty-two with only two bouts on my record. I admit to myself that I'm willing to leave my family, my country, and the man I love for a chance to be where women are allowed to box.

In October, eight months after the London underground match, I'm penning another batch of weekly letters. I've made the same request so often I could write in my sleep. In fact, I'm about to nod off when the phone rings and startles me.

"Is this—Deed-dra Go-garr-tee?" asks a drawling American accent.

"Yes," I reply, fingers crossed, hoping this is not another topless boxing freak.

"My name is Beau Williford."

"Oh, yes. Yes!"

"I got your letters. You mentioned Paddy Sower. He's a good friend of mine."

"Yes, I stayed with Paddy when I boxed in London. He's friends with my trainer, Pat McCormack."

"Your coach is Pat McCormack?"

"That's right. He was—"

"British light-welterweight champion," Williford finishes my sentence. "Brother of John, son of Spike. Yeah, I know who Pat is. Helluva fighter. Fought all over the world. Packed the house everywhere he went."

"That's him," I agree.

"So. You wanna come over? And box in the States?"

"Yes! I'll pay my own way. And fight anyone available."

"Well—I don't know any—um—women boxers."

Williford's slow, drawn-out words are hard to understand, but it's clear he has no interest in women's boxing. I'm disappointed he has no knowledge of the current female fighters. But I finish the call by offering to send him a tape of my two bouts. Surely, when he sees my skills he'll be encouraged to help me.

I have my fight tape transferred from PAL to VHS and posted to the States. An agonizing two weeks pass before Williford calls me again.

"Deed-dra, I just watched your tape. And you're one *baaddd* mother!"

Judging by what I've seen on American TV shows, I can only assume "mother" is short for motherfucker. And by his cheerful tone "bad" really means good. Shocked by his informality, I surprise myself and accept an invitation to his home in Louisiana.

"I can't promise anything," Beau warns. "I don't know shit from Shinola about women's boxing, but I owe it to Paddy Sower to try to help you."

I hang up and immediately cycle into the city to apply for a visa. With my Murakami Wolf money still tucked away, I'm able to book a flight. I choose early January so I won't impose on my new coach's family during the Christmas holiday. Now I just need to train hard (no problem) and explain my plans to loved ones (major problem).

I decide not to put off the hard part.

"What?" Mum exclaims when I tell her my plans. "Who is this fellow? Where did you find him?"

I explain Williford is a genuine boxing manager I found through a friend of a friend. And I tell her about writing letters to him until he finally called me.

"For God's sake! Are you mad?" she admonishes. "He could be a rapist. Or a murderer, for all you know."

The significance of my invitation to America means nothing to my mother. I'm finally taking a huge step to put right a lifetime of underachievement, and she can only react with fear and negativity. Away from Mum, I breathe deeply and can admit I might be a little off to want to move to another country and put my career in the hands of a complete stranger. I suppose I could be more patient with my mother.

Dad's reaction is more optimistic than Mum's. "Well, that's all very exciting," he says. "Maybe you'll find a graphic design job with one of the big companies over there." With Dad, it's always about art. He dodges the true purpose of my trip. But then I recall the pained look on his face as he scanned photos of my bout with Anne-Marie Griffin. Nevertheless, his attitude helps me, so I forgo the urge to correct him about my art. I am going to America for one reason and one reason only: the art of prizefighting.

Words spill from me thick with dread as I admit to Gavin that I've bought a ticket to Louisiana. But instead of the furious reaction I expected, after a long period of silence, he asks, "When will you be back?"

I tell him that I cannot give him an answer, and—another surprise—my veracity seems to draw us closer. It's as if Gavin expected this all along, and my honesty with him fills a space between us. And I'm ready for that space to disappear.

All Saint's Eve, Gavin and I strip off our clothes and devour each other in a fury of kisses and heat and skin. We roll and tumble on top of the sheets in my bedroom. I'm left with that guilty glow I feel after a fight. I am sore, but elated, and left wondering why what I've just done is considered so wrong when it seemed so right. I'd like to shout to the world that I'm defrocked, deflowered, and happy. Also, I am oddly relieved that I'll land in New York City an experienced woman, not a twenty-two-year-old virgin.

Mum, on the other hand, gives me no relief. She continues to voice her concerns about my traveling to meet a man I know nothing about. The only other Beau I've ever heard of is Beau Jack, an American lightweight boxer, famous for his four battles with Ike Williams. Despite numerous phone calls and questions, I've learned nothing about Williford and can't quiet Mum's fears. What if she is right? He could be a murderer or a gangster. The only thing I really know about Beau Williford is he'll be replacing someone who means the world to me: Pat McCormack.

On my last night at Saint Saviours, I share my fears with Pat.

"What if Williford is a gangster?" I ask. "What if I hate it there?"

"Just be careful," he says. "Don't do anythin' you don't want to."

"But I hate leaving you and the club. And I won't trust anyone else in my corner."

"You don't have a choice. You're openin' doors for other women—five, ten, or fifteen years behind you. But right now, you don't have a choice."

"I hope this isn't all a waste of time. Is it a waste of time?"

"Deirdre," Pat commands with a stern gaze, "there's no bigger waste than a wasted opportunity."

Those words help me, especially on the morning of my cross-Atlantic flight. I choke back tears as I tell Gavin goodbye over the phone. His voice is distant and solemn. Part of me wants him to burst through the door, rescue me from my madness, and declare his everlasting love—to tell me nothing will ever change between us—but I can tell in his voice it's too late for that.

"Who was that?" Mum asks as I hang up.

"Nobody," I tell her.

Mum will not allow Dad to accompany me to the airport. So I sit at a café in Dublin Airport with her, my sister, Adrienne, and my animation chums, Grace and Tanya. Mum buys us a pot of tea and scones. As my friends chatter, I can only nibble at my breakfast.

My beautiful mother sports a fashionable brown pantsuit with a white scarf and looks glamorous, the way she did before my father left her. She sips her tea and pretends not to be worried about me. This is the longest spell she has stayed out of hospital. Remembering those dark days when I pulled her from the River Boyne makes this moment truly remarkable. I wonder what she's thinking as she gazes back at me as though she wants to freeze my image forever.

At the security gates, Grace and Tanya embrace me and wish me luck. They both urge me to *beat the shite out of everyone*. When Adrienne hugs me, a lump strains in my throat and threatens to mortify me in front of my friends. Then Mum hugs me so tightly I'm surprised by her strength.

"Be careful over there, darling," she sobs. "I don't know what I'll do without you. I'll miss you so much."

"You'll be fine, Mum, really. And I'll be fine, too."

"If it weren't for you," she whispers, "I'd be dead."

"Ah, Mum—"

"I swear, Deirdre, when Des left me, I'd have killed myself if it weren't for you."

Mum and I embrace as the final boarding call is announced. I shuffle through the metal detector, and I'm afraid to look back. I push my way through the bustling concourse. At last I spot my boarding gate. The words JFK, NEW YORK liberate me as ghosts of hesitation and doubt and sadness give way to exhilaration.

On the one hand, I can hardly believe the reality of each step I'm taking closer to my dreams, to box in the United States of America, where it's not forbidden for women to fight.

On the other hand, I've never felt more alone.

CHAPTER 14
THE CRAWFISH BOILER

At last I am in the United States of America!

But no time to dawdle—I can't spare a moment to wiggle in wonderment. A snowstorm in Dublin delayed my flight and leaves me only minutes to make my connection to New Orleans. JFK Airport does not live up to the grandiosity of its namesake; it's disorganized and chaotic, with concourses in separate buildings and a maddening deficit of directional signs.

"You mean, N'awlins," the stout New York cop corrects me. But I'm in no mood for an elocution lesson. "Foist, you gotta claim your luggage. Second, you gotta go trew customs. Toid, for N'awlins, you're in dah wrong buildin'."

Huh?

No time to hustle a trolley. I haul my suitcase through a menagerie of ethnic headwear from cowboy hats and baseball caps to Middle Eastern headscarves and turbans. Urgency explodes in my head: *A complete stranger is driving one hundred and twenty miles to meet me in New Orleans!*

Outside, I lurch into the snow and figure there must be an easier path to Delta's domestic concourse. No one else is outside dragging their bags through the elements. And what the hell did I pack that's so bloody heavy? Faceless men in hooded coats approach and reach for my suitcase. "Help with the bag, ma'am?" But I politely refuse and tighten my grip.

My panic subsides when I find the right terminal. I am very late but once past the desk, I know I will make it. As I board my flight, an attendant urges me to my seat. I buckle my seatbelt and prepare for takeoff. I wait for my breathing to settle only to learn that the 727's departure is delayed by heavy snow and ice. As in Dublin, I sit on the runway.

It is midnight when I arrive in New Orleans, two hours late and so nervous I could vomit. What will I do if Beau Williford got fed up and left? Or didn't show up at all? My heart lurches, tapping out some weird Morse code of fear as I emerge into a deserted terminus. But then a tall, muscular man approaches and offers a nod of recognition. His badge of honor, a flattened, crooked nose, relieves me and I know I'm in the company of a former heavyweight boxer. Williford's battle scars contradict his dark, handsome features as he smiles and towers over me like the nose of a jumbo jet.

The Louisiana air is surprisingly mild considering the snow I just left in Dublin and New York. Williford effortlessly carries my cumbersome suitcase across the parking tower. He smells of cigar smoke and wears pressed blue jeans, a black polo shirt, a baseball cap, and loafers with no socks. When we reach his bug-splattered silver Mercedes, he tosses my suitcase into its cluttered trunk.

"I'm thrilled to be here!" I blurt. "I can't wait to see New Orleans!"

"Well, you won't see New Orleans tonight. We're heading west through Baton Rouge," he says as he pops open a can of Coke. "We'll be in Lafayette in a couple of hours."

As we cross the black expanse of Lake Pontchartrain, Williford points to a distant cluster of lights that is downtown New Orleans. He asks me about my home and then chronicles his world travels, which include a visit to Northern Ireland. It's a good thing he's a talker, because the view along this stretch of Interstate 10 threatens to lull me to sleep with its endless curtain of pine trees.

An hour into the drive, Baton Rouge brings my first look at an American city: animated signs, huge billboards, neon-lit shops, and cinemas. The bright lights help to keep me awake as I inhale fumes redolent of burnt toast, compliments of a booming chemical industry. Beau improves the stink of the city by lighting a sweet-smelling cigar.

Leaving the state capital, we cross the Mississippi River Bridge. I imagine steamboats rolling along as Huckleberry Finn trots barefoot on its banks. Beau points out a riverboat casino. He tells me they are illegal except on water or Native American land. How exciting for me to be among casinos, Indians, and the mighty Mississippi.

Trees surround us again, spectacular bare trees with broad bases that seem to float on the water. I wonder if the trees are dead. Or is this just the winter look for them, with their spooky limbs that jut erratically and drip thick-looking cobwebs.

"What's the stuff hanging from those trees?" I ask.

"Spanish moss," Beau says, pausing to relight his cigar. "Those are cypress trees. You can't see it, but we're actually on an eighteen-mile-long bridge over a swamp, the Atchafalaya Basin."

"Wow! We're traveling over a swamp? Have you ever been *in* the swamp?"

"Yeah, once. When I first moved here. Some guys took me waterskiing. I was having a great time 'til someone yelled, 'Watch out for that alligator!' And I said, 'Alligator? Fuck this shit. Get me the hell outta here!'"

I laugh and begin to relax.

We arrive in Lafayette at about two in the morning. It's a flat, sprawling town with wide streets and, even though it's January, lots of greenery. My accommodation is a fully furnished apartment at Canterbury Square Apartments on McDonald Drive. And thanks to Beau's wife, Teri, there are groceries in the refrigerator and sheets on the bed.

Beau carries in my bag, shows me the apartment, and then rushes home with a promise to pick me up tomorrow. Too tired to unpack, I open my overstuffed suitcase and yank out my pink flannel nightgown, a gift from Mum. After I clean up, I pull the gown over my head; the pattern of bunny rabbits tumbles down to my ankles. Then the split-wood smell of Mum's townhouse rushes up to greet me. I crawl into bed and stare at the oscillating fan attached to the ceiling. I've never seen a fan on a ceiling before. My mind drifts to thoughts of Mornington and Dublin and then spirals back to this flat, strange place I've come to. When I close my eyes, I see those ghostly trees that floated on a swampy lake. Then I drift into sleep where there's only the sweet, warm darkness.

Late the next morning Beau takes me to his home, an attractive bungalow landscaped by crepe myrtle trees and azalea bushes. His tiny office is plastered with framed boxer photos on panel board walls. Stacks of books and magazines cram the shelves with dusty, pugilistic figurines and boxing trolls. Ashtrays hold cigar butts and thick cylinders of ash.

Beau sits at his cluttered desk and explains each item as I explore the memorabilia. He has only been training and managing boxers eleven years, since 1982, but he's accumulated an outstanding number of champions. I recognize James "Quick" Tillis, who was the first to take Mike Tyson the distance, and English boxers Glenn McCory and Dennis Andries, who peer out at me through nicotine-stained glass. I pick up a tiny pair of red gloves with black cuffs stamped with the letters BBE. They are light and thin, more like bag mitts than competition gloves.

"Those are six-ounce gloves," says Beau. "That's the pair Kenny Vice wore when he knocked out Jim McDonnell. They don't use them anymore."

I'm surprised to learn Beau worked the corner for Kenny Vice during the fight. As he tells me the story, my memory flashes to the horrific McDonnell knockout I watched on TV. It was broadcast live from Royal Albert Hall in London over two years ago and left even the most hardened boxing fans unsettled by its brutality. Local favorite McDonnell was having a showcase bout before an expected shot at the WBO lightweight title. I was curious to watch the fight because McDonnell had retired my hero, Barry McGuigan. I even tried to dislike McDonnell, but he was just too nice.

As expected, McDonnell controlled Vice with excellent boxing skills in spite of a first-round knockdown. But the upstart American fought back and refused to play the role of stepping stone for McDonnell. In the fourth round Vice missed a right but then landed an astonishing left hook. Like a bird shot in mid-flight, McDonnell's left wing spun outward as he spiraled down. He crashed face first over the bottom rope and his head hung limp at the edge of the ring.

"Don't bother to count," cried the commentator. "That's a dreadful knockout."

South African Brian Baronet had died after being knocked out by Vice two years earlier. And for the agonizing minutes that McDonnell lay unconscious, Kenny Vice hung his head in tears and worried that McDonnell might follow Baronet's fate. McDonnell fully recovered, but was forced to retire because the British Boxing Board of Control revoked his boxing license. It's hard for me to believe I'm holding the gloves Kenny Vice wore in that brutal fight.

Beau takes me to see downtown Lafayette. It's a Tuesday, but unlike town centers in Ireland the streets are quiet. Mostly, there are office buildings, a sprinkling of bars and restaurants, and only a few places to shop. It's nice to sightsee, but I'm not interested in offices, bars, or shopping. I'm anxious to see the boxing gym where I'll hone my skills under Beau's expertise. But instead of the gym, we go to Hibernia Bank on Main Street to meet Beau's wife Teri, who is vice president.

Teri is a petite, attractive woman with short, light brown hair. And she is much more conservative than I'd imagined a former heavyweight's wife to be. She gives me a quick and Southern-sounding *Hey*. I can only imagine what she might think of her husband inviting a woman boxer over from Europe. She gives me no clue.

Lunch is at Antlers on Jefferson Street. Beau suggests I order crawfish étouffée, a buttery rice dish that is delicious but spicy hot. Beau notices my watery eyes and runny nose. "You'll be used to Cajun cooking before long," he chuckles, sliding over a tall glass of iced tea. I only drink hot tea at home, and the thought of cold tea appalls me. Sure enough, iced tea tastes awful, but the pecan pie is scrumptious.

After lunch, I begin to worry we will never make it to the gym. We pick up Beau's three blond sons from school. The twins, Leslie and Wesley, are eight years old, and Christian is three. The boys can't understand why this boxer from Ireland is not a man.

"Girls can't fight," says one of the twins.

"This one can," says Beau.

Until Teri returns from the bank, my coach plies his boys with Icees, horseplay, and affection. By the time their mother slams through the door, I'm bursting with curiosity to see my new boxing gym. At last, we are free and on our way.

This is the moment I've been waiting for. I've traveled from the Irish Sea to the Gulf of Mexico to work out American style. I wonder if the gym is downtown in an old brick building with faded fight posters pasting the walls. Or perhaps it's a modern suburban gym with high-tech endurance machines.

But my coach drives out of the city and its suburbs. We zip down country roads past rows of harvested sugarcane. After twenty minutes, Beau turns left onto Fortune Road, and we bump along for another mile and a half down crumbling, potholed asphalt. He then pulls into a farm with a small, redbrick house, a mobile home, and a shed. There's a medium-sized brown dog tied to a chain-link fence, and children's toys sprinkle the yard. I figure Williford has made yet another stop on our way to the gym, so after he pops out the car, I remain seated.

Beau pokes his head in the car window and asks, "Are you gonna sit there all night or what?"

Chickens scatter as we cross the cluttered yard toward the small shed. Inside is darkness and the smell of wet leaves. Beau flips a switch and florescent strips of light buzz and flicker to illuminate a homemade ring, a deflated speedball, and a busted-up heavy bag.

"Whatcha think? Just like Saint Saviours, eh?"

Dumbstruck, I stare at my new gym. The walls are swollen chipboard with thick, dark mold mushrooming down from the cobweb-covered ceiling. Black plastic trash bags replace glass in two small windows. Five or six children's bikes are stacked near a huge cooking pot on a gas canister. And the makeshift ring is only inches from walls on three sides. There is a shower but the drain is a hole in the floor, and the toilet has a bed sheet for a door. And the stench! The stink of mold spores seizes my lungs.

"Well, what's the hold up? Get your wraps on," Beau says, clapping his hands at me.

I swallow hard against the lump in my throat and mutter, "Okay," hoping he didn't hear the quiver in my voice. As I begin to wrap my shaking hands, the gravity of my decision to travel to Louisiana hits me full force. There is no way out now. No Saint Saviours, no friends, no family, no Gavin, and no train home. And to think, I left everything behind for a boxing career that begins in a stinking chicken shed.

"You don't need any fancy bullshit to make a champion. A champion is made in here," my coach says, pointing to his heart. "If you don't have *that*, you won't last two days in this place."

He watches me shadowbox as I try to loosen my travel-tightened shoulders. "I'm going to train you just like a man because that's the only way I know how. I've produced a lot of champions out of this tiny place, so I must know what I'm doing."

Even in January the shed swelters from the sun beating on its tin roof.

"You got lucky no one else is here today. Normally, we'd have that crawfish pot full of boiling water. Nobody has to worry about losing weight in this gym." He points to the cooking pot and says, "That'll really make you sweat!"

Beau works me until I can't move: six three-minute rounds of nonstop punching the heavy bag with thirty-second breaks, two hundred sit-ups, and ten minutes of jumping rope. "That's it for today," he finally says. "A light workout's all you need after that long flight. Tomorrow you'll spar."

After a night of restless sleep, I go for my morning run. I can't stop thinking about sparring and how badly I need to impress my new coach. Lafayette seems to have no pedestrians or pavements, and without distinguishing hills or steeples as landmarks, the streets look the same. Soon I've forgotten my running route. I'm lost!

"Big dummy. You must've run seven miles instead of three," Beau teases, already waiting at my apartment as I arrive home, panting and struggling to explain my tardiness.

With no time for breakfast, we head to the Williford house, where Beau works in his office. I'm ravenous after my marathon run, but I'm afraid to complain. My coach has not even offered a cup of coffee. Nerves, hunger, and homesickness have me in bits. I'm worried about sparring with no fuel in my body. Lunchtime comes and goes with no sign of eating. *Surely a big man like Williford must be hungry?*

Two hours before gym time, I decide to ask for something simple. Perhaps he'll realize I haven't eaten and take me for a lovely meal.

"Would it be okay if I had an apple. Or something?" I croak.

"What? Ya think it's your birthday?" he snaps.

Is he joking? I can't tell. But I never get lunch, or even an apple.

At the gym the crawfish pot is pumping clouds of suffocating steam into the damp, hot air. A familiar figure shadowboxes through the haze. He is slender and wiry, with knotted shoulders like the knees on cypress trees. He has a stone-carved chin, high cheekbones, and a nose so smashed that his profile is nearly a straight line from forehead to chin. His hair is light brown, his skin deeply tanned, and his hands move with an alligator's jaw-snapping speed.

"Dee-dra. This is Kenny Vice. Your sparring partner."

My stomach flushes with heat. I see McDonnell crash unconscious to the floor.

"Kenny Vice? Trains here?"

"Trains *here?*" echoes Beau. "He lives here. That's his trailer outside. We're on his property."

Jesus! I'm about to spar the man who *killed* a man in the ring, who *retired* the man who *retired* Barry McGuigan?

Just wrapping my hands I'm dripping with sweat because of that damn crawfish boiler. My body lacks fuel, and my nerves seem to amplify the growls in my stomach.

There is no need to give this guy a pop in the mouth to convince him to take me seriously. Kenny Vice, unlike most of the guys I spar, forgoes any gentlemanly pretense and goes right to work by shooting sharp jabs and straight rights. He is fluid and fast, a professional, a clear difference from the amateurs I've sparred with to this point. I manage to handle him fairly well by working jabs and executing as much lateral movement as possible in this tiny, cramped ring.

My jab wanes in round two and Vice's sledgehammer right drills my left temple. He traps me on the ropes as I try to slip away from his lethal left hooks. But a ramrod right scorches the tip of my nose and bores my head into the wall. Even the moldy chipboard wants to punish me.

I slink along the ropes to the open side of the ring, but Vice is on the hunt. He sees me wilting and shouts, "C'mon, bitch!" Indignant, I summon my last drops of energy and charge him with a barrage of left hooks and right hands. As usual, when I am angered, my muscles tighten, my timing is thrown off, and my energy drains. But my rage is sated when shots manage to penetrate Vice's guard and skew his head from side to side. He responds with a broad grin and hunts me again.

My only thought in round three is to climb out of the ring. *Did Beau say how many rounds he wants me to spar?* And then Vice's iron fists spark into my toast-rack ribs. A sickening pain devours my body. My legs are bolted to the floor.

"Quit standing in one spot! Do you own that piece of real estate?" shouts Beau. *"Mooove!"*

I desperately try to ward off a man who gave the great Julio Caesar Chavez trouble. Chavez had enough of Vice's insolence and finished the job. But I'm no Chavez, and Vice's punches are hurtful and draining me. My muscles have evaporated in the heat. I can barely carry my arms, never mind throw a punch. "Quit pitty-patting. Punch *hard*," yells Beau.

By round four I'm afraid to move for fear my legs will crumple. It's safer to take the bone-crushing shots than budge out of the way. I'm so exhausted I think I'll hit the mat for the first time—ever. Not from a punch, but from pure fatigue.

The torture ends as Kenny Vice slips out of the ring. Relief rushes through me. And then a young, black featherweight with tattooed arms steps before me. He is wiry, muscled, and grins to expose a few missing teeth behind a yellowed gum shield. This must be my test. Beau knows I have nothing left. But I must prove myself, so I don't object.

The featherweight beats me from corner pad to corner pad. I stick out my gloves but they are empty. To stay upright is all I can hope for. After six rounds I'm allowed out of the ring. Desperate to breathe fresh air instead of steam, I stagger for the door. If I had the strength, I'd kick over the obnoxious crawfish boiler and let the flames ignite this stinking gym.

"Get back in here before you catch pneumonia!" yells Beau.

On the way home I'm soaked in sweat, my head pounds, my torso throbs, and my limbs are dead. I'm aching, wrecked, battered, and hungry. How could I have ended up in such a place? And to think I traveled 4,500 miles to get here. I'm starting to think the worst—that maybe my mother was right.

"Ray's a dick-headed dawg!" exclaims Beau. "I told that little piece of shit not to take liberties. He knew you were dead tired after going four with Kenny."

"I should've been able to handle him," I moan. "I'm sorry. I boxed terrible."

"No sparring for a few days. Not 'till you're over the jetlag." After a long pause, Beau turns to me and says, "Then you're gonna spar Ray again, and you better kick—his—ass. You hear me? Kick his ass 'til his nose bleeds!"

The next morning Beau follows me in his van on my five-mile run. I alternate running three miles one day and five the next. My coach shouts, "Pick it up! Let's go! You're slow as molasses!"

Back at the Williford house, I call Mum and long to wail how homesick and lonely I am. But Beau is in the room. I don't want him to think I'm ungrateful for his hospitality. It takes all my strength not to burst into tears. Somehow talking to Mum makes me even more lonesome for Gavin. I miss him so much. My resolve to make the steadfast decision to come here seems as far away and foggy as Ireland.

After I hang up with my mother, Beau phones boxing connections to find me a bout. And just as I feel another surge of tears well in my eyes, he covers the phone's receiver and says, "You've been offered a fight. Next Monday in Kansas City."

And without hesitation I say, "I'll take it."

"Don't you want to know who you're fighting? And how much you're getting paid?"

"I don't care," I say. "Beggars can't be choosers."

Beau chuckles, shakes his head from side to side, and confirms the match.

My coach hangs up the phone and reminds me to bring my passport to Missouri. "And, of course, your protection," he adds. "The commission will check for it."

"Protection?"

"Yeah, your breast protector and foul cup."

"But I don't have any—"

"What the hell did you wear in your first two fights?"

"Nothing."

"Nothing? Are you fuckin' nuts!"

So we're off to a local karate shop. I purchase a foul cup for female kick-boxers that wraps under my crotch, and a pair of slightly cone-shaped plastic breast cups.

"You look like Madonna." Beau laughs and makes a hollow sound by popping my breasts with his fingers. On the way back to Beau's house, it starts to rain.

By the time Teri arrives home from work, which frees us to go to the gym, the roads are flooded. But I'm so sore from training, the floodwaters are a relief and allow me a chance to rest and rub muscle cream into my shoulders and limbs. I lather it on and suddenly can't breathe. My skin turns bright red. I'm on fire! Beau has to race me through flooded streets to Hamilton Hospital. Four days away from my American debut, I sit in an emergency room and gasp to breathe.

The day after my allergic reaction to an ingredient in the muscle rub, I have my rematch with Ray. The prescribed antihistamine pills make me groggy, but I'm over my jetlag and have been well fed. The only hunger in my belly is the hunger to prove I'm worthy of Beau's time, especially after the hours he just spent in the emergency room.

I plow into Ray and put him on the defensive with fast combinations and hard body shots. "You been practicin' at home or somethin'?" he yelps. But I ignore him and let my hands fly. When he dips under an attack, his eyebrow bumps into one of my breast protectors. "Whatcha got there, Dee?" he demands and then paws his left eye. But I will not afford him any excuses. Revenge is a great energizer. After four rounds of educating Ray, I'm ready for my American debut.

"You did the business this time!" Beau gushes and turns to Kenny Vice. "Whaddaya think, Kenny? Did she beat the piss outta Ray or what?"

"Yeah," agrees Kenny, "she fucked dat bitch up."

CHAPTER 15
STITCH HER UP, DOC

After two weeks of pounding the roads in thick humidity, sweating to the crawfish boiler, and surviving Kenny Vice, I take off with Beau to Missouri. Interstate 49 North stretches out in a straight line and disappears into the horizon. Cotton fields are sprinkled with oil pump jacks that look like giant prehistoric birds, dipping their heads to pick bugs from the grass. Eighteen-wheel cargo trucks blow past and rattle the van.

The fourteen-hour drive to Kansas City gives me an opportunity to learn more about my new coach. With great affection in his voice he tells me about his hometown of Fayetteville, North Carolina, and of his family. When Beau was seventeen, his father, a city court magistrate and mattress factory owner, died of congestive heart failure. After high school, Beau attended Wake Forest University and served in the Army. He moved to New York to pursue a professional career as a heavyweight in the golden era of champions like George Foreman, Joe Frazier, and Muhammad Ali. Beau sparred them all.

He finished the College of New Rochelle with a degree in business and moved to Lafayette in 1979 to work in the oil industry. His explanation of settling down in Cajun country: "I met my wife and got stuck here."

As we enter Shreveport, a cluster of downtown buildings emerges from the flat landscape. "Skyscrapers!" I exclaim. "I've finally seen skyscrapers!"

"Those aren't skyscrapers, you big dummy," quips Beau. "Those are only in places like New York or Chicago."

After we cross the Arkansas border, grain silos replace oil pump jacks until we reach Fort Smith and cross the Ozark Mountains into Missouri. On the other side of the mountains the road is hilly, but I can't see much because it's dark and snowing as we approach the city.

Kansas City streetlights illuminate dirty slush packed hard on the roadsides. Steam drifts from manholes and I spot our reflection—a snow-covered Ford Aerostar van—in the mirrored office buildings that lead to the Marriott Allis Plaza Hotel for our stay and my weigh-in.

The plush accommodation buzzes with people and energy. I'm impressed that everyone seems to know Beau. They greet him like an old friend, a next-door neighbor, a star. Everything about this place seems familiar to my coach.

Nothing is familiar to me, and even the weigh-in is surreal. Somehow, I've come this far without ever doing this part of the fighter's routine. For the first time, I step on a scale, sign a contract, undergo a pre-fight physical, and am granted a boxing license. My contract says I'll be paid three hundred dollars for four three-minute rounds against a local girl, Stacy Prestage, at the weight limit of 128 pounds.

After struggling to fight underground for six years in Ireland, I'm legally licensed to box in the USA.

As I'm taking a few minutes to absorb my newly legal status—*women are allowed to box!*—I hear Beau arguing with the desk clerk.

"But my fighter is a *girl*. The promoter knows damn well we need two rooms!"

"I'm sorry, sir," the lady says with a shrug. "There's only one room booked. The hotel is full."

We lug our things up to the room and I'm relieved there are two beds. My coach claims the remote and the chair closest to the TV. He then lights a cigar and turns up the volume on an old Western movie. I want to soak up America and I don't mind the smoke and the noise. And I can't imagine a better place for that to happen than a hotel room in downtown Kansas City, Missouri, with a view of a bronzed statue of Buffalo Bill rearing on a stallion to the soundtrack of television gunfire.

On fight day, en route to my dressing room, excitement gives way to nerves. What will it be like without Pat in my corner?

To make matters worse, my opponent and I are the only women on the card, so we have to share a dressing room. I never liked meeting my opponent before a fight, and I detest the idea of sharing a dressing room. Beau dashes in and out to chat with friends and acquaintances while Prestage and her team seize every opportunity to intimidate me. They joke they'll be washing my blood out of my opponent's white boots and sports bra. When Prestage finally struts out to the hall, Beau bounds in and says, "Hit her right in the titties!"

"Sorry?"

"I just watched her shadowbox. She's not wearing protection. Her nips are like this." He pushes his thumb through his fingers.

"But I want to win fair."

"Hey, it's the same target area as a man. Punch her right in the tits. You hear me?"

Beau leads me to the ring, and his friend Sean Gibbons, who has offered to assist in the corner, follows us. Prestage fans pack the hotel ballroom. Under an enormous crystal chandelier, I climb between the ropes.

"Jump on her like stink on shit," Beau instructs as Stacy Prestage hops into the ring to rowdy applause.

After the bell my opponent presses toward me with an aggressive, awkward technique. She fights with the classic American crouch style, bobbing and weaving and firing sharp hooks. To the delight of the crowd, I have trouble dodging her powerful right crosses before they sear into the side of my head. She lands three in a row. I consider my coach's advice to hit her in the tits. But it just seems too dirty. I have to figure out another way to win.

My jab keeps Prestage at bay and forces her to throw longer and riskier hooks. Soon I have her rhythm timed and can slip or roll under her right cross and counter with my left hook. When she misses, her punches loop behind my neck and pull me forward. The top of her head bumps into my face, but I retaliate with good shots to her midsection.

"Lookin' good," Beau tells me in the corner. "You won that round. Keep the jab in her face and dig those body shots."

In round two the crowd cheers for my opponent. But then I land a jarring straight right, knocking their hero off balance. I start to judge distance better and am able to push in close, land a power right, and step out of Prestage's reach before she can catch me. And then I step inside her reach. Up close, I relax and inflict more damage.

But then Prestage sweeps in low and—*clonk!*—her skull cracks my left eyebrow. My face stings with pain, but the referee is behind me and has not noticed the foul. I take back my distance and score with the jab. A white cloud of sweat or Vaseline obscures my left eye. I slide back each time her weight rocks forward to avoid her right hand. I can't even see the blistering punches before they whiz by my face, one after another. *Boom!* Prestage lands a right and snaps back my head to a loud *Ooohhhhh!* from the crowd. I never saw the right coming and might as well be wearing an eye patch. As we turn, the referee moves around us. He then steps in and escorts me toward the doctor. I paw at my eye with my glove and notice it's covered with blood.

"The blood's going into her eye," the doctor tells the referee. "She can't continue."

"No, please, I'm fine," I beg. "I'm fine —"

"Sorry, sweetie, I can't let you continue fighting half blind." The doctor apologizes as the referee walks away to wave off the fight.

In agony I circle the ring and kick the air like a brat. My energy drains from my shoulders and I drop my head onto the ropes. I don't even care about making a scene. I refuse to lift my head, so Beau has to coax me upright to place a towel on my cut. "Why didn't you give me a chance to work on the cut?" Beau complains to the referee. But the referee just mutters something and turns away. Beau refuses to be dismissed. "Hey! Why'd you stop it? Why didn't you let me work the cut?" he demands, louder this time.

"*I* run this fuckin' ring, not you, asshole!" shouts the referee.

"Fuck you, you fat piece of shit," snaps Beau. "Didn't you see the head butt? You blind cocksucker."

While the ref and Beau roar insults, a huge man rushes up with balled fists to knock my coach sideways. Our corner man, Sean Gibbons, jumps over the top rope and blocks the furious stranger. Bystanders, along with security, push into the ring to break up the scuffle.

I head to the dressing room and climb on a ballroom table to wait for the fight doctor to examine my eye. I must look a fright with my hair clumped with Vaseline, my clothes and limbs caked with blood. I'm a disheveled heap of disappointment when the physician arrives and prepares to stitch my cut.

"You can't get hit for at least six weeks," he says.

Beau stands beside me and I'm worried he's angry with me for my disastrous debut. The referee didn't see the head butt, so my record will read a loss by TKO in round two. But instead of anger, my coach's words are solicitous and doting. "Will you stitch her on the inside and the outside?" he asks the doctor. He then turns to me to explain, "So there's no scar."

A needle into my eyelid shoots a searing pain to the back of my eye socket.

"That was a better performance than the fight," the doctor jokes. "She didn't even flinch."

On the drive home, I tell Beau it would be best if I fly back to Ireland. No need to stick around here for six weeks if I'm unable to get hit. I'm not even sure Beau wants me to stay and worry he won't want me to come back. But the dread of going home with a loss on my record overrides my worry.

And the *I-told-you-so* I'm bound to receive must be endured. The searing pain of the needle to my eye socket was nothing compared to the constant ache of homesickness. I miss my family. And I miss Gavin, too. Though I intend to return to the States if Beau will have me.

After a fourteen-hour drive, Beau drops me off at my apartment around midnight. I imagine he's glad to be rid of me. I have been in no mood for conversation, and I've spent the entire trip in a pit of brooding silence.

Before I even unpack or brush my teeth, the phone rings. It's Beau. Missouri Boxing Commissioner Jim Hall had left a message on his answering machine. "They reviewed the tape," he tells me. "The decision has been changed from a TKO loss to a technical draw."

Now I can go home with my head up.

Back in Ireland I want to keep a low profile, but the media seems fascinated by my search for a fight in the States. My story is featured in the *Irish Independent*, followed by the *Irish Press*, the *Sunday Tribune*, and the *Star*. The publicity spate even spurs an invitation to appear on Gerry Kelly's chat show on Ulster Television in Northern Ireland.

I'm relieved Gavin seems happy I'm home after his cold reaction to my leaving. He's hardly left my side and travels with me by train to Belfast. At the station we are picked up by a chauffeur in a black Mercedes and driven to the luxurious Stormont Hotel. At the hotel my boyfriend and I share a suite and wrestle in crisp linen sheets, order room service, and pretend to be rich and famous. Gavin, though he's said nothing, seems to accept my boxing career now that I'm afforded such grand treatment and luxury to share with him.

My new status, however, does nothing to soothe my nerves before my first live television appearance on a chat show. They asked me to dress in character, but even dressed in a comfortable tracksuit, runners, and boxing gloves I'm still worried I won't make it to my seat without tripping. Gerry Kelly's other guests are seated across from him and include female rugby players from Northern Ireland, their coach, and the famous former BBC sports commentator, Frank Bough, who was sacked over allegations of drug use and sex scandals.

I sit to the right of the dashing Bough, who asks, "Do you spar with men?"

"Oh, yes," I answer.

Bough then looks me in the eye and says, "I can't go along with that. I'm sorry, I might be old fashioned, but I cannot go along. I mean, you actually spar with men who strike you in the face with their boxing gloves. How do you go along with that? I mean I have difficulty with the rugby, but this—" He points toward the women rugby players to his left and then to me.

Gerry Kelly shows a clip of my bout with Jane Johnson. Afterward, Kelly says, "In the name of God, Deirdre."

But Bough interrupts, "Can I, can I say something? The one thing that marks boxing out from every other sport is, there are dangerous sports and there is boxing. And boxing is the only sport where deliberately you intend to damage your opponent. I can't think of any other sport which you do that. And, and how do you live with that?"

Bough is in striking distance of my gloved fist and sits so relaxed with his legs crossed and arms spread apart, I want to sucker punch him in the solar plexus.

"Well," I say, "beauty is in the eye of the beholder, and to me, I think boxing is a beautiful sport." I look directly at Bough as I continue. "It's very hard for anyone who doesn't understand the sport. You can never explain to them why people do it and what the fascination is."

"Well, that's true," say Bough. "And I enjoy boxing enormously, but I don't like myself for enjoying it. And I just can't actually take-on-board the idea of a girl actually getting hit in the face with a boxing glove."

Kelly tries to take back the interview, but Bough cuts in again and asks, "But you have been struck, have you?

"Oh, yes."

"Have you had your eyes closed?" He points to his right eye and then above it. "A cut? Have you had a nose bleed?"

I'm thankful my cut is covered by makeup when I downplay my answer and say, "I got a cut, but that was an accidental head butt."

Kelly wins back control of the interview at last, but I'm relieved when it's over, since it felt more like a cross-examination. Toward the end I am able to express my intention to return to the States and continue my career in boxing, and I'm glad about that.

Backstage in the green room, Gavin is furious. At first I'm heartened, thinking he shares my anger at Frank Bough's prejudiced remarks. But I quickly learn his rage has nothing to do with the sportscaster's disdain. My words are what have him in a fury.

"Why do you want to go back to America?" he spits. "Look at what happened to your face. If you go back to America," he warns, "we're finished!"

The man I love sounds just like Frank Bough. During the three-hour train ride from Belfast to Dublin, I stare out the window.

Back at home, I'm jazzed to learn Sue Atkins and Mick Nairn have formed the British Ladies Boxing Association (BLBA) and will host the first-ever *licensed* all-women's show.

And I'm set to fight in the main event.

Sadly, not against Atkins for the British title—she is rumored to have retired and only plans to box exhibitions. I will fight her successor, Jane Johnson, once again. I look forward to the fight hungrily, not only for the rush of competition, but to stay busy and keep from thinking about Gavin.

Once my cut has healed, I'm back at Saint Saviours and training with Pat McCormack again. Jimmy Halpin works on my hook. He makes me practice turning my fist over to land a crisper shot with better leverage. Instead of my palm facing me, it faces the floor with my elbow up, so I can throw a parallel punch.

Fight day comes, and I am ready. The venue is in Tooting, South London, at the Foresters Arms, a rundown, seedy pub with red-velvet wallpaper stained with beer spills and vomit, judging by the cocktail of odors. The floor is dark and sticky but the patrons seem ready for a fight.

An impressive number of media folks have gathered for the weigh-ins. Johnson and I pose for the cameras and give interviews on this historic event.

"I heard you got outclassed over in the States," says an *Amazons in Action* photographer.

"Outclassed?" I retort, shocked by his insult.

"Yeah, you got stopped, didn't you?"

"The fight was stopped because of a cut. I wasn't—*outclassed.*"

The photographer disappears when Pat and Paddy Sower approach. They have brought athletic tape to protect my hands, which are injured from working the heavy bag. Paddy applies the tape directly to the skin across the backs of my hands.

The crowd pumps fists in the blue smoky air as Johnson climbs into the ring. I head to my corner to Tina Turner's "Simply the Best." Under ceiling fans, streaming lights, and blinding cameras, I look for my friend Grace, who lives in London. For the first time, I'll have a friend in the audience.

Gavin refused to come, proving it's over for us.

And then the fight starts.

In the first round I use my skills, my reach, and my movement to warm up and find my rhythm. In other words, I box. I take my time and wait for Johnson to attack and then counter with a left hook and straight right. I land a double jab, left hook, and right hand to wobble Johnson against the ropes. She doubles over as I move in and dig shots behind her elbows and into her ribcage. But the bell saves her, just like our last fight.

I pick up the pace in the second round and scam Johnson into dropping her guard by jabbing her midriff. A left hook hurts her again, so I unleash a combination of bad intent. This time the referee gives her a standing eight count. But her reprieve doesn't last long, and she grabs onto me. Johnson is helpless on the ropes and at my mercy. I am swept up in the intensity of controlling this fight. And off goes the blasted bell again.

I'm in a nice rhythm in round three. The left hook Jimmy Halpin helped me to develop punishes Johnson. I'm convinced I can stop her with headshots alone. I nail her with straight rights to knock her sideways and pummel her for the entire round. She's not catching me with anything like the hard right hands Prestage slammed into my face.

I double jab and box in the fourth round. My hands throb, but I'm not concerned, because this is a one-sided bout. Pat wants me to stay to the body. But the body shots only produce standing eight counts—I want a spectacular knockout. So I continue to nail headshots confident, she will crumble. But round four ends and Johnson has made it farther than our last fight.

In the fifth I decide to move and circle the ring to let my opponent come in. Her forward momentum will allow me to land a harder shot. Sure enough, as I box and move, Johnson charges. I catch her with good uppercuts but find myself on the ropes to escape trouble. Johnson knows she must knock me out to win, and her supporters urge her to do so.

I can't believe "Rocky" Jane is still going in round six. Last time I had her out by four. And now I'm feeling weak—not fatigued, just weak—as I box to allow her to run into something big. She swings a backhand at me but misses. I work the jab as she attacks and I'm impressed by her doggedness. She swings another looping backhand but this time she nails my right temple. The referee warns her for the foul, and I box to the finish. The bell sounds, and the ref, the sole judge, raises my hand as the crowd tosses coins into the ring.

Back at Paddy's flat, I'm perplexed by my performance.

"I can't believe I didn't stop her," I complain to Pat.

"The body shots!" he pleads. "Where were the bleedin' body shots?"

I made a terrible mistake. My plan to win with a spectacular knockout backfired. By not sticking to basics, I risked being the one knocked out. I swear to never disobey my coach again.

"Just enjoy the win. It was a good, disciplined boxing performance," Paddy says. "Worry about your mistakes later."

"But I almost had her stopped in the second round."

"I know, I told the timekeeper to ring the bell early."

"What? Why?"

"Well, you said you needed more experience. Now you've got another six rounds under your belt. Be happy with yourself. And let's give Beau a ring."

"That's great, Dee-dra!" Beau gushes across the telephone. "A win is a win. Paddy says you boxed bee-u-ti-ful. Now get your ass back over here."

"Really!"

"Yeah, I've got a fight for you in Arkansas in twenty days. And then you're going to rematch Prestage in June."

I'm thrilled Beau still wants to coach me. And I'm a little surprised how desperately I want to go back after the loneliness that engulfed me in the States—and Lord knows I'm apprehensive to return to the pain and sweat of the chicken shed. But my passion for boxing trumps all else. Not to mention the sweetness of revenge; I get another shot at Stacy Prestage. So it's back to Louisiana.

And back to the bloody crawfish boiler.

CHAPTER 16
THE HANGING JUDGE

After eighteen hours of travel, I'm exhausted when my plane lands in Baton Rouge. But Beau informs me we're driving directly to Fort Smith, Arkansas. Nine hours in a car. No shower. No bed. And a fight in two days.

Before I can hardly blink I'm unpacking in a hotel room in Arkansas. The next morning I'm out of bed and preparing for a phone interview with a local newspaper reporter. Beau talks to the journalist first because he's the show's promoter and has four boxers on the card.

My coach boasts to the press, "Well, of course, fighting in the main event is local hero, heavyweight Bobby 'The Fightin' Hillbilly' Crabtree. Even George Foreman says Bobby hit 'em harder than anybody. Returning from Liverpool, England, we have the knockout puncher, light heavyweight 'Killer' Kenny Rainford.

"Also a crowd favorite, we have the sensational lightweight 'Bad' Chad Broussard, defending his 28-and-0 record. And all the way from Dublin, Ireland, we have the exciting female featherweight," Beau pauses, clearly thinking, and then says, "'Dirty' Dee-dra Gogarty."

Did my coach just call me "Dirty" Deirdre? Whatever happened to "Dangerous" Deirdre, the name given to me in London when I fought Jane Johnson? Surely the reporter knows Beau is joking and won't plaster it in headlines. It sounds too much like the name of a sleazy topless boxer.

After a workout and lunch, Beau and I amble toward the Arkansas River to a popular tourist attraction. Inside a walled-in grassy area are the rebuilt gallows. Painted white wooden steps lead to a platform where six hangman's nooses dangle from the center beam above trapdoors in the platform. In the late 1800s, seventy-nine criminals were hanged at the order of the infamous judge Isaac C. Parker, nicknamed the "Hanging Judge."

"Tomorrow night, I want *you* to sentence this girl from Oklahoma," Beau jokes. "You be the hanging judge." I try to decide which is a worse nickname, the judge's or mine, and find them to be close contenders.

On fight day, I lounge in my hotel room and watch reruns of *Cheers*. My only workout is to practice the left hook Jimmy Halpin helped me to develop. I wait until the last minute before I sprint downstairs. Fight fans pack the Holiday Inn lobby and line up for tickets into the ballroom. In the dressing room my teammates shadowbox and offer their hands to be wrapped in gauze and taped for battle. But "The Fightin' Hillbilly" Crabtree appears to be dozing in a chair.

I figure Crabtree hasn't slept in a week, has narcolepsy, or is supremely confident. Whatever it is, I'm envious of his ability to nap before a match, because there are no peaceful nothings in my head. Last time I was here, I spent the next twenty-seven hours agonizing over the referee's TKO. Even the commissioner's phone call to reverse their mistake did not erase the sting.

My redemption—rather, my lust for revenge—has to wait until June for the scheduled rematch with Prestage. For now, I focus on tonight's opponent, Jane McGehee, the women's division winner of the Oklahoma Toughman Contest. A win tonight is essential for my busted self-esteem.
While "The Fightin' Hillbilly" dozes, I slip into the bathroom and pop the cold, hard breast cups into my sports bra. I try to sneak past Crabtree on my way out, but he must hear me because he peeks through his sleepy lull and blurts, "Damn, Dirty Dee! Your titties growed!" Great. And, he used my awful new nickname, which was printed in the newspaper.

I make my way through the ballroom, rowdy with fans, and into the ring.

At the ding of the bell McGehee barrels toward me. I circle my slightly shorter rival and shoot a jab into her forehead. She flicks a blinder jab and whips a wicked overhand behind it. I dart to my left and twist back with a left hook, elbow up, palm down, arm parallel to the floor while I pivot my weight on the ball of my lead foot. *Bam!* My fist crashes into McGehee's jaw and neck below her ear. She drops like the gallows' trapdoor.

I'm about to raise my gloves in a rush of victory when Beau yells at my fallen opponent, "Get up! Get up! You better get up or you won't get paid!" Why does my coach want my opponent to get up? Doesn't he want me to knock her out?

But it doesn't matter what he wants. This fight is over, twenty-seven seconds into the first round. Jimmy Halpin would be so proud the winning punch was the left hook he taught me. Still, my new coach fumes as McGehee clutches her jaw and, with assistance, lumbers out of the ring.

In the lobby McGehee sits with an ice pack tucked between her neck and right shoulder. She sucks an orange ice pop and mumbles, "You knocked out my back tooth." What can I say? I shrug and let Beau do the talking.

"I'm sorry I threatened not to pay you," he apologizes. "I was mad because I thought you were taking a dive. I didn't realize how hard you'd been hit."

Four days later he next day we pack up the van and drive to Bay St. Louis, Mississippi, because Beau is the matchmaker for a televised boxing show at Casino Magic the following night, May 18, 1993. I don't have a match, but I'm along for the ride and to learn from the champions scheduled to fight.

The Gulf Coast casino floats under a sliver of moon in a stingy, star-sprinkled sky. But inside, the casino is lit up with bell-ringing slot machines and spinning roulette wheels. Not keyed up for a pending bout, I'm able to take in the scenery. Colorful stacks of chips and rolling dice add color and excitement to my road trip.

Beau introduces me to famous boxers: Sean O'Grady, Reggie Johnson, Emile Griffith, and the former heavyweight champion, Larry Holmes. Holmes is confident, boastful, and friendly. He sends his personal physician to examine my sore hands. The doctor explains the ligaments in the backs of my hands have been overstretched from impact and will need total rest in order to heal. Not the diagnosis I was hoping to hear.

But the buzzing casino drowns thoughts of a setback. Just trying to keep up with Beau leaves me no time to think. Five of the six scheduled fights fall out the day before the televised show. Holmes, the main event, has the only intact bout, against Paul Poirier. With a flurry of shuffling, Beau manages to fill the card and save the show with last-minute replacements. But his stress is not over. His middleweight prospect, Jason Papillion, fresh from camp with Roy Jones Junior, gets knocked down early. But then Papillion recovers to TKO his opponent in round three. Whew! And of course, Larry Holmes does not disappoint. He wins the main event when Poirier does not answer the seventh-round bell. We drive back to Lafayette still caught in the ebb of adrenaline.

My apartment was leased to a new tenant while I was out of the country, so I'm to stay with the Williford family. But I feel like an intruder, as three-year-old Christian has to vacate his bed for me. Two days later, Beau hits the road for another show. I'm left behind to prepare for my rematch with Prestage.

Beau's wife Teri rises before daybreak. Somehow she manages to feed and dress her boys while attending to her own hair and make-up. As bank vice president she has to dress up every day. I slip out of the chaos of their morning routine and go for a run as the wet Louisiana heat deepens with the rising sun. By the time I return, the house is empty. I slap together a bologna sandwich for breakfast. Then I shower and dress and write letters to home in an effort to quell my loneliness. After another bologna sandwich, I flop on the couch to watch daytime TV, American style. Phil Donahue and Oprah Winfrey talk about issues we never discuss in Ireland.

My homesick blues retreat when I train at the chicken shed with the suffocating crawfish boiler. I'm back to sparring with iron-fisted Kenny Vice, plus up-and-coming prospects Jason Papillion, "Bad" Chad Broussard, and Timmy Rabon. It's good to have a variety of sparring partners. And they've all been kind enough to give me lifts to the gym and back while Beau's on the road. Still, I wish I were traveling with my coach. A road trip would really defeat the awful homesickness that tracks me like an opponent in the ring.

Famished and soaked in sweat, I drag myself home after an evening work out. Teri glances at me with uncertainty as she lays out an extra dinner plate. After the first serving, she asks if I want seconds. "I wouldn't say no," I say. She, the twins, and Christian seem surprised yet entertained by my large appetite.

Finally my coach returns, but my loneliness holds on even in Beau's presence. It's as though the stillness between fights unlocks a door on my feelings. But the Prestage fight is three weeks away. Surely I can last three weeks. I raise my spirits with thoughts of redemption. I'm also looking forward to a trip back to Ireland to visit my family.

Then I learn the rematch has been postponed for two months. "You'll have more time to let your hands heal," Beau tells me. But he knows I'm depressed and desperate to stay busy. He wrangles with various promoters to find me a fight, but no one's interested.

After a month crawls by, Beau leaves for another out-of-town show. The Williford children are freed from school and home all day for summer holidays. I have to cut short my morning runs because the boys follow me. They are unable to keep up, and I can't leave them abandoned on the street, though I fight back wild thoughts of doing just that. After four or five attempts, I sneak out the house for a proper run. And then I come home to discover the twins rummaged through my belongings. They have uncovered my bras to great hilarity.

Adding to my misery, red blotches bloom in bright patches across my face. I've visited various doctors with no diagnosis. I'm only told that the rash is not acne, and sun exposure activates it even more. I knew *that* already.

"Why are you so white? Is there no sun in Ireland?" one of the twins pesters.

"Why is your face always so red?" the other chimes in.

When I discover acne medication planted in my suitcase, it sets off a good cry. My lack of privacy is as disconcerting as the noise and activity. The kids' incessant energy and questions wear me out. While I'm privately thinking I never want children, Teri wants to know why I would leave my family in Ireland to become a boxer. Am I not ready to settle down at the age of twenty-three, she asks?

But I don't answer her questions. I've been down this road before. I know I cannot explain my desire for boxing, and especially to such a normal woman, a natural wife and mother, juggling a career with ease. She's good at her job but family is her world. Boxing, however, is the only thing that makes me feel whole. And defeating Prestage is what I need right now, not a husband and kids. I wonder if any other woman could understand that.

I hide in Beau's office in the comfort of silence. Every evening the sound of Teri's pointy heels—*click, click, click*—across the kitchen floor gives me a fright. She cooks dinner and then goes to bed. Christian asks why his mother and I never talk to each other and, once again, I'm unable to answer him. How can I say to a four-year-old that I admire his mum's hospitality but I'd rather be alone?

At last I'm offered a reprieve when Beau's friend, John McGovern, invites me to train and stay at his home in Cottonport, Louisiana, an hour north of Lafayette. I'd first met John at the casino in Bay St. Louis and liked his dry wit. A boxing fan and former golfer, he works as classification director at the Avoyelles Correctional Center. He thinks he can arrange for me to spar with inmates in the prison's boxing program.

Since Beau is still out of town, McGovern picks me up on his day off in a shiny, dark-green Mercury Cougar. My rescuer is an attractive man with brown eyes, thinning dark hair, and a well-trimmed mustache. During the hour-long drive, he tells me he once lost a golf scholarship. As he talks, I discover the setback left him cynical and sarcastic. I understand better why he's nicknamed "Moan 'n' Groan." But to me, he's wonderful company because his sour attitude is sweetened with humor.

And he doesn't ask me probing questions that I cannot answer.

When we arrive at John's weathered wooden rent-house, he shows me to my small bedroom with a view of a weedy field and a pretty brown-and-white filly. Nice, I think, until I pull back the bedspread and discover my sheets are sprinkled with tiny v-shaped insect legs and wispy cockroach wings. But with a little brushing off, I settle in. It's nowhere near as bad as the chicken shed.

At six the next morning, I run along Bayou Rouge to the tropical clatter of crickets and frogs. Fog lifts as egrets take flight toward the rising sun. Cottonport-to-Bunkie commuters honk their horns, and I'm not sure if they're being friendly or just want me out of the way.

Back at the house John explains that news travels fast in Cottonport. The locals already know I'm a boxer from Ireland and that I'm here to train for a fight. So they are just being friendly. But I don't venture outdoors after noon because of the heat and swarming mosquitoes. Again I miss the cool air and tranquil hills of Ireland, where nothing will sting or bite without provocation.

My second day in Cottonport, John's Baton Rouge girlfriend barges through the back door with suitcase in hand and plans to stay until I leave. Jackie is pudgy with short, bayou-brown hair and sun-damaged skin. She cooks and cleans with an ambition to marry. She is nice and tries to engage me in conversation, but I hate small talk and have nothing to say. My reticence seems to make her uneasy, and she complains to John that I don't like her.

At work John tries to cut through the red tape preventing me from sparring with inmates, but it's not looking good. After my morning run, I punch the air, pump a stationary bicycle, ignore Jackie, and eat my way through my benefactor's groceries. By the time it's apparent Avoyelles Correctional Center will never allow me to spar, I'm pre-menstrual and bloated and eight pounds overweight.

When Beau picks me up in his brand new Chevrolet Suburban, I immediately whine about my weight gain. My coach is furious and scolds John for my lack of training. But blame doesn't drop an ounce for me, and now I must lose eight pounds in a week to prepare for my match with Prestage.

Back in Lafayette I spar daily with two-time national Golden Gloves champion Timmy Rabon. After six rounds, Beau works me to exhaustion on the punch-back mitts to make up for my lack of sparring. En route to Missouri, torturous hours of starvation begin. To quickly drop weight not sweated out at the gym, I swallow a handful of laxatives.

"Don't worry," soothes Beau, "after we cross through Arkansas, we'll stop and get you a hobo sundae."

"Oh, yeah. What's that?" I ask, my mouth watering at the thought.

"You'll see. Be patient."

Twelve hours later, stomach stuck to my spine, Beau reveals the mouthwatering contents of a hobo sundae. "A glass of water and a toothpick," he chuckles.

Beau's laughter is cut short when a truck darts out in front of us, and we slam into the passenger side of its cab. My head hits the rearview mirror and cracks the windshield. I flop back in my seat feeling stunned and dizzy. The truck driver skids to a stop, inches from the edge of a thirty-foot drop into a concrete culvert. And he doesn't seem the least bit thankful to be alive. He's in a rage as if the accident was our fault. But Beau is calm even though his new Suburban is ruined.

Unlike my coach, I'm in a panic. If we don't make the weigh-in on time, or if my injuries are visible, I won't be allowed to box. But Beau takes care of everything. He hires a car, and we make it to Kansas City only a few hours late. I've missed the weigh-in, but the commission understands that we had an accident and allows me to forgo stepping on the scales. It seems starvation was in vain. And it's a good thing, because the laxatives did not work.

Until the morning of my fight.

Diarrhea and nerves leave me weak and shaky. And now the bump on my forehead has swelled and is more visible than the day of the crash. I worry the fight doctor will spot it and pull me off the card. But he doesn't even glance at me, and Prestage and I are gloved up in the ring. Announcing legend Michael Buffer introduces us to an eager crowd.

Prestage fires hooks to start the fight, so I use my jab to keep her on the end of my punches and to force her shots to fall short. I land a straight right and follow with a harder right. She shoots back with right and left hooks and rushes me to the ropes. I fight back and turn her by rolling my upper body to slip her arcing punches. When she misses, my counterpunch rocks her head and I attack her body. In control of the bout, I pick up my punch rate and slip under another left hook to score body shots. I then land a barrage of punches to finish the round.

I continue to outbox Prestage in the second round by exacting my jab. "Angles, Dee-dra, angles!" shouts Beau. My opponent's attacks are ineffective as I jab and pivot to keep my distance. A couple of times Prestage moves to the ring's center as if to avoid running into punishment from chasing me.

In my corner I watch an athletic round-card man in black-and-white striped shorts incite whistles from women and jeers

129

from guys in the crowd. My mind drifts in amazement to the radical changes in women's boxing. In men's matches, bikini-clad women hold up cards with a number to announce the next round. This is the first time I've seen a man do the job.

I quickly reprimand myself for thinking about anything other than this fight. But everything is going well, and I feel at peace with my place in the world after months of frustration.

At the beginning of the third round I land a straight right that forces Prestage to drop her head and cover up. But she bursts out of cover with an attack. Sharp shots penetrate my guard. She jars my head back with a right hand to cheers from the crowd, but I pivot off the ropes and catch her with a solid left hook. Her nose spouts bright blood as she gasps for air. I then land a crisp jab and she staggers. So I nail her with clean straight rights, left hooks, and more unanswered jabs. The bell rings and I'm impressed with the amount of punishment my opponent can take.

This time an unimpressive skinny guy with a mullet carries the round-card and is booed. I'm in the blue corner and breathe easily through my nose. I purposely keep my mouth closed as I stare at Prestage, who pants in the opposite red corner. Crestfallen, she stares back at me.

Early in the fourth round I land a beautiful one-two punch. I then circle Prestage and notice her pretty brown eyes sink into her face. The glaze of despondency has dulled her usual bright countenance. In contrast, I feel lit and aligned. I can't miss! It's as if everything I've worked for has come together—right now—in this moment.

"You're nailing her with the jab every time," Beau yells from the corner.

He's right, but I to wonder how many more jabs it will take to stop her.

Prestage comes out hard in the fifth as though she knows she's behind on points. She charges after me, so I turn her on the ropes and dig a right hook into her ribs. Too straight with her feet, she's off balance, so I shift to my right, smack her with two right hands, and follow with a left hook that drills into her forehead. She staggers backward and Beau yells, "On her. On her!"

In the final round I move, give angles, and box. The only interruption to my rhythm is when I slip onto my back in Prestage's soaked corner. She runs into everything I unleash. At the sound of the bell I'm thrilled I've won so decisively. Triumphant, I embrace my coach, whose smiling face reflects my own delight with a dominating performance.

Michael Buffer begins the formality of calling the scores. "After six rounds of action, here are the score totals: 59 to 55 for Prestage. 58 to 57 for Gogarty. And the final score is 57 to 57. Ladies and gentleman, this bout is a *draaawww!*"

Are you kidding me? I can't believe this. The referee raises our hands as the crowd boos the decision.

"You won the fight," Prestage tells me. She touches my arm and trudges away, hanging her head.

Beau confirms her words when he says loud enough for everyone to hear, "The three judges must've been Ronnie Milsap, Ray Charles, and Stevie Wonder if they couldn't see the ass-whippin' you gave her. They're the real hanging judges, 'cus they just hung you."

Whatever they want to call the decision, I know I won. And thankfully, the disappointment doesn't diminish my performance or my desire to box. If anything, it drives me to plan my future. My tourist visa is expiring, so I'll need to leave for Ireland in a few days. But I decide to return with a green card in order to work and rent my own place. My best shot for a career is here in America, and I am now certain that I intend to live here permanently.

Of course, I make this decision without consulting Beau. When I tell him, he is less than enthusiastic. He seems open to the idea but is quick to remind me he's not my manager and has just been helping me out. "The guys will always have preference," he tells me. In other words, if I have a bout scheduled elsewhere, on the same night as one of the male boxers, I will go it alone. But his words don't discourage me. I've heard it all before, and by now I believe I'm on a path that cannot be blocked.

Back in Ireland, I doggedly pursue tedious paperwork and gather photos, garda station forms, and lung x-rays to obtain a

Morrison Visa Green Card. And then in September, Beau calls to tell me in November I may have a world title fight in Florida with Christy Martin. The title will be the first Women's International Boxing Federation Championship, created by Jimmy Finn and Barbara Buttrick. Originally from Yorkshire, England, Buttrick—known as "The Mighty Atom of the Ring"— boxed in booth shows in the 1950s and became the world flyweight and bantamweight champion.

Word spreads about my possible title fight and Channel 4, Europe's cutting-edge TV station, wants to do a documentary about women's boxing. Producer Ann Lalić flies over from England and meets me at Mum's townhouse for an interview. She wears sensible shoes and a pantsuit and wears her jet-black hair in a blunt-cut bob. She's professional and efficient and asks lots of questions. We watch a few tapes of my bouts, and then she rushes off to the airport, enthusiastic about the possible documentary.

A few weeks later Ann Lalić returns from England, but this time she brings a camera crew. She interviews Mum and then films me training at Saint Saviours with Pat McCormack and Jimmy Halpin. The crew sets up a little track to allow the cameras to circle the ring.

But the world title and subsequent documentary are in jeopardy when the Martin match falls apart a few weeks later. Since the WIBF is newly formed, there is no champion of women's boxing. Christy Martin, Stacy Prestage, and I are considered to be the top three female contenders. So Beau gets on the phone and replaces Martin with Prestage.

For the third time, we are scheduled to fight in Prestage's backyard in Kansas City, the territory of my hanging judges.

CHAPTER 17
SHOT FOR THE TITLE

November, the month of my title fight with Stacy Prestage, I'm back in the States and camped in a Lafayette hotel room. Since I'm featured in the upcoming Channel 4 documentary, Hotel Acadiana provides me with a room in exchange for advertising they'll receive in the film. I'm on my own for now; my coach is in Las Vegas with "Bad" Chad Broussard, who is boxing on the undercard of Evander Holyfield and Riddick Bowe's main-event rematch.

Without Beau to advise me I run alone in the mornings near the hotel on Pinhook Road. To escape heavy traffic, I run along La Rue France until I reach Tower Plaza, a large glass office building with lush landscaping and a lovely hill sprinkled with trees. I keep running until I reach the railroad tracks and tear down a sloping road to the sounds of a train's whistle and the roar of a jet preparing to land at the nearby airport. When I reach General Mouton, I sprint by an underpass behind Dependable Dodge and the biggest American flag I've ever seen. My route takes me across a bridge over the Vermilion River, past a Masonic cemetery, and finally back to the hotel.

When Beau returns from Vegas, the Channel 4 producer, Ann Lalić, calls to verify her crew will arrive in ten days to resume filming the documentary. So we clean up the chicken-shed gym and slap fight posters over the mold stains. But the posters do little to hide the burgeoning black masses on the walls and the ceiling.

Beau leaves town yet again, so Jason Papillion and "Bad" Chad Broussard provide lifts to the gym. Some nights, for extra sparring, Chad takes me thirty miles to the Frog Capital Boxing Club in Rayne, Louisiana, where I box ten rounds, fighting a fresh man every round.

The day after my coach returns, Ann Lalić and her Channel 4 crew arrive from England. Cameras shadow my every move and capture my coach working punch-back pads with me. They then follow us to lunch at Pete's Sports Bar. A reporter asks Beau why he decided to take me on. He tells the reporter about the letters I sent him from Ireland.

"I got her letters all right, except I threw 'em in the trash."

My salad stops in my esophagus at Beau's shocking revelation. "Then Paddy Sower called me," he continues, "wanting to know why the hell I hadn't contacted this Irish girl. I told him the truth, that I threw the letters away because I had no interest whatsoever in a woman boxer."

I'm frozen, the salad stuck in my throat. I had no idea how much Beau didn't want me to come here. I can't seem to swallow as he finishes his story.

"Well, Paddy reminded me of the times he'd taken care of me in London and asked if I'd do him a favor and help this girl, adding that she could *really* fight. So I watched some tape and invited her over, figuring she wouldn't last long. The training and the heat would be too much for her.

"On the first day I put her in with world-ranked Kenny Vice, and boy, he gave her a good spanking. Then a promising featherweight, Ray Ryan, beat the snot out of her. I really felt kinda sorry for her but figured it was best in the long run, you know, make her realize what she'd gotten herself into. Well, it shows how dumb I was. A few days later she beat the absolute dawg outta Ray. That was eleven months ago and we've never laid eyes on him since," my coach brags. "So, she really had to prove herself to me. And here we are, on the verge of a world title. But, you know, that comes from dedication. Nobody stuck a shotgun up her behind and said she had to do this. Nobody said it was gonna be a rose garden."

Gulp! I'm finally able to save myself from choking.

The next day, the Channel 4 crew flies to Kansas City to film footage of the town. Beau and I catch a later flight and are there when Barbara Buttrick arrives with the first ever WIBF World Title Belt. I want to own that belt more than anything in this world. I know the belt's tacky, gold and oversized with a buxom woman on it. But I don't care. The belt represents my life's primary ambition to be a championship boxer.

On the eve of my title fight, Beau sends me to bed early. But the TV crew clamors into my room with lights, camera, and sound boom. They push my bed in front of the window for a view of the city. I lie down and pretend to relax while a camera zooms in on the bump on my nose (not caused by boxing). Ann

Lalić asks for insight into my thoughts the night before a big fight.

"It's great to win," I tell her, "it's a great feeling. That you've put yourself in such a predicament and come out on top, and that your opponent is doing everything to prevent you from doing that, and you get through it. So, eh, you know, it's very exciting. It's worth it in the end, but in the build-up, you're kind of wondering, 'God, I must be crazy. What am I doing this for?' But afterward, it's worth every drop of anxiety."

The producer must be satisfied with my rambling answer because she orders the crew to pack up their equipment, push my bed back into place, and leave me alone with my pre-fight jitters.

The morning of my shot at the title, I try to force down a traditional American breakfast of scrambled eggs, sausage, and pancakes. But I'm too self-conscious to eat with Channel 4's camera on me. I push away from the table and escape outdoors. I walk around the corner to a convenience store and buy a Fifth Avenue candy bar. The cashier, a young blonde woman, recognizes me and asks, "How d'ya think you'll do in the fight?" In an uncharacteristic outburst, I blurt, "I think I'll stop her this time." I don't know what came over me. I leave the store uneasy and embarrassed by my hubris.

That evening, a few hours before my bout, I approach the dressing room area and overhear Beau and Joe Gallegos, Prestage's trainer, arguing about the gloves we'll use to fight. And then I spot my opponent milling around with a blonde woman—*the* blonde woman from the convenience store. Christ! The cashier is giving me hard looks, and I'm embarrassed she's told my opponent I bragged that I'd stop her.

More edgy than ever, I try to psych up for my match. People always talk about "psyching up" for a fight, but I've never really known what that means. I assume it means to think nonstop of the bout. But when I think about my bout too long beforehand, it creates nervous energy and negative scenarios play out in my head, so I do my best to empty my mind until the last possible moment. The arena is where it gets real for me. I can see, feel, and imagine the crowd, as though gathering external knowledge will help me internally. Then I head to my dressing room and try to visualize my strategy.

In the dressing room I'm glad to see Sean Gibbons is here and will assist Beau as cut man in my corner. I remember that Sean worked the corner of my first Prestage fight when a brawl broke out, and he blocked a furious stranger from attacking my coach. But even the presence of a proven ally does nothing to calm my nerves. War is waging in my head. Both outcomes, a win or a loss, fight for center stage as bloodied men return from the ring.

As Beau wraps my hands, my head settles; the tightly bound gauze and athletic tape transform me into a professional boxer. With wrapped hands I feel strong enough to punch through a locked gate. Beau rubs Vaseline on my arms, legs, and face. "If only you knew where my hands have been," he jokes to ease my anxiety. Too nervous to laugh, I force a snicker for the cameras.

When it's time to glove up, I rush to the toilet and discover a crimson shock. Pain in my abdomen should've warned me of my period, but I tried to deny the ache in an effort to keep menstruation away. A heavy bleeder, I always use the highest absorbency tampons and, as backup, stitch a sanitary napkin into my knickers to ensure stability. But there's no time for stitching. And, to make matters worse, my hands are too slippery with Vaseline to grip the tampon's applicator. Cursing my female body, I finally manage to insert the damn thing.

In the ring I slip my hands into the compact eight-ounce Reyes gloves. It seems Beau won that argument. As I wait for the introductions, nerves and period cramps mesh into one concave throbbing. Then a cold sweat comes over me as I stare toward the red corner.

In most fight venues the red corner is for the house fighter, and the blue corner is for the visiting opponent. The only time I've fought in the red corner, a head butt cracked my skull open. My first piece of good news all night—Prestage is already in the red corner when Sean Gibbons signals me to make my entrance toward the ring and my favorite blue corner.

A rowdy crowd of spectators makes way for my team as I jog behind Beau to U2's "The Real Thing." The crowd's cheers and excitement energize me. But just as I climb through the ropes, I hear the officials tell Prestage she's in the wrong corner.

They make us switch sides.

I have to give up the blue corner and wait while the Channel 4 crew scrambles to reposition their equipment to the opposite side of the ring. While waiting, I notice the ropes sag and are far too loose. Then Beau yells, "Stay off these ropes, Deedra!"

In the red corner I stand and listen to the announcer introduce the judges, the referee, Prestage, and me. Then the fighters are asked to meet center ring. Prestage and I stand face to face as the ref instructs us to fight clean.

In the first round I give angles to probe with my jab and catch my opponent with hard rights and follow with a left hook. I'm able to block her attacks, so I shoot a left hook to her body. Prestage counter-punches, so I counter right back with hooks to escape her wildly thrown retaliations.

My rival lands a powerful right to my face in the second round. She then charges me toward the ropes. But the ropes are so loose I can't gauge where I'm standing. I do manage to pop her with a few straight rights to even the score. But I'm worried an even score won't be good enough to beat the hometown favorite. And then someone chants my name and I wonder who it is. My focus evaporates.

Prestage must sense my lack of concentration. She bounds into the ring's center to start the third and digs me hard with an illegal blow to the hip. My leg muscles weaken and die. I can't tell if the hip blow was deliberate, but it left me immobilized. She then pushes me into the ropes, leans hard, and pushes off me as referee Kevin Champion breaks us apart. I fight back against her crude tactics and raise a swelling under her eye. I finish the round on a weak leg but am boxing well enough to break even.

My opponent bulls me to the ropes again in the fourth and nails me with a hard right. She jams her thumb into my left eye socket, and now I can't see. A blurred disk obscures the buzz saw spinning toward me from all angles. *Is my retina detached?* I'm cracked with another powerful right and pushed into the loose ropes. Panic grabs hold of me. I've lost the round.

Beau growls at me as I return to my corner. I hate to disappoint him and try to explain that my vision is blurred. But he misunderstands my Irish accent and asks, "What's wrong with your arm?"

"No, my eye. My left *eye*. She thumbed me in the eye."

"Well, thumb her back then," he snaps as if the answer is obvious. Beau squeezes a wet sponge over my eyebrow. "You wanna win the fight?" he asks.

"Yes."

"Okay, then. You gotta do something. Because if you have another round like you just had, I'm stopping it."

"No, please."

"Hush!"

"Don't stop it," I beg.

"Don't talk back to me!" he barks and slaps me across the face.

What is happening? Why is this all going so wrong, so fast?

"All you gotta do. Listen to me! All you gotta do is what you're capable of doing. You're letting her run all over you. Like an amateur."

Awakened, I start the fifth with a sharp jab that snaps back my opponent's head. I plant another hard jab into her nose to open a gush of dark blood that indicates a break. Beau shouts, "Press!" Prestage flails back and charges into me with a head butt. But I don't care. I'm boxing my way back into the fight, enough to win the round.

After the bell to start round six Prestage pushes me into the ropes again. But this time she shoves hard enough to send me right through. I land on my bottom, and the ref has to grab my arms to pull me inside the ring. Back on my feet I try to regain my composure but I've lost the snap in my punches. Prestage lands a few shots to tighten the score. And a tight score means a loss on the judges' cards.

Early in the seventh round I penetrate Prestage's guard and bury rights into her face. Her nose continues to gush and her face is a swollen, bloody mess. I'm back in control and confident I've won this round. But in order to win the fight, to become champion of the world, I need to keep Prestage from bullying me and continue to outbox her.

And that's exactly what I'm doing in the eighth when Prestage smacks my face with her head. I paw at my eye and swipe blood. But the amount of blood doesn't signify a bad cut so I'm not alarmed. I'm clearly out-pointing my rival. And then she bowls me into the ropes and shoves her elbow into my neck. Prestage forces my torso over the top rope. My back strains under her weight. I'm about to fall out of the ring when I feel large hands on my back pushing upward to save me. I've won the round despite my opponent's dirty tactics.

In the ninth I aim to take Prestage to the trenches and beat her at her own game. I've had enough of her shenanigans and go straight to work, up close and on the inside. Kenny Vice taught me a thing or two in the chicken-shed gym where I had no choice but to master the nuances of up-close survival under his relentless pressure.

As I manipulate inside and dig body shots and uppercuts, my opponent spits out her mouthpiece. The ref waits for a clinch to halt the fight to allow Prestage to replace her gum shield. After the break I go right back inside to land more good shots to win the round.

"Okay, great work. Now make this a big round," Beau urges. "Don't leave any question to the judges. Knock her ass out, Deedra."

In the tenth and final round I go straight to battle. Toe-to-toe, I hustle and repeatedly fire hard left hooks to Prestage's battered head. My mind hungers for the tacky belt and commands me to push harder. I've transformed my opponent's face into pulp. A tennis-ball-sized swelling juts from her right cheekbone. Her nose is flattened and spurting blood.

The final bell rings and I return to my corner. Beau gives me a sip of water, removes my mouthpiece, and wipes my face. He then unlaces and removes my gloves. I walk in circles and wait for the call.

"Ladies and gentlemen, we have a majority decision," begins the announcer.

"Aw shit!" blurts Beau.

"One judge saw the fight 95 to 95. The others, 98 to 92 and 97 to 93. The winner by majority decision—Stacy Prestage!"

"You can't get a decision in someone's hometown, ya know," cut man, Sean Gibbons complains to the press. "You're fightin' in her hometown. It's about the third time they did it to her. She come up here before. She got head-butted. Then, they called the last one a draw when she won easily. And now, you've seen this. Man, look at her," he points to Prestage's distorted face, "and look at her," he points to me. "Her face looks beautiful."

"It's two times she beat the snot out of her up here and they stole the fight," Beau states as he stares into Channel 4's camera. He then turns toward me and rubs my shoulder and tussles my sweat-soaked curly mane. "C'mon, c'mon, sweetheart, you're alright. We know who the real champ is. C'mon." He turns to the camera and says, "I'm pissed off! All of Ireland, England, Wales, Scotland," he stops talking, looks down, and starts to walk away. But then he aims his anger back to the camera and adds, "Kansas City can kiss—my—ass!"

But my coach's outrage doesn't change one simple fact: I had the chance of a lifetime and blew it. I cracked under pressure early in the match. I panicked and let the fight get too close. To win the world title would have validated every risk, every busted relationship, and every morsel of angst. I would have been proven a winner, not just a hopeless dreamer. But there will be none of that. No congratulations or pats on the back for me.

I'm exposed as a failure.

And on national TV.

CHAPTER 18
COURAGE TO CHANGE

I've been gone so long, I feel like a tourist as I stroll down Grafton Street in Dublin. But then I spot the tiny plastic reindeer flying in circles behind the huge display windows of Brown Thomas. Familiar elves and snowmen repeat mechanical motions at Switzers and merge with my childhood memories. I recall the innocent girl who once trembled while waiting to share wishes and dreams with Saint Nick. But all grown up and toting a box of my possessions to sell, I'm utterly aware that wishes and dreams sit in my own failing hands and not in the hands of a white-bearded old man in a red suit.

"Gloves Gogarty!" a voice calls from the busy street, another sure sign that I'm home.

I easily spot my friend Declan, a former coworker from Murakami Wolf and the only person to use that nickname. His hair hangs in long, bleached yellow strings with black roots. A tinge of black eyeliner, a single looped earring, and a leather rope necklace decorate his stark white skin. His black leather jacket is as scratched and worn as his black jeans and stained tie-dye T-shirt. He holds a lager and wears the scent of pot.

"Deckers!" I scream.

"Where the fuck 'ave you been?" asks my old friend. "I haven't seen you in yonks!"

"I've been traveling back and forth to the States to box," I explain. "I'm moving there permanently and already have a deposit on a flat."

"Moving over with the Yanks?"

"That's right. But first I need to collect my art portfolio and find a pawnbroker to sell my belongings."

"You're seriously into this shit?"

I wish I could tell him I'm world champion so he'd understand. The documentary will not air for several months, so for now, I'm spared the public humiliation of my disastrous title loss. My black eye has turned a faint yellow, and my cut has disappeared into the crease of my eyelid, but shame hangs over me like the holly strung above the street.

"I hope you're using that great ring name I gave you," he says.

"You mean Gloves Gogarty?"

"No, I mean, Ferocious Vagina!"

"Yeah, and you should be the Impenetrable Prick," I quip, and we both choke with laughter.

After we chat for a while and catch up on old times with the Ninja Turtles, I show Declan my collection of wares for sale. My tapes and CDs, Walkman, camera, even an expensive watch I purchased with my first Murakami Wolf paycheck. The perennial joker's face turns serious.

"I need every penny I can get," I explain. "My traveler's checks are gone. And I used my fight money on the flat and the flight home."

"Are you really sure you want to do this? I mean, what if it doesn't work out? You'll be left with nothing."

I try to explain to Declan that it's no longer a question of whether I should do this or not, it's only a matter of how. And then I reluctantly tell him goodbye. Recognition on the streets is such a rarity back in the States. I'm hesitant to leave the company of an old friend. But I'm pulled away by a stronger desire to find a pawnbroker and raise funds to support my career in boxing.

In a seedy basement I accomplish my mission. A balding, olive-skinned man glances at my belongings with acute boredom. "Therty pownds for de lot," he grunts.

Luckily, my sister Adrienne gives me a much better deal on my TV, video player, and stereo system. But the hardest things to part with are my boxing books and videos, which I take to Saint Saviours' gym to sell or give away.

Dad visits and insists on taking me to an art shop for supplies. He still thinks I'm intent on landing a fabulous graphic design job. But I don't want to spoil his excitement by telling him my intention in the States is to be a prizefighter, not a graphic artist. I don't say a word as he forages through art supplies and pays a ludicrous price for a few sketchpads, one of every class of pencil, and a protractor. What I really need is cash. Then my father whisks me away to his home in Julianstown near Drogheda, where he lives with Jean. It's the same house where I'd stop over to chat with Jean before their affair became public knowledge. And it's the same house where Mum found them together six years ago. But I'm too desperate for my father's company and affection to decline the visit.

At the top of the driveway stands one of Dad's sculptures, a life-size Viking with windblown hair cemented in motion. The warrior grips a drawn sword and impresses visitors upon entering the garden. Christmas roses and winter clematis burst in blooms against a garnish of golden beech hedges. Together with finely trimmed grass, the scene reveals a horticultural passion I'd assumed Dad lacked, for he never stepped foot in Mum's garden nor paid her the slightest compliment. I feel guilty being here, and I hope Mum never finds out. To make things worse, most of my father's sculptures on the ivy-covered walls are images of Jean. It's my first visit to their home as a couple, and I can't swallow how awkward I feel.

We go inside for tea and toast and Jean must sense my discomfort. I offer her pleasant chat and jovial quips, but she is dismissive and withdraws. I return to Mum's house in Dublin feeling like a fool and a traitor.

My mother's chatty and upbeat when she sees me. I'm glad to learn she continues to visit the psychiatrist. She seems stable but still complains about Dad's departure. And it's clear she doesn't want me to move to the States, although for Christmas she gave me a Louisiana travel book and an Al-Anon publication titled *Courage to Change*. The books are a fine gesture, especially since I know my leaving is so difficult for her. I tuck the books into my suitcase, sip tea, and listen to Mum's stories on my last night in Ireland.

CHAPTER 19
DUST OF THE DUNES

This trip back to the States is more cheery. I don't have to stay with the Willifords or in a hotel room. I've rented a flat that looks like the set of a '70s TV series, with dusty, fake wood paneling on the living room walls. Curtains in various shades of brown, yellow, and orange block any hint of sunlight. The furniture mismatches from Lego blue to mossy green and is punctuated by a bright gold vinyl recliner that leans to one side. And it's all nestled on a cowpat-brown shag wall-to-wall carpet. But it's cozy. And it's mine.

In my job search I quickly learn an Irish education and work experience mean nothing to potential employees. No one recognizes the companies on my *curriculum vitae* or wants to call Ireland to check references. It's as if I had no life before coming to the States. Desperate, I ask Beau to help me. So he asks a friend to hire me as a waitress in his sports bar. I'm given the job but I hate waiting tables. The exhausting pretense of cheerfulness confounded by my painful fear of strangers leaves me in a constant state of distress. When Beau gives me a lift to work, I beg him to let me sit in the car until seconds before my shift.

Inside, a windowless cavern of flickering TV screens bans me from daylight—and calm—for hours. My first duty is to clear empty beer bottles left on dirty tables from the night before. I tediously fill tiny plastic tubs with mayonnaise and ketchup under the critical eye of the busybody bartender. And then I brace myself for the dreaded lunch-hour barrage of customers.

I scribble down demands, I deliver the orders to the kitchen, but I'm confused and can't read my own scribbles. I get a furious glare from the chef, and I know I'm not cut out for this job. Back out on the floor, a picky child sniffles and asks, "Where are my extra pickles? I said I didn't want tomatoes. Ugh! I *hate* lettuce. I can't eat this!"

I want to tell him to pick the fucking lettuce out with the hands God gave him, but his parents glower at me over my shameful mistakes.

At the end of each day, my tips are pathetic and confirm I am a lousy waitress. But I am due a basic wage payment in a couple of weeks, so I continue to work. I stare out a side-door window that leaks sunshine into the dark bar. Just like in school, I dream of my escape to the outdoors to bask in the light of day.

The hostility of other wait staff is palpable and competition for tables is fierce. But I don't care. They can have my tables. I cringe when customers sit at my station, so it's no surprise that after paying the busboy and taxes, only a few dollars remain. I take solace in knowing my basic wage check is due and go to collect it. But I'm told I haven't been clocking in properly. There's nothing to collect.

To add to my disappointment, a large group arrives the same afternoon. Thankfully, they sit at another station. But the boss, watching the floor from his elevated throne on a shoeshine chair, clicks his fingers, pointing at me to spring into action. Humiliated, I dole out menus. I start for the kitchen, take a detour, and escape through the side door. I am in the sunlight. My apron is in the garbage bin. I am flat broke.

But I'm free.

Another month of unemployment passes before my portfolio opens the door to an interview at an advertising agency. I'm worried because my works of pencil illustration, Letraset typography, photo bromides, and animation cells are dangerously close to industry extinction. The interview goes well until my handsome interviewer, Larry Sides, notices my lack of computer experience. But I'm desperate for income, so I put on my best act until he believes I'm capable of microchip wizardry. In truth, my tiny bit of computer experience encompasses a few hours a week at my FÁS course, time I spent in dreamland or flirting with Adam.

The first two weeks at Sides & Associates, I struggle to learn Quark and Adobe Illustrator. I blame glitches in the computer and printer for my slow output, smile reassuringly, and somehow earn a handsome nine dollars an hour. I have a payroll check in hand for the first time in ages, but cashing it is impossible without a driver's license. The bank teller says my green card is not valid identification. Finally, Beau's wife Teri sorts things out with the bank, and I purchase a second-hand bicycle.

My new life in America has settled into a routine. I wake up at five-thirty to go for a morning run, alternating three miles one day, five miles the next. Then I shower, eat a bowl of cereal, and cycle three miles to work. Even in February, the Louisiana humidity soaks my clothes, so I arrive to work dripping with sweat. This must be why nobody bikes to work in Louisiana, though it's normal in Ireland. Here, I feel like a freak. Coworkers shoot me looks of sympathy or suspicion.

"Where's your car?" the receptionist asks. Then she whispers, "Is your license suspended? DWI? Don't worry, I won't say anything."

"That's nice," I tell her, "but I don't even drink."

In the evenings I bike from work to Beau's new gym on Rayburn Street. The gym has no ring but is quite large with fresh paint, carpeted floors, workout equipment, and a wooden platform for jumping rope. After the rigors of sparring, I drag myself home to my shag-carpet sanctuary. I love having my own place even though the floors and walls are paper-thin. I tread lightly and try not to disturb the downstairs neighbor. The neighbor offers no such courtesy, and I'm forced to listen to the screams and rumbles of sex and Southern rock. But tonight I'm thankful for the noise because it helps with the wave of loneliness that rises and threatens to drown me as I drift off to sleep.

I awaken to a hard, slanting rain that beats on my bedroom window. Unable to cycle to work in a storm, I'm relieved when Beau shows up to give me a lift. He brings news of an out-of-state visitor arriving today: a twenty-eight-year-old man, a heavyweight and former cocaine addict who is to stay with me. He's been sent here so that Beau can help him get into shape. And Beau's putting him up in my apartment.

Is he kidding? It's hard to tell with Beau, but he seems serious.

My coach explains I am to let the heavyweight sleep on my couch for a couple of weeks until he finds his own place. In exchange, the heavyweight will pay half a month's rent. I'm shocked Beau expects me to share my small space with a strange man, especially since the only access to the toilet is through my bedroom. I could use the extra rent money, though, and I try to look on the bright side. Maybe everything will turn out okay. Perhaps I'll make a friend for life—maybe the guy's even a soul mate. Who knows?

Some soul mate.

The heavyweight, who's name I can't bring myself to say, is a droopy-breasted beast with a large hairy mole jutting from the side of his head. It's hard to believe this huge body, settling its girth onto and into my couch, is an athlete. He immediately claims my favorite spot by the phone, shamelessly hogs the remote control, and talks incessantly.

"So, you a boxer?" he asks.

"Yes," I say. At least we have something in common, some mutual topic of conversation.

"A woman ain't meant to be no boxer," he says.

"Huh," is all I can manage, so I excuse myself to prepare for bed, where I sink into the mattress and watch the ceiling fan as it goes round and round.

On Monday the new roommate is at the gym when I get there. Beau has to persuade, cajole, and yell at him to finish his exercise routine. Back home the sweating blubber plops onto my couch. And then he removes his putrid sneakers, which sends me into my bedroom for the rest of the night.

Beau wants the heavyweight to run with me every morning. So, the next morning, I wait outside while my new roommate hauls himself off the couch. As we start to sprint, I find temporary relief as I leave him farther behind with each step. With all his other infringements on my life, why should I hold back my roadwork for this slowpoke?

This is a three-mile-run day, and the heavyweight is far behind as I approach Girard Park. Cypress trees are wrapped in a hazy fog that rises from the pond. Reeds and lilies loom in the mist. Fat black-and-white ducks squawk and waddle their way onto the shore. Enormous nutria rats nibble on something close to the water and startle me. And then a baby-pig-like animal scuttles across my path. It is an armadillo, with shiny ridges of scales that curve into a shell. It looks prehistoric, like a possum from the dinosaur age. I also discover possums are not the cute little furry creatures I imagined. They look mean, with sharp teeth, thick rattails, and fleshy feet. All this Louisiana wildlife is so different from the foxes, badgers, and rabbits of Ireland.

The next day, on my five-mile-run, I choose Bendel Gardens, a peaceful and hilly residential area. The heavyweight doesn't even attempt to keep up with me. It's still dark and the air is crisp and clean, mine the only breath stirring, it seems, on this new day. Not even the birds bother to fluff about as I step on twigs and pinecones. But by my second pass near the Hilton Hotel's glowing red letters, I'm tired and drenched in sweat. I'm still a long way from my flat, so I run as fast as I can the rest of the way home and wonder where the heavyweight is hiding. He's nowhere in sight, yet he always turns up at the apartment shortly after I arrive.

Sure enough, as I leave my bedroom, heading for work, he's "home." As I prepare to leave the apartment, the heavyweight says, "Everyone comes 'ere from their shithole countries to steal from our taxpayers."

"But I have a green card, so I'm totally legal *and* paying tax," I explain.

He grunts with disdain. Then, with an effeminately high-pitched giggle, he says, "Well, it's a known fact the Irish are stupid—that's why they were used as slaves. Just like niggers." He rolls on the couch with another pig squeal. And it occurs to me that I hate him. What he doesn't know is that I'm horrified by his comment but not insulted. In fact, thinking of my diverse array of friends in the gym—the boxers who are, unlike him, men I admire—I'm thrilled to be put into a category apart from his. We may both have white skin, but I've no relation to him.

After his stupid comment, our living arrangement continues to deteriorate. In my bitter letters home, I refer to the heavyweight as Phatchit. Running and working are my only escapes from him. He's at the gym, at the Williford house, and at home. Weekends are the worst. So I beg for overtime and flee to the gym on Sunday when I'm supposed to be resting.

Phatchit is still overweight, but today he is confident enough to go shirtless. A festering cyst oozes from his hairy back. I catch him trying to squeeze the zit and cringe when he lies back against my couch. Unable to eat, I hide in my bedroom, listen to the radio, stare at the walls, and cry. I could not possibly have a worse roommate if I were in Hell. I manage to be grateful that he never barges into my bedroom to use the bathroom, though some mornings I'm convinced I smell piss in the kitchen sink.

Four weeks pass before the heavyweight finds a job that includes a rusty company truck. Though his job is not far from mine, I insist on cycling. When it rains, and Louisiana rain is usually torrential, Beau makes Phatchit give me a lift to work.

"You ain't shit in this country if you don't have no car or you can't drive," he taunts, even though he's driving a rattling, oil-stinking, tin box of a company truck. "You're a foreigner. I was born in this country. So all I gotta do is make one phone call and you're outta here."

My brain shuts down under his attack. Shocked by what he tells me and fearful he has the power to end my U.S. boxing career, I say nothing.

"If I wanted, I could drive out to the woods and kill you," he chides. "No one would ever find you."

Every private moment with Beau, I complain about the heavyweight's verbal abuse. "He told your twins I'm really a man," I cry. "What could be the point of a person like him in the world?"

"Don't you see he's jealous?" Beau explains. "You work your behind off, and he's just a lazy, fat piece of shit. And ugly as a bag of assholes. It's because he doesn't feel good about himself. That's what makes him such a jerk. But maybe if I can fix that, teach him some self-worth, he'll change."

But I'm beyond caring about his self-worth and convinced he'll never change.

The heavyweight continues to crash on my couch even though it's been six weeks since he showed up. For a few days, though, I'm enjoying a bit of mental relief. I'm in Fort Smith, Arkansas. Phatchit is here, too, but I've got no room for him in my thoughts today. I've got a fight.

My opponent is Missy Buchanan, a tall, longhaired blonde from St. Louis, Missouri. She has an entourage of biker-looking friends. To intimidate me, they slowly eye me up and down and then flaunt bearded smirks. But I'm not intimidated. I'm excited.

This is my first bout on neutral ground. For once, I don't have to fight in my opponent's backyard.

In the ring I'm gloved and ready. Beau says, "Get this motorcycle bitch outta here, Dee-dra. They think they're a bunch of badasses, trying to intimidate you. But Dirty Dee will show 'em how to fight!"

Soon into the match, after a few jabs and straight rights, I force my opponent to close her eyes and bend at the waist, a sure sign this bout is mine. As she grabs onto me, the referee whispers, "Ease up. Let her go a couple of rounds." But I've been screwed in too many fights to let anyone ride. I'm going to get this over with as quickly as possible. So I dig a straight right to my opponent's solar plexus and make her groan and fall into the ropes. I unleash a barrage of punches, and Buchanan is reduced to tears. The referee stops the fight, one minute twenty-eight seconds into the first round.

On the ride home to Lafayette I learn Phatchit is moving out in a week. When the blessed day rolls around, five weeks longer than promised, I speed his departure by packing his food into boxes and even throw in my own groceries to make sure he doesn't come back to split hairs. He owes me a hundred and fifty dollars in rent, but he throws a twenty on the table and slams the door on his way out. I'm so happy he's gone, I would have paid *him*.

Unfortunately, his new apartment is not across town or down the street. It's right below me. But at least he's not on my couch. The minute he's out the door, I drench the furniture with antibacterial spray. I sanitize every surface of my reclaimed sanctuary. I can't seem to stop cleaning. Apparently, the beast can hear my incessant vacuuming and responds by blasting the Guns N' Roses' album *Appetite for Destruction* at full volume. But it's fine by me. The music fuels my mania, and I clean and clean and clean into spring, until Channel 4 airs the women's boxing documentary across Europe, showing the world my title loss to Stacy Prestage.

I'm unable to see it here in the States. But Mum, my sisters, and my brother Shane gather to watch it at Mum's house. As soon as it's over, Sheena phones me. I can hear my family shouting cheers and clinking wine glasses in the background. "It was brilliant!" my sister exclaims. It's nice to know my family finally celebrates my career in the ring.

And I would, too, if only I'd won the title.

Now I spend my days fielding phone calls from the press, boxing associates, and friends back home. When my copy of the documentary arrives, I relive every second of drama and heartbreak. I'm stunned when a reporter questions Prestage before the fight, and she vows to make it "brutal." The film proves she certainly kept her promise.

Reliving the painful defeat, I vow to train harder and not allow my job at Sides & Associates to interfere with my time at the gym. It's difficult to work fifty hours a week even though I'm considered a part-timer. Demanding deadlines force me to add overtime at a moment's notice. I like my boss and co-workers, but I'm constantly torn between earning money at my career in graphic design and earning no money working out at the gym.

I'm especially keen to be at the gym one day because boxing legend Alexis Argüello is visiting Rayburn Street. But I'm busy sketching an illustration—a rare opportunity to escape the computer and display my true artistic abilities. The illustration is not going well. In my haste to meet Argüello, I misjudge the perspective. I'm hours behind schedule. I watch the clock and know a champion boxer is at the gym while I'm hunched over an illustration. So I leave the papers and pencils scattered on my desk, hop onto my bicycle, and take off for Rayburn Street, work unfinished, pedaling fast so no one can stop me.

I've jeopardized a well-paying job, but standing here with three-time world champion Alexis Argüello, "The Explosive Thin Man," is worth it. He is warm and kind, and I'm bursting with pride as Beau snaps a picture of me standing beside him. Argüello even takes the time to critique my sparring and says, "Doze boys, dey hit you hard!" I can't believe Alexis Argüello, a champion, who boxed his way out of abject poverty in Managua, Nicaragua, is watching me spar.

No surprise—the next morning, I'm fired.

So I set off on my bicycle and apply to every advertising agency, sign shop, print shop, and copy center in Lafayette. Days turn to weeks and then two months of applications with no job. Out of options, I call home for help. My family collects seven hundred pounds and wires it to me. Their collection saves me and makes me miss them even more.

By July I manage to pick up a few days of freelancing at The Foster Agency. I'm struggling with an oil-field brochure and cursing myself for shunning typing lessons when Beau calls. "You wanna fight in Vegas in sixteen days?" he asks.

All I manage is one word—*yes!*—before Beau hangs up with no details of my match. My heart gallops. All I can think about is the chance of a lifetime to showcase my abilities in Vegas.

My supervisor is not interested in my boxing career. He groans in exasperation at my anemic henpecking, barges to my desk, and types the document himself.

But I don't care.

I'm going to Vegas.

The strip in Las Vegas is like an adult amusement park with the MGM Grand Hotel & Casino's giant lion and the medieval castle-like Excalibur Hotel. Easter Island fronts the Tropicana, and a black pyramid and sphinx adjoin the Luxor. Massive electronic message boards advertise Vegas superstars, Wayne Newton and Siegfried & Roy. Beau and I take in the sights as prostitution flyers flutter down the streets like tumbleweeds in the warm desert breeze.

We check into the Aladdin Hotel and notice Stone Temple Pilots will perform tonight. Plenty to do in this town, lots to see, but I'm here to fight, which doesn't mix well with Vegas nightlife. I do enjoy walking around when the sun goes down. The heat evaporates into a nice chill, and the stars seem to reflect the city's never-ending stream of twinkling lights.

Back at the hotel I learn the Dunes Hotel across the street is set to implode at five in the morning. With so much excitement, it's hard to unwind. Just as I fall asleep a massive *BOOM!* rattles me awake. I dash to the window and see nothing but dust. The south tower of the Dunes Hotel has been erased from the landscape. I watch the leftover powder as it mushrooms and swirls to cheers from neighboring guests and a large crowd across the street.

Unable to sleep, I lie in bed and think of all the boxers who have come to Vegas to fight. How did they manage to doze off? Pre-fight jitters alone are enough to keep me awake, not to mention the energy of the city. As the minutes tick by, my head aches and my nose starts to drip. Great. I thought people traveled to the desert to escape allergies.

The next day, at the press conference, it's clear I have a full-blown head cold as I take my place beside boxers and trainers at a table flanking the podium. I sit between Beau and Olympic boxer Robert Wangila, who won a gold medal in 1988 for his homeland of Kenya. Wangila's muscles twitch like a stallion's beneath his suit. A supreme athlete, he is the perfect model of health and fitness. The Olympian exudes calm and poise, and bears all the confidence of his gold-medal status. His mere presence commands respect. I'm thrilled to learn that I'm scheduled to box on his card.

I need to figure out a way to project some of that Wangila-like confidence when I face my opponent, Mary Ann Almager, a tall, well-built Latina from New Mexico. But it's Almager who radiates confidence as she swaggers into the room with her brother, who is also her coach. Since she smiles while she fights, her moniker is "Gorgeous." And she seems to be popular and connected to the show's promoter, as she shakes hands with numerous well-wishers.

"Stop sniffing," Beau whispers. "We don't want Almager to know you're sick." I try to resist wiping my nose, and snot shoots toward my top lip. Great.

Jimmy Finn and Barbara Buttrick of the WIBF are here with women's boxing fan Doug Duncan. I'm finally face-to-face with Duncan, who calls me often to ask countless questions about my career. He speaks with an inflated Scottish accent, and his insatiable curiosity moves me from flattery to suspicion to unease. I've acquired several male fans that have somehow acquired my address and phone number.

After the press conference, Beau, Doug Duncan, and Jimmy Finn circle around me.

"Do you have a bit of cold there, Deirdre?" asks Jimmy Finn.

"It's just allergies," I lie. "Some Afrin spray will fix it."

"Almager's won all her fights by knockout," Duncan boasts. "How're you going to handle her power?"

"I'd say Mary Ann easily walks around over one-fifty," says Finn. "Wouldn't you, Beau?"

"Shut the fuck up, Jimmy," mutters my coach as he rescues me from further interrogation.

Before the weigh-in Beau encourages me to gorge at the value-packed Aladdin buffet. Overfed and fully dressed, I climb on the scales and manage to top off at 133. Almager strips to her underclothes and tips the scales slightly under 140.

"Great! I can eat!" she blurts and then skips away from the scale.

Side by side, Almager and I pose for photos. I feel puny next to her. When she clenches her fists, the muscles in her forearms, biceps, and shoulders knot in rock-hard attention. I'm petrified but try to convince myself otherwise. I've been blessed, after all, with a granite chin that's been tested time and again in the gym. I've been shaken but never dropped.

On fight night Mary Ann "Gorgeous" Almager dances into the spotlight sporting a cowboy hat. Her long black hair is tied back in a thick braid. She's garbed in red-velvet trunks and a black top with diamond-shaped gaps exposing the skin on her wide back. Mexican music blares from the darkened corners of the Aladdin arena. I'm struck by the lack of intimacy I feel with the crowd in this enormous place. It's nothing like the close settings of my previous fights, where I could hear shouts of insults and praise. Here, the crowd emits a hum that is sucked into the vacuous cave.

At the bell Almager ploughs toward me.

I'm surprised to see that she is a southpaw. Surely I knew that, so why am I surprised? My reaction is to attack, and I land a series of good shots to score points. I escape her booming left hands by rolling under her fists. Lunging at me with wild punches, she seems certain she can knock me out. But she leaves an opening, and I counter with blistering flurries. Unaffected, she pops a left hand against my mouth and spawns a roar from the crowd. Almager is strong and knocks me around the ring, shoving me into the ropes and onto the floor. I jump up quickly to show it was not a knockdown. My nose fills with mucus as I elude more bombs. My lungs burn as Almager leans on me, and I wrestle my way free. The bell rings.

In the corner Beau presses my nostrils one at a time as I blow into a towel. He tells me to move to my left, away from Almager's powerful left cross. So I box behind my jab and move to my left as instructed. I try to catch my opponent lunging in, but when my fists find her head, the impact seems to evaporate. She falls into me and shoves me into the ropes. Carlos Padilla, the referee, breaks us up and cautions my opponent for pushing.

Almager circles so I slide left to force her to step into my left hook. I follow with a hard right, which inspires my first *Ooohhhh!* from the crowd. But Almager only smiles at me around her huge wet mouthpiece. I try to make her miss so I can counter punch, but my counters cause little effect. Her wind-up punches provoke chants of "Gorgeous! Gorgeous! Gorgeous!" I'm bending at the waist and can barely breathe. My legs are weak. Inadvertently, I stumble to my corner, my head clogged with snot.

Again, Beau tells me to blow into the towel. Padilla sprints to Almager's corner to scold her for pushing. The second was a close round but my opponent's strength has sapped my energy. I have four more two-minute rounds to keep her off me, escape her bombs, score enough points to win, and somehow breathe.

Almager grins behind a triple jab in the third and traps me on the ropes. I nail her with a right, and she lands a sickening right hook to my body and a dizzying left to my temple that knocks me sideways. I spin out to the ring's center and land another right. She counters with a wild right hook, so I duck and rise to catch her off balance with a left hook. She charges me toward the ropes, so I peg her coming in with a right that forces her to fall against me and grab the ropes. I dig body shots until the ref breaks us up, and my rival backs away. So I attack and land a stiff jab that leaves Almager unsteady and squared up. As I back her to the corner, she bends forward and I dig into her face with a right uppercut. My late rally should be enough to win the round, or at least break even.

In the corner I scan my body for damage. My entire upper torso aches and is bruised from body shots. My neck is wrenched from a blow behind my left ear. My lungs feel pea-sized. My head is so blocked, I'm unable to hear the crowd or my coach's instructions.

So I coach myself. *Step it up. Show what you're made of. Find a way to win.*

I jab and use footwork to survive and score points in the fourth. I can't breathe through my nose, so I try to suck air through my mouth. But with every breath my lungs tighten up. Fortunately, Almager appears to be resting as I claw out the round. But her rest serves her well in the fifth. She rams me with a left that shoots a flash of white light behind my eyes. And then she pushes through my heavy counters. It feels like I'm punching underwater. I'm losing the round, so my opponent mocks me with another spit-spurting smile.

Slumping onto my stool, I gasp for air and inspiration. Beau says, "Come on now, one more round. She's got nothin' left. You're winning! You just gotta finish big."

An unknown man interrupts Beau and asks, "Are you all right? Do you have a headache?"

I ignore the question and try to focus on my coach, but then Beau says, "Answer the doctor."

I turn to my side and am horrified to find a suited man.

"Do you want to continue?" he asks.

"Yes!" I answer, offended by the question. I must look awful to propel the fight doctor into my corner.

In the sixth and final round, I drag my feet. Drained, snot-filled, and gasping for air, I try to attack. My opponent can barely move, too, so I manage to catch her with a few shots. But she doesn't even blink. And then I run into a few ramrod blows. The doctor's concern has left me in a panic to heed Beau's advice and prove I'm okay with a big finish. Confident my chin can withstand Almager's hardest punch, I take a foolish risk and charge her. I'm hoping to find a weak spot when the bell rings.

Almager embraces me with respect, but her weight nearly buckles my knees. I feel a bear has mauled me for six rounds. Beau greets me with a smile. Then my opponent climbs out of the ring. Boxers know they're not supposed to leave until the decision is announced, but she's gone, hugging her family. The referee motions for her to return and she slips back into the ring.

"All three judges have an identical score of 60 to 54," says the announcer. "The winner, and still undefeated, Maarry Aannn Al-maa-geerr!" The winner leaps with delight and beams as she embraces her team. She then grabs the microphone.

"I wanna congratulate Deirdre," she says and gestures toward me. "I can honestly say, she is the toughest opponent I ever met." The rowdy applause soothes my defeat. At least the crowd appreciates my efforts. They praise and pat my back all the way to the dressing room. But 60 to 54 on all three scorecards? They didn't give me a single round. Almager's congratulations and the crowds' reassuring applause quickly fade from my mind, and self-pity and pain flood in.

A couple days later, I learn Olympic gold medalist Robert Wangila, the man I sat next to during the press conference, died from injuries sustained in his fight. How can someone so supremely fit and confident be dead and gone? We fought on the same card. I cringe at the thought of media debates and the inevitable outcries to ban boxing. I'm prepared to defend the sport, but how can I convince anyone that boxing saved my life, when death hangs so close to fighters, and Robert Wangila, like the Dunes Hotel, is nothing but dust.

CHAPTER 20
LA POETA DE RING

It's been five weeks since the Almager match. Half my fight purse was spent on a pelvic exam required by the Nevada State Athletic Commission. I haven't found employment. My money is nearly gone. In a day, September's rent is due.

Beau is out of town, so I manage to track down the phone number for his hotel.

"I'm short a hundred and fifty dollars for the rent," I say.

"Don't worry. We'll sort something out," he assures me.

But what can he do on such short notice?

By nightfall I'm a bundle of worry, and then someone knocks on my door. Surely it's not the landlord so soon? What will I tell him?

But it's worse. It's the heavyweight from downstairs— probably here to gloat over my Las Vegas loss.

"Beau called," he grumbles and reaches for his back pocket. He pulls out his wallet and removes crisp bills, one at a time. "Said you gotta borrow my money to make the rent."

"Thanks a million," I mumble. "I've had terrible trouble finding work."

"The Irish ain't good for nothin' but back work," he replies. "Chicks don't got strong backs, so ain't nobody never gonna want you. Best you find a kitchen job. Oh yeah, I forgot. You can't cook!"

Why did he have to spoil my relief by opening his mouth?

"I seen how you treat money," he grunts, "all scrunched into your pockets with no respect. That's why you don't got none."

I want to remind him he still owes me a hundred and thirty dollars for the rent he never paid. Some distant voice in my head says I'd rather live on the street than take a dime from this man. But I keep my thoughts to myself.

"I'll pay you back as soon as I possibly can," I say instead and close the door.

I manage to find a job at a trophy shop. For five dollars an hour, I'll design awards on a computer. After I've completed the design, I'll engrave, sublimate, or sandblast my creations onto metal or glass. I hope boxing money will supplement my income, but at least I've got regular work, and it's creative. It's also within biking distance of my apartment.

My Cajun French boss is short with dark hair and a mustache that accentuates his large nose. He is funny but unpredictable. He laughs one minute and then snaps at me the next. He looks at me with disdain when I arrive to work dripping in sweat from cycling in the heat.

"Lean *away* from the computer," he orders. "You'll short out the keyboard."

I need a car in this big, hot landscape called Louisiana. But I can't pay my rent, much less buy a vehicle. I do as he asks.

Four weeks into my new job, I'm scheduled to fight in Tampa, Florida. I tell my boss I need three days off.

"You don't work for Beau Williford," he barks. "You work for me."

Does he really expect me to turn down palm trees, an ocean breeze, and a fight? In exchange for what? Eight hours a day in his windowless sweatshop with low ceilings, dark paneling, and a temperature gauge set steadfastly at eighty-two degrees? But I keep those thoughts to myself and simply give my boss the dates I'll be leaving and the date I'll return. It's not subject to debate, so I don't invite one.

Beau is in London but plans to join me in Tampa the day of my fight. So I fly to Florida alone for my scheduled eight-rounder against Gail Grandchamp of North Adams, Massachusetts. Grandchamp, I learn, has spent eight years and her own money to win a court case to allow women to box as amateurs in the States.

I respect my opponent for fighting to advance women's boxing, but it doesn't mean I want to share a dressing room with her. Without Beau here to represent me, that's exactly what happens. My inability to state my preference pisses me off. Frustrated, I scrape a heavy chair out to the hallway. This makes me even angrier. I will not argue for my own dressing room, but I will move furniture?

The handsome security guard must feel sorry for me sitting alone in the passageway. He checks on me often and gives me dressing-room updates. "That's the fifth time your opponent's gone to the restroom," he tells me. "She must be nervous."

Maybe, but her bathroom habits are of no interest to me. At least Grandchamp has a coach to keep her company. I have no idea why Beau is late. He should be here by now. How can I face eight rounds without him?

Then I learn Beau's flight is delayed in New York, and that he's organized another trainer to take his place. But I don't want anyone taking his place—no one can. For three hours I pace and worry, my head full of superstitions. Then, just as the music blares and I jog into the arena, I hear someone shout, "Dirty Dee!" Beau sprints up behind me with a suitcase in each hand. He tosses his bags to the side and follows me to the ring. It's amazing how much calmer I am with Beau at my side. His presence is like an injection of adrenaline and confidence.

As I step through the ropes, I am ready to take care of business.

Stalking my opponent, I start the fight by landing sharp jabs. Grandchamp circles cautiously but with style. She shoots quick lightning strikes and switches back and forth from orthodox to southpaw with unsettling poise and a cool demeanor.

I fire a nice jab to snap back her head and take control. She circles but I step in to cut down her space and catch her with a straight right. Grandchamp juts backward to lessen the impact of my shot, but I have maneuvered her toward a corner. A searing left hook traps her against the corner pad, and I drown her in punches.

"You better punch back or I'm gonna stop it!" referee Brian Garry yells to my opponent.

Up and down, I fire nonstop punches—*pop-pop-pop*—body to head, head to body.

"You gotta punch back!" the referee screams again.

My rival tries to escape along the ropes but I slide with her.

"Punch back!" shouts the referee.

But Grandchamp is bent over and wailing in pain from a right hook to the ribs. The referee jumps between us just as I rout a right to my opponent's temple. The fight is over before the end of the first round. I leap straight into Beau's travel-weary arms. It is a good thing he catches me, or we'd both be on the mat.

Back home, the building Beau rented to use as a gym has been sold. So the workout equipment has been moved from Rayburn Street to Beau's garage. There's just enough room for a bag, a speedball, and Teri's car. Beau's wife scowls as she considers the situation. Who can blame her? She recently gave birth to a fourth baby boy and works full time. Teri must be exhausted by the time she rolls her car into the tiny boxing gym.

Few boxers show up to train in the garage because of the cold. Beau still uses the chicken-shed gym, but he's too busy to go out there because he often takes care of Alex, his newborn son. I don't have a car, and the shed is too far to travel by bike. So Kenny Vice picks me up a few times a week to hammer me in the bloody chicken-shed ring as he trains for an upcoming world title fight. Mostly, I prepare for my next match alone as I pound the heavy bag and exhale steam in Beau's garage.

On Valentine's Day, 1995, I travel to participate in the first-ever women's boxing match in Louisiana history. Beau and I drive south on LA 1, parallel to Bayou Lafourche. The road is so close to the bayou that we seem to glide on the same tide as shrimp boats and barges on our way to Cut Off, a small town whose name is not hard to figure out.

My opponent, Isra Girgrah from Atlanta, Georgia, weighs in at 149 pounds. Louisiana State Boxing and Wrestling Commission Chairman Leonard Miller doesn't want to approve the match because Girgrah weighs twenty-five pounds more than I do. A differential of more than seven pounds is not allowed. But because I have experience, and this is Girgrah's professional debut, and Beau is a good talker, the chairman eventually agrees to the match.

No matter her weight advantage, I cannot allow this greenhorn to last the scheduled six two-minute rounds. I answer the bell by staying out of Girgrah's reach and nipping her with nice jabs. She manages to catch me with a mediocre right, but then someone shouts, "C'mon, do something, ya sissies!" That's all it takes for me to ignite.

I send my opponent into the ropes—three times—before the bell.

By the second round Girgrah's heart seems to waver, so I break her down with good technique and repeatedly land my left hook. After a sharp right, I shift in and out to counter her every move. I take her apart, piece by piece.

A loud yelp from a body shot in round three signals my opponent's near defeat. I give her a heavy beating and a booming right pummels her sideways into the ropes for a standing eight count. To my disappointment, she survives until the bell. But in the opposite corner, Girgrah's coach waves his arms to signal surrender.

Two months after beating Girgrah, I'm offered another WIBF lightweight title shot. I'm twenty-five and have a solid record of seven wins, two loses, and two draws. And this time, instead of Kansas City, the fight is scheduled to take place in Las Vegas at the Aladdin Hotel. Of course, the out-of-state fight means more time off work. Once again, my boss is not impressed by my opportunity, though he does seem to realize nothing will stop me. "Be back first thing Monday morning," he snaps.

Stacy Prestage retired, so my opponent for the title is Laura Serrano, also known as "La Poeta de Ring." Serrano is a lawyer and poet from Mexico City. I've never met her, but I know we have faced the same exile and jeers, because women are not allowed to box in Mexico either.

Serrano and I are to fight in the main event of an unprecedented all-women's world title card arranged by Barbara Buttrick and Jimmy Finn. Eleven other women from the States, Belgium, the Netherlands, Norway, Germany, Northern Ireland, and Mexico are here to fight in six weight classes. All for belts.

And the WIBF belt is no longer the tacky trinket Prestage and I scrapped over. It's completely redesigned and, to my eyes, beautiful. But in truth, even if it were the most garish and tacky adornment in human history, I would want that belt more than anything in my life. In my eyes, it would be a symbol of validation for every bruise and cut, every drop of sweat, every tease and insult.

Two days before my fight, Beau has not yet arrived in Vegas. He is babysitting, if that's what you call a father minding his own. I need my coach by my side and am worried when Mum phones to say two of my siblings, Katherine and Sheena, are on their way from Ireland to support me. As I hang up the phone, there's not a punch in any fighter's arsenal that could knock the grin off my face.

Sure enough, my sisters arrive from the airport in a taxi. They meet me upstairs and toss their suitcases onto the beds in the room we will share. We hug each other and they tell me about their flight. Katherine admonishes me for being so skinny. Still chattering away, they change out of their boots and into sandals. Then they peel off their long-sleeved sweaters and slip into summery tops.

Sheena seems more excited than Katherine, but she has always been that way. Sheena is bubbly and lighthearted. Her ash-blonde hair spills over her bare shoulders, and her hazel eyes seem to smile with perpetual delight.

In contrast, Katherine's almond-shaped eyes are calm. Her thick swirl of shiny dark hair is cut short and flatters her pretty face. Maybe being older is what makes Katherine more serious and nurturing.

I'm thrilled to be reunited with my sisters, but their presence puts more pressure on me to win. Maybe it's good that I have so little time to spend with them. Instead, I spend the entire afternoon and evening of their arrival doing press conferences, interviews, and workouts for the cameras. That leaves me precious little time to worry I'll disappoint my family.

The next morning, the day before my fight, most of the reporters rush off to cover a terrible tragedy. Bombs have ripped through the Alfred P. Murrah Federal Building in Oklahoma City. The excitement surrounding the fight has shifted to shock and horror at the bloody images on TV. And Beau's flight is delayed. I call the airline, though I know he is nowhere near the disaster.

Beau's still not at the hotel as I head to the evening's weigh-in. It is all so surreal. Everyone's discussing the bombing. We are going through a process that seems to be happening in another dimension. Nothing seems normal as Serrano steps onto the scale for a reading of 130 pounds, the lightweight limit. I'm told it's my turn to weigh in. The official announces my 124 pounds, but I am thinking about people dying. Then Beau arrives and reprimands me for weighing one pound under the featherweight limit in a lightweight fight. He tells me I have given the shorter Serrano a psychological advantage. But I'm so relieved to see my coach; his scolding doesn't upset me.

The next morning, Katherine, Sheena, and I join Beau at the Aladdin Hotel buffet for breakfast. Yesterday's bombing stunned my sisters. Terrorism is not supposed to happen in the United States. But they have traveled all this way, so I try to encourage my sisters to explore Vegas. At last they grab their purses and head for the streets. I'm glad they've chosen to shop and relieved I'll have time alone to mentally prepare for tonight's match.

Since I can't work out on fight days, the minutes drag on. Beau always advises me to take a short walk after breakfast. Then he wants me to rest in my hotel room and watch TV. But it's hard to clear my thoughts with the gut-wrenching images of the Oklahoma bombing. So I shut off the television, focus on my breath, and try to empty my mind. Time slips by until I'm summoned backstage to prepare for my fight.

In the dressing room I change into my white trunks adorned with a wide green stripe down the right side and a wide orange stripe down the left—the tri-colors of Ireland. Sheena has enjoyed the hotel drinks and is a bit tipsy. Katherine assembles the Irish flag on a staff to wave as she follows me into the ring. She is wise to keep herself occupied, because the tension in the dressing room is thick—only Sheena does not notice. But even Sheena lapses into silence as the undulating roar of the crowd floods into the dressing room and grows louder and louder while we wait for my call to the ring. Judging by the crowd's applause, the first all-female world title card is a hit.

So far, Belgium's Daniella Somers, along with Bonnie Canino and Delia Gonzales of the United States, have claimed belts. My former opponent, Mary Ann Almager, has stopped the Northern Irish girl in the second round for the light-middleweight title. And another American, Yvonne Trevino, upset undefeated Regina Halmich of Germany by pasting a grotesque gash under her opponent's right eye.

My call comes and Beau leads me out to the metal beat of "She Sells Sanctuary" by The Cult. My sister Katherine parades the Irish flag behind me. Sheena is beside Katherine and, I hope, steady on her feet.

As soon as I settle in the red corner, Serrano bounds into the ring with her fists in the air to the jangle of Mexican music. Suddenly it's déjà vu of the Almager fight. Not only am I standing in the ring at the Aladdin arena, I'm about to fight another Mexican southpaw. To make matters worse, Team Almager is working my opponent's corner.

After our teams clear out of the ring, Serrano and I stand in our corners. Serrano wears black trunks with a gold band. Her dark hair is cropped short in a bowl cut with bangs that she pushes out of her eyes just as the bell dings to start the fight.

To score and to keep Serrano at arm's reach, I move in behind my jab. I expect Serrano's stocky build to make her a pressure fighter, but I manage to back her to the ropes. Slipping her shots I land left hooks and draw back my arms to block her counters. As usual I've had a strong first round and Serrano looks concerned. But my lungs burn as they did in the Almager fight.

In the second round Serrano tucks her chin and peers at me as she tries to come forward. I shift and change the distance to stop her from unleashing. Toward the end of the round, she ignites with a flurry of punches. So I bob and weave to give angles and counterpunch. But my lungs burn and strain for air.

In the third, Serrano pours on the shots and gains momentum. I dip and roll, slip and counter. But I'm afraid if I box and counterpunch too much, I won't get the decision. I need to stand my ground and fight aggressively. Launching a big combination, I trap my rival into her blue corner and fire an attack. But then, just as I unleash a right hand, my foot slips and I kiss the mat. I spring to my feet, but referee Kenny Bayless begins to count. "It's a slip, a *slip!*" I plead, knowing I'll lose a point on the judges' scorecards. But Bayless continues to count the mandatory eight. And then Serrano attacks and forces me to block, roll, slip, and sidestep as I try not to get hit.

I'm off to a good start in the fourth, but the burning in my lungs increases. I suck air just as Serrano pounds me with body shots to freeze my movement. Rooted to the spot, we stand toe to toe and exchange blows.

"C'mon ya Republican bitch!" someone shouts. *Where the hell is my concentration?* I'm in the fight of my life, I can't breathe, and I'm listening to some asshole in the crowd taunt me? Just like that, doubt erases my self-esteem. *But Beau believes in me. So maybe... maybe I'm thinking too much!*

Serrano nails me and snaps my head side to side. *What must this look like to Beau and the ref?*

Then the referee jumps between us. "No, no!" I cry as Bayless motions me toward my corner. Has the fight been stopped? But Beau is putting the stool in. The ref was signaling the end of the round.

The fight doctor pushes up beside me. "Do you want to continue?" she asks. I want to scream, *I'm fighting for the championship of the fucking world! What the hell do you think?* But "Yes" is all I muster. Beau pours me with cold water and begs me to use my reach.

I know I need to box, follow technique, instead of fighting Serrano at her own game. But I'm so physically drained. I can't rally the energy to move quickly. I cannot deflect worry for what the fans think. To have the doctor in my corner is humiliating. I've barked at the referee twice, and someone in the crowd hates the Republican Irish. I want to tell everyone this isn't the real me. *I'm much better than this! Don't you see? I can't breathe in this damn altitude!*

In the fifth I fear the doctor will stop the fight. I push myself to the limit of collapse, beg my body to function, but it wants to die. I manage to squeeze enough energy to stay upright and even catch my opponent with stinging head shots. Combinations ripple up and down my head and torso so I rip combinations right back. Exhausted, my lungs struggle for breath, my muscles scream with pain. But we stand head to head, toe to toe. So many punches are flying that it's hard to know who's winning this round.

My air comes back and I'm landing clean shots in the sixth; my rival slows down, so I catch her with a left hook. She tries to escape along the ropes, but I slide with her and nail another left hook. Then she unleashes combinations. Again, we stand toe to toe and exchange blows as sweat seems to float and spray like Mum's garden sprinkler in Mornington. The flicker of that image helps me to escape the rapid-fire pain of Serrano's gloved fists. And then I sense the excitement of the crowd as they leap to their feet, seconds before the bell.

Beau urges me to stay on my stool until the start of the seventh round. Once I'm up, my adversary springs an attack. I desperately try to fight her off but she presses me to the ropes. My legs are gone. Serrano plants her feet and rips into me. Don't stop punching back! But my arms are dead. I can't move. *Keep punching back or they'll stop the fight! Keep punching back or they'll stop it—*

The referee jumps between us and waves his arms. I'm about to protest when I glimpse a white towel on the ring mat in my corner. *Has my coach stopped the fight?* This cannot be happening. But then I see Beau climbing into the ring, and there's no doubt about it. I've caused my coach, my most ardent supporter, to throw in the towel.

Beau maneuvers me onto the stool in my corner. "You just had nothing left, sweetie," he says. "You have nothing to be ashamed of. You just had nothing left."

The fight doctor, Margaret Goodman, urges me to stay on the stool. Her concern is evident as she questions my physical pain. But the worst injury is so deep in my heart she cannot possibly see it. I'm unable to speak.

"After a *bruising* six rounds of action," begins the announcer, "at the one-twelve mark of the round, the towel is thrown in. And the referee, Kenny Bayless, elects to stop the fight as the corner of Deirdre Gogarty said the fight can continue no more. So by virtue of technical knockout, the new WIBF lightweight champion of the world, *Laura 'La Poeta de Ring'* Ser-ra-noooooo!

"And ladies and gentlemen, let's hear it for a valiant effort. Giving everything she had in probably one of the greatest women's bouts ever staged, in any continent on the face of the earth, Deirdre Gogarty!"

The crowd springs to their feet with applause. But Beau has to raise my left arm because I've fallen into an abyss of disappointment.

I am utterly defeated.

Too early the next morning, Katherine and Sheena wheedle me out of bed to go sightseeing. We travel beyond the brutal heat of the Mojave Desert and up to a snowy Grand Canyon. As my sisters admire the earth's deep, eroded wound, I'm overcome with shivers and muscle pain. Unable to share the devastation of loss, or explain my desire—my need—to validate my existence on this Earth with a title belt, I can't take in the splendor of the third natural wonder. It's like I'm not even here. I'm back at the pier of the fishmeal factory.

Chapter 21
The Coalminer's Daughter

Fire has swept through the chicken shed, leaving only a smoldering heap of cinders. And it wasn't even the crawfish boiler's naked canister of flames that did it. An electrical short set the hovel ablaze. I'm relieved I no longer have to endure lung-drowning beatings in the steamy shed, even though I was only working out there a few days a week. I'm back to full-time training in the Willifords' cramped and weather-prone garage.

Beau no longer has a gym to train boxers, and Peter "Hurricane" McNeeley is traveling here from Boston to prepare for a fight with "Iron" Mike Tyson. The controversial competition has stirred the press because it will be Tyson's first boxing event since serving three years in prison for a 1992 rape conviction.

Beau doesn't want to risk injury for the heavyweights by allowing them to train on concrete. So squads of volunteers scramble to erect a boxing ring in the driveway of the Willifords' suburban home.

When McNeeley arrives, he seems unfazed by the outdoor ring. Ready to work out, he immediately strips off his shirt to expose a lawn of chest hair as thick and dark as the mullet on his head. He's accompanied by Vinnie Vecchione, his basketball-bellied, cigar-chomping, go-to-hell-talking manager. His nickname is "Curly." A skully cap tops Vecchione's bald head, and I assume his nickname comes from *The Three Stooges* character.

Garing Lane, whose build and style are similar to Tyson's, has flown in from Florida. In a gold Chevrolet hatchback stuffed to the roof with clothes and belongings, Lorenzo Boyd rolls in from Tulsa, Oklahoma. Boyd pushes open the driver's side door, and I notice a screwdriver jammed into the car's ignition.

Beau's wife, Teri, arrives home to find shirtless heavyweights pounding each other in a full-sized ring in her driveway. Forced to park on the road, she manages smiles for curious passersby and neighbors who have planted coolers and deckchairs on her lawn. She cuts through the yard, her heels sinking slightly with each step, and disappears into the house.

Outside, a lawnmower whines in the distance and the July breeze carries the scent of newly mowed grass. Crepe myrtle blossoms cascade into the ring like confetti. Children play with dogs and zigzag between onlookers and parked cars. Babies in prams sleep, even though they are parked close to the ring.

At six the next morning, "Hurricane" McNeely meets me at the entrance to Bendel Gardens subdivision to join me for a run. Our coaches, Williford and Vecchione, puff cigars and follow us in Beau's Suburban. As I leave McNeeley and the coaches behind, my running partner yells, "Go on and fuck off. Leave us in the dust."

I finish my run at McNeeley's hotel, which is across the street from the subdivision. I have to wait several minutes for him to appear. He arrives panting and spitting and then squeezes his abdomen and farts. I look away, embarrassed, but he laughs like a kid ripping one at his big sister's sleepover. His frequent burping and gas makes me rethink the origin of his "Hurricane" nickname. When I turn toward him, he spreads his legs and aims a steady stream of piss into the flowerbed beside the hotel's entrance while our coaches search for a parking space.

Back at Beau's house, reporters arrive and seem puzzled by the unconventional location of McNeeley's training camp. The *Daily Mirror UK* has sent boxing writer Fred Burcombe with a photographer, whom I secretly nickname Michael Caine because of his resemblance to the English actor. Caine scouts out the garage and asks to borrow Beau's wooden ladder to enable a better view for his shots.

"I wouldn't use that ladder if I were you," cautions Beau. "It's rotten through."

"I'll only be up it a jiffy," says the photographer. He manages only a few shots before the rung he's standing on splinters and snaps. He clutches his camera, falling down a step and pausing only a moment in the air before the next rung snaps. And the next. All the way down until the ladder's legs fall in opposite directions.

"Are you okay?" shouts Beau. But the shooter has landed on his feet. And he's still snapping shots. Practice comes to a halt as fighters and observers burst into laughter. "Now that's a true professional," chuckles Beau, shaking his head.

In three weeks training camp ends, and the outdoor ring is dismantled. Everyone goes their separate ways—except Lorenzo Boyd, the fighter with the Chevrolet hatchback and screwdriver ignition, who's too broke to leave town. Even Beau flies off to Vegas to work the corner for McNeeley's Tyson fight. I stay behind to prepare for an upcoming bout with Jessica Breitfelder in Jefferson City, Missouri, at the end of November.

Beau returns slump-shouldered from Vegas after McNeeley's first-round loss to Tyson. McNeeley charged and Tyson answered. After Tyson knocked McNeeley down a couple of times, Vinny Vecchione jumped into the ring to save his stunned fighter—a save that's created a huge controversy. But there's no time to second-guess Vecchione's decision. I have a match coming up and flashbacks from the Serrano fight make me edgy.

I order myself to stay composed, but I'm wound up by something more insidious than my usual thirst for redemption: I'm intent to destroy my opponent, to annihilate her, to unleash my pent-up anger and frustration at losing to Serrano. Never have I felt such a surge of emotion before a fight. And the feeling doesn't dissipate as I train.

My anger rises as I stand in the ring with Jessica Breitfelder to await the bell.

I explode in the first round with a torrent of punches and then land three left hooks to bend Breitfelder sideways. I bludgeon my ponytailed opponent into a spiraling fall. A final right spins her to the mat in my corner. She rises onto her hands and knees and sobs. With anguished doe eyes, she glares at Beau. He shrugs at her sheepishly as she struggles to stand and then stumbles to her corner. The referee waves the fight off forty-four seconds into the first round.

Beau is so excited when he gets home, he sends the tape of my win to the local television stations to air on the news. He's proud that I landed fifty punches in thirty-six seconds. I'm thrilled, too.

But, for the first time, I'm bothered by the tough time I gave an opponent in the ring. I unleashed pent-up anger from my Serrano loss on Breitfelder when I could have taken my time and boxed my way to a win. I'm also frustrated that my win only paid a hundred bucks.

Three months pass and I'm not offered another fight. My bank account is overdrawn. Financial worries keep me up at night, so I'm awake when the phone rings after midnight.

"You got offered a fight in Vegas with Christy Martin on the Tyson card," Beau whispers. I figure Teri or baby Alex must be asleep beside him. I want more details but Beau hangs up. All I know is that I have ten days to prepare for a fight with the most famous female boxer in the world. This is the chance of a lifetime. And I need the money.

Christy Martin is from Bluefield, West Virginia, and is nicknamed "The Coalminer's Daughter." She's promoted by Don King and is a regular feature on the big boxing shows. Her only setback in six years is a controversial draw with Laura Serrano.

When I tell my boss I'll be fighting on the Mike Tyson/Frank Bruno card, his mustache raises to one side. He scoffs, "You'll never find a hotel room this close to the match. I'm sure they've been booked for weeks."

"But Don King Productions is taking care of the rooms, the flights, the meals, everything," I boast. My boss stomps away on short, stiff legs.

This time, I meet the Vegas altitude head on. In order to acclimate to the thinner air, I'm sent to Vegas eight days early. Beau plans to join me later, so Bill Folliard, cut man for my Las Vegas fights, picks me up at the airport. Bill is short and sixtyish with white hair and a white mustache. He wears large eyeglasses, a thick gold necklace, and a massive gold ring. And he insists on carrying my bag to the car.

Folliard drives me to his house in the high-desert valley town of Pahrump, Nevada, a mobile settlement with few permanent structures and no irrigated greenery in sight. It's the ugliest town I've ever seen, which leads me to wonder why Bill and his wife would choose to live here. But in his backyard I meet an excited pack of rescued dogs, mostly greyhounds, and Bill tells me Las Vegas has a pet-limit ordinance. I look at Bill and give him a nod of respect. He lifts his chin and grins, then carries my bag inside.

For my road work the next morning, Bill takes me to the edge of town. I run in the searing heat and struggle to squeeze a decent breath from the air around this rugged red and brown landscape. Even the twisted branches of mesquite trees are black and scorched by the sun. Cactus offers the only green, but it's a thirsty shade of green, not at all like the lush foliage of Ireland and Louisiana. For four days I run. I hit a heavy bag every day. I share meals with my cut man and his wife in a house filled with sweet, slobbering canines.

Four days before the fight, I return to Las Vegas and check into the lion-guarded MGM Grand Hotel & Casino. Huge screens animate the lobby with images of Mike Tyson and Frank Bruno. The deep boom of theater speakers vibrates through my body, electrifying my heart and increasing my excitement.

For the press conference, crowds pile into the MGM Grand Theatre. English fans chant and wave Union Jacks, the flag of Great Britain and Northern Ireland, in support of Frank Bruno. Bruno is here to defend his WBC heavyweight title against the American, "Iron" Mike Tyson. Foreign and domestic photographers jostle for position in front of the stage.

I stand beside Tyson while we wait to sit down. I'm daunted by the size of the man, remembering that I'll be fighting the woman known as the Tyson of women's boxing. But for all his muscle and bulk, his bravado in the press, "Iron" Mike is quiet and shy. I don't say anything to him. But Tyson's camouflage-outfitted friend Crocodile shouts threats and insults at Frank Bruno, which ignites Bruno fans into a frenzy of boos and obscenities.

Promoter Don King presides at the center of linen-covered tables that line the stage. His house fighters convene to his right and include Mike Tyson, Christy Martin, Bernard Hopkins, Michael Carbajal, Ricardo Lopez and Miguel Angel Gonzalez. Frank Bruno and I are seated to King's left, along with the other opponents.

During the press conference, each fighter is asked to speak. Nervous without Beau to talk for me, I keep it short. "I'm thrilled to be here. This is a great opportunity. Christy got her foot in the door first, but I hope many more women get this kind of exposure." Immediately, I sense that in my nervous state, I've said the wrong thing.

"I just didn't get my foot in the door first," Christy Martin spits. "I got my foot in the door because of my fists! And I'm going to show that Saturday night when I stop Deirdre Gogarty in such a spectacular fashion that everybody's going to leave talking about it."

Yep, I said the wrong thing all right.

And I'm glad Beau isn't here to retaliate and cause a big scene.

The press motions for Martin and me to stand for face-off photos. It's the first time I've seen my opponent up close. Her dark brown eyes dart away from mine, and I understand why King signed her on. She is thick, muscular, confident, and glamorous. And she owns the one-punch knockout power that is extremely rare in women. Martin's got all she needs to back up her huge self-esteem.

The novelty and excitement of a big-time press conference wanes after a ninety-minute Don King speech. I've grown tired of catching wry smiles from reporters and fans that say they are sorry for me. They believe Martin will stop me in "spectacular fashion."

Even Tyson exposes a gold tooth, giving me a coy grin as if to say, *You're* fucked!

Beau finally arrives the day before my fight, just in time to learn of a last-minute decision to add the women's bout to the televised portion of the pay-per-view show. Suddenly, reporters want an interview with me. I'm content to stand beside my coach while he does the talking.

Beau and I are summoned for a pre-fight interview with Showtime commentators Steve Albert, Bobby Czyz, and Tommy Morrison. Czyz and Morrison are former boxing champions, and I'm delighted to be in the company of such distinguished and handsome hosts.

During the interview Beau brags about me as though I'm the greatest fighter who ever graced the ring. He pours over my family background and calls Dad "a world-renowned oral surgeon." I picture my humble father squirming from such accolades.

My coach is a great salesman, but soon they'll want to talk to me.

Under the table I fidget with a fight program. I look down and notice my record and Christy Martin's record. Even upside down, it's easy to tell them apart. My record is a short list while Martin's thirty-one bouts continue onto a second page.

Steve Albert finishes questioning my coach and then turns to me. "How do you pronounce the city you're from?" he asks.

And with deliberate enunciation, I answer, "Dub-lin."

There's a moment of unnerving silence. And then everyone bursts into laughter.

"He means Drogheda, dummy," Beau corrects, and my face warms and glows. I'm mortified I've seemed like a half-wit in front of the star of Showtime Boxing.

"Christy has a lot of experience over you," Bobby Czyz proceeds. "You have a record of thirteen fights. Christy's had fourteen first-round knockouts." He scans his notes. "Actually, she's had almost twice as many knockouts as you've had fights. How do you plan to deal with that?"

"Well, Martin's defense leaves a lot to be desired, so I plan to box and move to find the weakness in her guard."

My interviewers are respectful and friendly, and I manage to answer the rest of their questions without further embarrassment. They seem fascinated by my story. But as I prepare to leave the pressroom, my active imagination tells me they're also expressing something akin to pity.

A few hours before the weigh-in, Beau wants to check my weight. The fight is set for 135 pounds, and I weigh 124 pounds. "Jesus Christ!" he blurts. "There can't be more than a seven pound differential. The commission will pull the fight. Go straight to the buffet and eat. Don't leave until I get back."

While I pile my plate, my coach heads for the casino. He reappears with a cloth bag and plunks it on the table. He explains that inside the bag are rolls of quarters. Not for the slot machines, but a way to make weight.

For the weigh-in I stuff the quarter-filled paper tubes into my pockets, socks, knickers, and bra. While I anxiously await the scales, a doctor calls me over for a physical. "But Doctor Homanski did one yesterday," I protest. If the quarters are discovered, I'll surely be disqualified. In a panic I shoot to the restroom and remove the rolls and dump them into a plastic MGM souvenir bag.

After a simple blood-pressure check, I rush back to the restroom and jam the quarters into position. But they're calling me to the scale, and I have to hurry. I'm afraid I'll be found out. The coins make it awkward for me to walk and they are noisy, so I'm relieved by the crowd's raucous roar as my opponent steps onto the stage.

"Take off your shoes," says the commissioner in front of a tent filled with spectators and reporters. I bend forward to untie my runners and eight rolls of quarters plunge out of my sports bra. My heart stops. But the elastic of my tracksuit jacket catches the rolled coins like a net. As I step onto the scale, the cylinders in my socks slide down my ankles, eye level to the press.

"One hundred and thirty pounds!" proclaims the scale master.

Relief floods me as I escape the platform.

Christy Martin strips down to her underclothes before she climbs onto the scale.

"One hundred and thirty-five pounds!" declares the scale master to an eruption of cheers and applause. And I cheer my own little victorious weight gain as I head off to shed the pounds just as quickly.

On fight day a sell-out crowd of fifteen thousand streams into the MGM Grand Garden Arena. Hundreds of people line the long hallways and wait to glimpse the fifty celebrities scheduled to attend. I scan the impressive list of sports stars like Boris Becker and Tommy Hearns, musicians Kris Kristofferson and Snoop Dog, and actors Jack Nicholson, Eddie Murphy, Gregory Hines, George Clooney, Forrest Whittaker, Drew Barrymore, Jim Carrey, Kevin Costner, and Bill Cosby. I'm especially thrilled to see Pierce Brosnan is here, because he grew up near my hometown of Drogheda.

Backstage in my curtained-off dressing room, I slip into a white top and trunks with a wide, sparkly green stripe down each side. Pre-fight nerves peak backstage among the fighters. With so many boxers preparing for their fights, the atmosphere thickens with anxiety. Escorted by an entourage, boxers breeze past my curtain on their way to the ring.

Dressed and ready, I'm called to step on the scale for the unofficial weigh-in, a routine the Nevada commission uses to track weight gain between the official weigh-in and the fight. In my case, I've lost weight, so Beau tells me to put on my robe. But even with the full-length terrycloth-lined satin robe, I'm fifteen pounds lighter than Martin.

Cut man Bill Folliard and assistant corner man Abdullah Muhammad join Beau to lead me into a packed arena. The undercard bouts have been lackluster so the crowd is restless for the main event. They groan at the idea of a female fight and begin to boo and shout obscenities.

As I jog toward the spotlighted Showtime ring, I imagine I am being sucked into a giant television screen. I climb through the ropes into an onslaught of media. A man wearing a headset escorts me to the blue corner, where I'm surrounded by cameramen and soundmen and heat that radiates from the equipment.

Christy Martin swaggers into the ring surrounded by four corner men. She is dressed in Grant-sponsored pink trunks, a pink track jacket, and pink boxing boots. Even her corner men wear matching pink jackets with Christy Martin's name monogrammed in black script on the backs. The fact that four men of boxing, including legendary tough guy and cut man Johnny Tocco, are willing to wear pink is a sign of respect for Martin.

To avoid intimidation, I glance away from the Martin team and out to the ringside crowd. Staring back at me are the famous faces of boxer Tommy "Hitman" Hearns and actor Pierce Brosnan. My heart stops and then leaps. So much for keeping my cool. I'm used to watching them perform—and here they are watching me.

As announcer Jimmy Lennon, Jr., introduces the fighters, I'm relieved to see the referee is Carlos Padilla. Padilla refereed my Almager fight, so I figure he knows I can handle a bigger opponent and won't be so apt to intervene.

Padilla motions for Christy and me to meet center ring. I try to glare into my opponent's eyes, but she's too experienced to make eye contact with me. On Padilla's instruction, I offer to touch gloves. But Martin slams down my outstretched hands with her fists and marches back to her corner.

In the first round I work behind my jab and bounce on my feet. Bouncing enables me to change distance quickly and avoid Martin's dangerous right hand. She moves in and tries to attack but I slip away. Circling to my right, my foot catches a high spot in the canvas and I stumble. But I catch my balance and my opponent stalks me, so I sting her with jabs to keep her at bay. She then lands a rib-crunching body blow and follows with a left hook to my face.

Christ! She hits like a man!

I feint a right and then land a jab. But she answers with a crunching overhand right and follows with a solid left hook. Lightning sparks behind my eyes. And then she nails me with another overhand right. And another.

Instead of evading, I roll under the next shot and slam her with a solid left hook and follow with a right. The force rocks her off balance, so I jump on her to catch her again as she tries to cover up. Indignant, she steps backward and drops her hands to reveal a broad grin as if to say, *That's all you have?* I leap toward her and land a series of punches.

She stops dead, digs to my body, and fires a right uppercut.

I spring out of reach and then back inside to fire another left hook. But my glove catches the rope tie and I have to move back. Back inside, I connect with a right. At the end of the first round, instead of boos and obscenities, the crowd leaps to their feet in cheers and applause.

As I move and circle in the second round, I sense my opponent's intention to destroy me. I search for psychological weakness, but I'm unable to find a smidgen of caution or intimidation. Instead, I see a right coming for me. Bam!

Martin's fist crashes into my face. *I saw it coming—why didn't I move?*

I move backward to catch her with a left hook. But just as I unleash, another booming right sends me crashing. My butt hits the mat. I push off the floor with my left glove. *What the hell? Did I just get knocked down?*

A man knocked me down once, but never a woman. At least my legs are steady as I march toward my coach. I'm disgusted with myself for hitting the mat. Beau is yelling at me to pivot when she attacks. Padilla finishes the mandatory eight count and wipes my gloves on his shirt.

And then Christy jumps on me. I grab on, turn her to the side, and push her into the ropes. Padilla breaks us apart. Using all my chicken-shed survival instincts, I smother her onslaught by pushing in too close for her to effectively throw a punch. Inside, I manage two right hooks to her ribcage. "No holding!" Padilla shouts as I tie up Martin's right arm so she can't step back. But she springs forward and batters me into the corner. I manage to turn her slightly to push forward and stifle her shots.

Despite my survival tricks, I'm taking a beating.

Desperate, I try the crossover defense made famous by heavyweight champion Archie Moore. With my arms folded and parallel in front of my upper torso, I successfully dip under her right. But I miss with a counter right. I'm lucky not to be anesthetized by Martin in this moment of madness as I attempt a move I've never practiced. Martin continues to batter me until the bell rings.

"C'mon, you gotta get some life, baby girl," says assistant corner man Abdullah Muhammad. Then the fight doctor says, "You all right, honey? You okay?" And I am pissed off for drawing such pity.

"Courage, Dee. Just a little more courage," says Muhammad.

But I've been sent to the mat and handed a one-sided beating.

Still shocked by the knockdown, I doubt my ability to fight on a par with Martin. I know I've been blessed with an iron chin. But I'm not sure it can save me from the humiliation of a knockout on a prime card for women's boxing—in Las Vegas, on the most prominent stage in the boxing world.

What possessed me to fight someone with thirty-one fights and fourteen first-round knockouts? My opponent outweighs me by fifteen pounds and hits like a man. She is the "Iron Mike" of women's boxing. Who could blame me if I stay in my corner and not answer the bell?

"Tell the doctor if you want to continue," urges Beau.

"You want to continue?" the doctor demands.

I nod yes.

Rising for round three, Martin is poised to finish the job. But I move, circle, and box my way back into the fight. As I bounce around the ring, I'm surprised by how good I feel. I am physically stronger than in my previous Las Vegas fights.

And then it occurs to me that I can breathe.

Training in the high desert altitude has paid off.

My breath inspires me to be assertive. So I circle slightly forward to the left and close the distance between Martin and me. Then I fire a powerful straight right into the bridge of Christy Martin's nose. The impact shoots a sting through my forearm and rocks back my opponent's head to a loud *Ooohhh!* from the crowd.

As Martin continues to press, her nose pours blood. She fires a double hook to my kidney and cheek. I whirl outside to escape under another hook and she's left facing a corner pad. Beau yells for me to jump on her, but I miss the opportunity. Martin spins around and rapid-fires bombs. I counter her missiles and target her injured nose. By the end of the round, my opponent's face and tank top are smeared with dark blood.

In the fourth round I relax and my feet find their rhythm.

Martin unleashes but I tag her with a straight right and left-hook combination. For the first time I notice a slight waning of her confidant swagger. I manage to time my head shots with precision and counter with several left hooks. Martin's nose starts to bleed again. The rusty smell makes me thirsty for more. The possible broken nose has me back in the fight.

My opponent tucks her gloves against her jaw and, like Tyson, shifts her head side to side. She drives me into the corner with a ramrod right and then lands a couple of left hooks. I escape by rolling out and stepping to my right under another booming left hook just as the bell rings.

Beau sits me on a stool and gives me sips of water, wipes my face, and rubs Vaseline on my eyebrows, nose, and cheeks. Cut man Bill Folliard checks for injuries, and Muhammad Abdullah holds the spit bucket for me. At the sound of the ten-second warning, Beau tells Muhammad to wait for the bell to remove the stool, so I can rest until the last second.

After my coach and cut man leave the ring, Muhammad says, "For Ireland, Dee. Do it for Ireland."

And I think, *What've I got to lose? I'll just go for it. I'm decked out in green and white. Saint Patrick's Day is tomorrow.* By the ring of the bell I've got a gut full of determination to make Ireland proud of this fighter, the way we rallied behind my hero Barry McGuigan.

Christy Martin starts the fifth with a succession of jabs but only lands one. She follows her jabs with a right hand bomb but misses. Every shot she unleashes has knockout intentions. And each shot is emphasized by a yell of *Hhuaah!* Soon we're nailing each other in a seesaw battle. Repeatedly, I score by slipping her whizzing rights, which allows me to rotate back with snappy left hooks.

Martin thrusts me to the ropes again but I weave to my right. This time, instead of backing to center ring, I trap her on the ropes. My hands fly in a combination. The crowd surges in excitement for the underdog gaining the upper hand.

Do it for Ireland!

A right snaps her head back to a roar from the crowd. Martin's face is masked in blood, but she retaliates with body shots and a scorching uppercut. We finish the round by punishing each another in the middle of the ring. The fans are on their feet.

Back on the stool, I assume my face looks like pulp. But my cut man only needs to treat my nose with a giant Q-tip. While Beau smudges Vaseline on my face he stops to make eye contact and says, "Okay, sweetie. You go out there and back her up. She's so tired, she can hardly stand up."

The sixth and final round I follow Beau's instructions to back her up, forcing Martin to back-pedal with one-twos. She pants heavily. Her pink shirt has turned scarlet.

Bam! I land a right to her face and move in to work her midsection.

We exchange blows and I notice her shots have weakened, but my muscles are getting the oxygen needed to unleash nonstop. I land a right and she missteps, so I stab her with sharp left hooks. I throw a string of punches.

For Ireland, Dee!

Martin tries to slide along the ropes, but I step across and stop her with a left hook. At the bang of the ten-second warning we are center ring and trading leather. I land the last punch—a right to my opponent's bloody face—before the final bell.
Martin turns away and throws her fists above her head.

"Put your hands up!" Beau yells. "You won the fight!"

I raise my hands to please Beau but figure the knockdown cost me a win, though I'm hopeful for a draw.

As Jimmy Lennon, Jr., announces the scores I can't believe how far off I am. Two of the three judges didn't give me a single round. Beau motions for me to give my opponent a customary handshake. But "The Coalminer's Daughter" is engrossed in celebration. She ignores my extended hand until her husband, Jim, nudges her to turn around.

"Good fight," I say.

"Yeah," she begrudges and whips back to her supporters.

On a backstage TV, I watch Tyson climb into the ring. It only takes him three rounds to crush Frank Bruno. Then I see Tyson return to the dressing area with his fists raised in victory of his second world title. The referee for the fight, the famous Judge Mills Lane, follows Tyson's entourage. Lane spots me sulking on a concrete bollard and kneels in front of me. He puts his elbows on my knees and says, "Great job, kid. I've never seen anyone back her up like that." He strokes my nose with his thumb. And I'm thrilled he has taken the time to cheer me up.

Back at the hotel Beau convinces me to dress up to face the press. But Martin outpoints me again by wearing a stunning leather suit and six-inch spiked heels. I feel dowdy next to her in my modest skirt and sensible shoes in the outdoor media tent.

I'm baffled by the tremendous buzz surrounding my fight. Irish reporters Gerry Callan of the *Star*, Vincent Hogan of the *Sunday Independent*, and Tom Humphries of the *Irish Times* anxiously await an interview.

Beau tells the Irish press, "I hope those officials who won't let her fight in Ireland get to see this. They're like ostriches. Their heads are stuck in the mud. Deirdre is as good a fighter as Wayne McCullough, Steve Collins, or Michael Carruth. And her heart's the size of her country."

Dozens of people stop to compliment me. Even Nick Charles with CNN's *Sports Tonight* interviews me and boasts an estimated 80 million people in 180 countries have viewed the fight. I can sense Martin behind me as I answer his questions. Afterward, Beau says, "You should've seen Christy when Nick interviewed you and not her. She shot us a killer look and then stomped away."

The following day I enjoy Beau's description of Christy all the way home. When I arrive, my answering machine blinks. To my shock, complete strangers have left messages that range from telling me I got my ass whipped to saying I got robbed. Quite a few messages are complimentary, and I enjoy listening as I lie back on my bed and fall asleep.

The next morning I wake up in a panic. I forgot to set my alarm. It's Monday. I'm going to be late for work. Beau phones while I slip into my slacks.

"People are goin' nuts over the fight," he says. "I'm getting calls from all over."

"So what?" I tell him. "I lost and nothing's changed. I'm still late for a job that I hate."

Pushing hard on my pedals, I have no idea why so many people are honking and waving to me on the streets. Did they watch my fight? Is it possible that on Saturday night I fought at the MGM Grand Garden with Christy Martin to open for Mike Tyson and Frank Bruno? It doesn't seem real as I roll into work twenty minutes late.

The only signs of Saturday's fight are the bruises on my face and the stubborn Vaseline patches in my hair. The best sign will show up soon in my bank account. I made three thousand dollars but had to pay my manager and corner men, so I took home about fifteen hundred. Martin's purse paid fifteen thousand minus expenses—a pittance compared to Tyson and Bruno's split purse of 36 million.

"C'mon, snap out of it," my boss says. "Get your head out of the clouds and on to your work. Boxing's taking you nowhere. I'm the one who's paying your bills and putting food on your table."

My tasks piled up the week I was gone. I'm calculating how many hours of overtime it will take for me to catch up when a coworker breaks my trance.

"Quick! Quick!" Winfred says. "They're talking about the Tyson fight on *The Howard Stern Show.*"

I rush into the screen-printing room and hear Howard Stern's scathing commentary on Frank Bruno. "I fell for the hype," Stern says.

"I knew Bruno couldn't fight," says co-host Robin Quivers.

I hope they don't talk about my fight. The shock jock will surely rip me to shreds.

Stern: "So the girls come on and fight." *Oh God, is he going to make fun of me?* "And that was great. That was the best fight of the night."

Robin: "I'm telling you, they make great boxers. That was the most exciting fight."

Stern: "Yeah, these two women got on and bashed each other's brains in. One of them had her nose broken. Her blood was running down her face. The one who *won* had her nose broken. I say the one who bleeds the most should lose."

Background voice: "Were they big? Like heavyweights?"

Stern: "No, no. One was real thin and wiry. And the other was kinda heavyset, stocky, not fat. And they were punching hard. You would *not* wanna fight one of these girls."

Robin: "And punching constantly. They never stopped. They never slowed down. There was no dancing around. They were beatin' each other from beginning to end."

Stern: "Like if they threw a punch in someone's face, the other would clip 'em in the jaw. So my wife and my daughter were like visibly shaken during it. It really showed the brutality of fighting. Because not only was it a brutal fight, it was *girls*. The whole time you're sittin' there goin', 'A guy gets his face bashed, you can live with it. But a girl? It's her face'!"

Robin: "At first I was like, 'Girls fighting? I don't know how I feel about this. I don't know what I think.' When that girl started bleeding, I was like '*Oh—my—God*'!"

Out of the corner of my eye, I glimpse someone listening to the program from the doorway. I figure it can't be my boss. He'd be fussing at me to get back to work.

Stern: "And you know what else was weird? Wouldn't you punch them in the chest?"

Robin: "That was interesting to me too because nobody got punched in the breasts. I would've thought that'd be your primary target."

Background voice: "What do they wear, like bathing suits?"

Stern: "No (laughs), like bras with tank tops over them. And shorts."

Robin: "It's funny they put one in pink."

Stern: "Yeah, to make it more feminine. The blood clashed with the pink though. It was pretty wild. There was a lot of blood."

Background voice: "Did anyone get knocked out or anything?"

Stern: "The Irish girl kinda buckled, went down a little bit."

Robin: "The other thing that cracked me up, the announcers at the very beginning when they were talking about the fight, they said there was a lot of controversy in this women's boxing field because of the damage that could be done to the women's breasts. I thought to myself, 'Men get their brains knocked out, but we're worried about the women's breasts'?"

Stern: "Well, the breast is an important part for a guy. I kept thinking about the breasts and that girl's face. Because she looks like a pug fighter now."

Robin: "Yeah, they said that nose was probably broken."

Stern: "Yeah, that's it. I don't think you can rebuild that."

Robin: "Would you really want the face of a boxer?"

Stern: "Not if you're a broad."

The conversation revolves back to insults of Bruno and Tyson. I'm thrilled my match was praised and not ridiculed. If *The Howard Stern Show* endorsed my fight, then countless others around the country must also be impressed. Despite the disappointment of losing, my perception has drastically changed. A major barrier has been broken. Now I can enjoy knowing that I've played a key role in proving to the public that women can fight.

As I turn to bolt back to my desk, I notice the person standing in the doorway is my boss. Incredibly, he is silent. And, for the first time, he looks at me with something resembling respect.

185

CHAPTER 22
ALL THE KING'S HORSES

Christy Martin faces the camera without a smile on the cover of *Sports Illustrated*. She is cast in shadowed lighting with her chin slightly raised. Gloved fists rest on her hips in a commanding pose. The heading reads, "The Lady Is a Champ."

The article and photos chronicle Martin's career and include our bloody battle. The interviewer proclaims our Vegas fight overshadowed the Tyson/Bruno main event and has lifted women's boxing into the spotlight. Martin responds by insisting she is only out for herself and is not interested in championing the sport for women. Nevertheless, "The Coalminer's Daughter" is the first female boxer to be featured on the cover of such a prestigious magazine.

In Ireland, the Tyson/Bruno match was televised on Sky Sports while my match with Martin was usurped by a men's bout in Germany. Newspapers' ringside reports are the only way residents of Ireland can learn about my fight. I have no way to read the articles, so Dad sends me a parcel of clippings. He jokes in an enclosed letter that he's no longer identified as "Dr. Desmond Gogarty." Now he is known as "Deirdre Gogarty's father."

I examine a clipping from the *Irish Times*, a newspaper I once used to stuff my homemade punching bag. The headline reads, "Irish woman loses thrilling fight." Tom Humphries writes, "It took five, maybe ten seconds for the beery, testosterone-charged crowd in the MGM Garden to realize they weren't watching a novelty act... The mixture of ferocity and serious boxing skills left the most chauvinistic ticketholders gape-mouthed. The fight developed into perhaps the best boxing match of the night."

My favorite part of the article is Humphries' admonition of the Irish Boxing Union for not allowing me to fight: "It is a pity indeed that outmoded paternalistic attitudes have denied her an opportunity of fighting in front of a home crowd. The question of whether or not women should box is purely up to the women themselves. But *can* they box? Watch five seconds of tape from Gogarty versus Martin. End of argument."

Like Humphries, Vince Hogan of the *Irish Independent* and Gerry Callan of the *Star* rave about my fight. But I'm crushed to find another article in the *Irish Times* that slaps me with the scathing headline, "Female fight obscene." Sean Kilfeather writes about his "shock and profound concern" over two women, "one from Drogheda," being allowed to box on the Mike Tyson/Frank Bruno card. Kilfeather continues, "As someone who has been watching boxing in a professional journalistic capacity for some twenty years, I can only suggest that whoever allowed this so-called contest to take place should be in prison, and possibly sharing a cell with the convicted rapist Mike Tyson and his manager, the convicted killer Don King."

Am I reading this correctly? Is this man saying that allowing women to box is a criminal offense equal to rape and murder? Kilfeather's archaic public statement boils up the most primitive anger from deep inside me. This is precisely the kind of attitude that banished me from my homeland in the first place.

In the States, positive media overshadows Kilfeather's condemnation. The magazines *Time* and *People* cover Christy Martin and me. The articles include photos of our now-famous battle with anecdotes from our fight. *The Ring, Boxing Illustrated,* and *Boxing News* also give Martin and me varying levels of enthusiasm in their coverage, proving women's boxing can no longer be ignored.

After two months of publicity, Don King Productions offers to sign me, with the possibility of a rematch with Christy Martin. I want another shot at Martin, but I am not willing to cut Beau out of my career. I'm fearful that will happen if I sign with King. Beau reassures me he'd never permit the most powerful promoter in boxing history to push him aside.

A flight to Florida and a meeting with Carl King, Don King's stepson, proves Beau to be right. We fly home with an agreement and a contract stating Beau and Carl will co-manage my career and split the managers' purse evenly between them. I am guaranteed a minimum of three fights a year and a possible rematch with Martin. Now I'm in the starting gate alongside an expansive stable of Don King fighters.

To celebrate my new contract, I resolve to end two and a half years of cycling through Louisiana's torrential rains and stifling heat. I decide to buy a car. And Beau has just the one for me. It's a white 1982 Cadillac Fleetwood limousine with a black vinyl top. Beau had accepted it as payment for a promotion. Now the limo is mine for a mere one thousand dollars. I figure I'll become an expert driver by practicing in a vehicle twice the length of a normal car. Plus, when people recognize me on the street, instead of a sheepish gesture from my weatherworn Raleigh bicycle, I will honk back from the giant steering wheel of my big Cadillac.

At work I've made friends with a couple of co-workers, Kelly and Sandi, and look forward to showing them my new set of wheels. It'll be nice to go out with friends to watch bands at Downtown Alive or grab a bite to eat and answer strangers who approach me and ask, "Are you that girl who fought on the Tyson card?"

It happens so often that Sandi jokes I should wear a T-shirt that says, "Yes. I *am* that girl."

As I pull into the parking lot, my friends spot me and rush outside for a look. Kelly and Sandi seem genuinely happy that I'll no longer arrive for work soaked in sweat or rain, but they also seem baffled by the car I've chosen.

At five o'clock I escape the doldrums of graphic design and rush out to my newly waxed, long-bodied car. I can't help but admire its gleaming silver bumpers even though they are pockmarked with dents. The vinyl top is cracked but glows with an oily ArmorAll shine. I'm giddy as I slide into the torn black-leather driver's seat. Instead of handlebars, I grip an enormous steering wheel and marvel at the luxury of a roof to shelter me from the day's spitting rain. The battery is low, but after a couple of cranks the engine roars and the air conditioner vents blast a cold breeze on my sweat-beaded face. Queen's "Don't Stop Me Now" pumps from the speakers.

One of my coworkers watches me back out of my two parking spaces. *Bam! What the fuck?* I've hit the metal dumpster belonging to the animal shelter across the street. I've shoved the obstacle several feet, and the racket has made the dogs bay hysterically. The spectacle has also sent my colleague into a fit of hysterics. I swing my contraption around and barely miss a pole and fence on opposite sides of the street.

I make my way down a side road to Johnston Street, one of Lafayette's busiest thoroughfares. The limo's engine coughs as it idles while I wait to cross four lanes of rush-hour traffic. Halfway across Johnston, the engine cuts out and my monster rolls to a halt. I block the turning lane and two driving lanes. Brake-slamming drivers scowl at me, and middle fingers shoot up from every direction. I should be able to jump the battery with the charge from my embarrassment.

Fortunately, after a few seconds, I'm able to start the engine.

But every time I stop at a red light, the limo sputters and dies and I have to crank it back to life. I finally park at Beau's house for training much later than if I had cycled. But at least I'm not wet. I hop out to inspect my poor limo's damage from the dumpster, but, to my surprise, there's only a small impression on its back bumper. The dumpster lost that battle. As I study my vehicle, a man with dark hair and a mustache pulls into Beau's driveway in a navy blue Mercedes. He introduces himself as Keith Menard and asks, "Are you that girl who fought on the Tyson card?"

Menard signs up to train and, within a couple of months, we move the gym to a new facility in a commercial strip mall he owns on Kaliste Saloom Road. The space is small but pleasant with freshly painted walls, a wooden floor, and a soft-carpeted ring.

I'm relieved I no longer have to inconvenience the Williford family by training in their garage and driveway. The new gym provides a safe place for me to work out and spar with Olympian Eric Griffin. I'm not thrilled, however, that my former couch crasher, Phatchit, spends most of his time in the gym. When new kids arrive to sign up, if Beau's not around, he props his boots on Beau's desk, looks the kids up and down, and scoffs at their scrawny size.

Despite Phatchit's shadow on the gym's atmosphere, I quickly settle in and enjoy training in the new facility. As I prepare for an upcoming bout in Denver, Colorado, I learn my fight date clashes with one of Beau's promotions in Fort Smith, Arkansas. I have a fight in both cities and have to choose between Fort Smith and Denver. Beau devises a brilliant solution: I will box in both fights. After the afternoon Denver show, I will fly to Fort Smith, Arkansas, and fight again in the evening. Beau says, "I don't know *anyone* who's boxed two pro fights on the same day in different states." I'm sold on the idea.

In Denver I'm joined by my Las Vegas cut man, Bill Folliard. Because I have no time to acclimate to Denver's altitude, Beau has chosen Jessica Breitfelder as my opponent. She is the woman I stopped in Jefferson City with fifty punches in thirty-six seconds.

At the weigh-in, without Beau here to encourage me to stuff myself with food, I step on the scales at my true unaltered weight of 122 pounds. Breitfelder weighs 137. An even thicker girl accompanies my opponent from her gym. I'm told the larger girl is my next opponent in Fort Smith, Arkansas, later tonight. But I don't care about the size difference. In the past I've had to wait months—years—for a fight. Now I have two bouts in one day.

Fight day, Bill and I enter Denver's Mammoth Events Center and head for the dressing room. Even though I destroyed Breitfelder in our last match, nerves churn in my stomach and it seems clear I'll always have to deal with pre-fight jitters. For this fight, I've added the fear of high altitudes, since my lungs deflated in Las Vegas against Almager and Serrano. Even though I did much better against Christy Martin, I'm scared of burning out.

As I stand in my corner, I notice Breitfelder isn't pumping her fists the way she did before our last fight. Instead, she waits in her corner and shifts her weight from foot to foot. Standing beside her is my next opponent.

I begin the first round by firing a snappy jab and straight right to Breitfelder's solar plexus. She retaliates with a right, so I bend my knees and roll under the punch. I then fire a body shot and follow with a solid right to her head. She tumbles to the canvas.

While the referee counts over my opponent, I tell myself to work and box to extend the match if she returns. But as soon as Breitfelder indicates she wants to continue, she's wide open for a right fist. I twist my hips, fire a sharp right, and drop her hard. This time she is counted out.

It's announced that the knockout came at the one-minute-eight-second mark of the first round. But there's no time to soak up the thrill of the win. I'm pressed for time. I need to change and rush off to the airport. But Breitfelder and my ashen-faced Fort Smith opponent are standing off by themselves and seem in no hurry to leave.

Jessica Breitfelder motions me over, and I immediately know tonight's bout is in jeopardy. She tells me her friend refuses to fight me in Arkansas. I promise to go easy and take my time in the fight. But all I get in return is a no. Fort Smith is off.

In September, I travel to Fort Lauderdale, Florida, a few days before Wednesday Night Wars, my first show on a card with Don King Productions since signing the promotional contract. Beau meets me at War Memorial Auditorium the day of my fight.

Bob Walshak, a businessman and admirer of my boxing, also arrives from Miami with a set of green T-shirts he's had custom made for the event. The T-shirts have white letters that spell "Diedre Gogarty." A large four-leaf clover adorns the front center of the T-shirts with a #1 symbol in the middle of the clover. It's a kind gesture, so I don't have the heart to tell Walshak that the symbol of Ireland is a shamrock, not a four-leaf clover. Or that he's misspelled my name. But my coach is not one to hold back.

"You spelled her name wrong," blurts Beau, and Walshak's tanned face turns a deep shade of red.

It's odd to watch a green team with my name, albeit misspelled, emblazoned across their chests. My crew is eager to give me water, towel my face, and fetch things Beau and I need. Not long ago Beau often worked my corner alone. He put in the stool and the bucket himself. I'm amazed by how a bit of TV exposure can spur change.

My opponent, Shawnise Davis from College Park, Georgia, is tall and muscular with dark hair that shoots straight up just like Don King's. She's dressed in black and has a sultry demeanor. According to rumored trash talk, Davis is determined to knock me off my number-one-title-contender pedestal and get in the King stable herself.

The bell rings and, within seconds, I drop Davis with a fast left hook. My opponent scowls, climbs to her feet, and pumps her fists to demonstrate a willingness to continue. I move in to finish her off, but she stands toe to toe and faces me. She then crashes into me, charges me backward, and fires wicked right hands. Davis shoves me with her left forearm and I fall to the floor.

Confident I can land a knockout bomb, I ignite a violent combination of punches. But a roundhouse right slams into my head and is followed by a thunderous left hook that smashes my face. *Shit! This is getting out of hand.* And then Davis rams me backward while the referee barks at her for using dirty tactics to shove me around.

Steady on my feet, I nail Davis with a few shots and a hard right, but she doesn't budge. Her wildly thrown punches arc toward me like sling blades. Even when I roll under her shots, she crashes her forearm into the back of my head, bends me over, and leans on my back.

With a backhand she shoves me again. My butt hits the mat while my back pushes against the ropes. I jump up, and the referee wipes my gloves while the crowd boos Davis, who glares at me.

The bell rings to end the first round. Weak-kneed, I find my stool. Pound for pound, I've never battled a woman this strong. I've fought harder punchers, but never anyone knotted with this kind of strength. I wonder if her brute force is why the customary two-minute round seems to last so long. I can't possibly survive five more like the last one.

"You gotta get inside her shots," says Beau. "You're giving her too much room to punch. Stay in her chest and work up and down."

In the second round I keep my hands tucked near my chin as Davis's roundhouse punches storm my defense. Staying in close to minimize the damage, I manage to roll under her looping shots. I counter with a solid right that forces Davis to stumble and fall into the ropes. She tries to get away, but she sidesteps and turns her back to me. I move in and catch her with two left hooks that send the crowd into a burst of cheers.

Seemingly unfazed by the crowd, my opponent grabs onto me and pushes and leans until the referee breaks us apart. I charge her and land a left hook while her back is half turned. She starts to weaken, so I batter her into the ropes and dig shots up and down.

But Davis will not quit. She rages back with hard blows and smacks my left eyebrow with her elbow. She spins off the ropes and pushes me diagonally across the ring. I'm on the ropes with a powerful Davis trying to finish me. A right punch to my face draws an *ooohhhh* from the crowd as they shout and stomp, a thunderous racket from the bleachers.

Another sharp elbow stabs my eyebrow. The referee spots the foul, breaks us apart, and warns Davis. But it's too late. I'm cut above my left eye. Now I'm worried the bleeding will blind me and force the referee to stop the fight.

Davis smothers me again, but I break from her hold and find my range. *Bam!* The impact of my right hand to her jaw sends a vibration through my arm and down to my toes. There is a slight delay before Davis slowly tumbles, and I throw a left hook that catches her after she's collapsed on her back.

Lightheaded and weak, I wait in the neutral corner to see if my opponent returns. Horrified, I watch as Davis rises to her feet. The referee stands in front of her and counts. He motions her forward but she staggers sideways. The ref waves the fight over.

"In two-thirty-eight of the second round," the announcer begins the call. But I don't hear anything else he says. Now I know why the rounds seemed so long. We were fighting three-minute rounds instead of the usual two. No one told me, though that is no excuse for my weakness. Still, I'm sure I've pleased King by executing a solid right punch to end a crowd-pleasing thriller.

Unsteady, I climb through the ropes and descend the ring. Dozens of people surround me to admire the weeping cut over my eye. I can barely stand as fans recount their favorite moments of the fight. Slowly, I make my way to the dressing room. I guzzle water and rest for about twenty minutes. When I can finally stand up without feeling faint, Beau finds me a ride to an emergency room to get stitched, and then we fly back to Lafayette.

With money in the bank, I decide to sell my limousine for a more practical car. In the used-car section at Service Chevrolet, a sleek, dark blue 1988 Lincoln Continental entices me with its dignified lines and classy authority. The Lincoln seems to float as the logo crosshairs guide my drive from the dealership to the mechanic shop for inspection. The mechanic tells me the car is a steal for four thousand dollars. And even though it breaks down on the way back to the dealership, I willingly slap down a check for the deep-shine, the leather seats, the air-cushion suspension, and a digital display to give me important messages such as how many miles are left in the tank.

With a Lincoln Continental and a Don King contract, I tell myself I should be content with the way my life's going. But I'm anything but satisfied. Only winning a title can breach the huge gap that I must fill. That's what boxers do when they reach for their personal best. They want to fight to be world champion. I am proud of my accomplishments so far, but I have farther to go. I have taken stock of the person that I am and believe I have one gift. I am a boxer, and I want to prove I'm a champion.

One quiet November morning, I'm up so early it's dark and chilly outside as I jog onto Beverly Drive in Bendel Gardens. It's Tuesday, so it's a five-mile-run day. Beverly Drive is a mile-and-a-half circle I sprint around twice. Add to that the mile to and from my apartment, and it's a perfect five-mile route.

Halfway into the first circle, I turn on my yellow Sony Walkman to listen to U2's *The Joshua Tree*. Wiping sweat from my brow, I run my fingertips across the slender line of scar left over from the Davis fight. The cut has been put to the test in the gym and has healed, unlike my aching ambition. On that count I feel gutted. "I Still Haven't Found What I'm Looking For" booms through my headphones.

As I near the end of my route, I increase my speed. But instead of whizzing by, live oaks and magnolias seem to reach out to catch me. My foot snags a rough patch of blacktop, and I'm going down. I shoot out my hands to break the fall, but I'm holding the cassette player in my right hand. The Walkman slips away on impact, and my face smacks into the grating tarmac. Turning upright, I pull myself into a sitting position. I'm in a daze as blood drips onto my thighs from my face.

Light trickles through the trees, and the blood on my legs has coagulated by the time I awaken from my stupor. I'm embarrassed by my clumsiness and don't want curious residents to see me covered in blood and prone on the street. I drag myself upright, though my right knee is swollen and throbs with pain.
I limp out of the subdivision and onto South College for the long hike back to my apartment. Traffic is heavy with morning commuters who stare at me, eyes wide with surprise. I know I must look awful when I notice a man's jaw drop. Despite my swollen knee, I break into a run because I don't want anyone to stop and assist me.

As I climb the stairs to my apartment, my knee feels as heavy as a medicine ball. Once inside, I peer into the bathroom mirror. My left eye socket and cheek are scraped raw and ooze spots of blood. The bridge of my nose pours blood and is deeply gashed. So despite the pain in my knee, I limp down the stairs and into my Lincoln. I only have to drive a few blocks to the Oil Center to visit my physician.

As soon as the receptionist sees me, I'm told to bypass the waiting room and go straight to a holding room. Dr. William Bernard is always calm, but he seems as stunned by my appearance as the morning commuters. His nurse Gayle cleans and dresses my wounds as he prepares to suture the cut on my nose.

"I have a fight in ten days," I mumble, trying to hold my head still as Dr. Bernard pulls silk thread through my skin. "In fact, I have two bouts coming up. Do you think I'll be able to fight?"

"You need to ice that knee and rest it," he advises. "And if you get hit, the cut will reopen, so no sparring. But if you're crazy enough to want to fight, I doubt you'd listen if I told you not to." He chuckles and calmly finishes sewing me up. He then tells me the cut on my nose will most likely leave a scar.

Nine days later Beau and I fly Continental Airlines to Houston and then on to snow-covered Cleveland. Beau rents a sedan from Avis and drives me to Parma, Ohio. The first of my back-to-back fights is tomorrow—the day before Thanksgiving. If all goes to plan, I'll fight again the day after the holiday in Saint Paul, Minnesota. Because the fights are only two days apart, it's imperative I end my Parma fight early and not sustain further damage to my nose or reinjure my knee.

Against doctor's orders, I've sparred to prepare for my upcoming matches, but wore face-saver gear. Even with protection, punches grazed the bridge of my nose and opened the cut to a bright ooze of blood. I've tried to hide the wound with heavy make-up, but apparently my ruse doesn't work, because my coach has to convince the venue doctor to allow me to fight.

"She won't get hit, I promise you," Beau tells him.

My dressing room at UAW Hall is the corridor space between interior and exterior doors. Trying to warm up, even with the outside doors closed, I watch snow whip past the gaps in the frames. I shiver, but I think it's more from nerves than the freezing temperature. Beau sticks his head into my dressing room to tell me Cleveland native, former light-heavyweight champion Joey Maxim, is here and waiting to watch "the Irish girl."

On the way to the ring I'm anxious to impress Maxim, who is a legend and beat the great Sugar Ray Robinson. At the ding of the bell I immediately deliver a hard right to the face of my opponent, Sharon Yates, also from Cleveland, Ohio. Her panicky reaction tells me this will be a short night. She smothers me but I tussle and turn to find my range. Stepping back, I find enough room to land a good uppercut. I work her up and down as she reaches around my neck to try to minimize my blows. I manage to make space for a four-punch combination that knocks her down.

Desperate to survive, my opponent grabs me around my torso and wrestles me into a hold. The referee tries to break us, and I feel his foot under mine. He trips and hits the mat while the crowd erupts with laughter and applause. The ref, who blushes and grins, springs to his feet to break us apart.

Yates attempts a last ditch effort by charging me with power punches. But I unleash a finishing combination. As she crumbles to the floor, she pulls me with her. I fall face first and land hard on top of my head in an effort to avoid my nose. Now I'm the one embarrassed. But my nose is intact, and I've won the fight by technical knockout at one minute, thirty seconds into the first round.

Two days later I'm in Saint Paul, Minnesota.

I hope to end my second bout as early as the first one. When the bell rings, I notice Patricia Sims holds her elbows too wide, so I send a straight right into her body. She also stands square on her feet, which leaves her wide open. But the worst thing she does is to take her eyes off me. I move in and batter her until she cries, and the referee stops the fight. It seems two fights in three days have given my nose more time to heal than working out in the gym. Back-to-back wins get me into just the right mood to enjoy the holidays.

Christmas is spent with the Williford family. I no longer feel like an intruder—more like part of Beau and Teri's family. New Year's Eve, Beau tells me about a possible world title shot at Madison Square Garden against Bonnie "The Cobra" Canino from Miami, Florida. This time I'd be fighting for the WIBF Super Featherweight Title in my true weight class of 125 pounds.

Excited about the possibility of a title fight, I celebrate New Year's with Sandi and Kelly at Ray's Sports Bar. The cut on my nose has healed but left a scar, as Dr. Bernard predicted. I'm glad I covered the scar with make-up when an attractive guy comes over to chat with me. He's clean cut with dark eyes and hair, and he's dressed in grey slacks and a buttoned-up Oxford shirt. Nice, but not my type—I'm usually attracted to scruffy, edgy-looking men. Still, I like something about his smile.

"Are you that girl—" he starts to ask.

"That fought on the Tyson card?" Kelly finishes for the handsome stranger.

In this type of social setting, I'm uncomfortable when recognized as a boxer. The sport is as much a part of me as my blue eyes. But when I'm somewhere other than a fight venue or working out at the gym, my first instinct is to deny I'm a boxer. I'm not sure why—perhaps it's just a reaction to bad past experiences. But this man is enthusiastic when he says, "Yeah, I know who you are. I always see you running on South College. One morning I saw you covered in blood. I honked the horn but you didn't look up."

"I was afraid someone would stop," I explain. "I had just, literally, fallen on my face."

"Oh, I figured you just got back from a fight or something," he says, and we both laugh.

We continue to chat, but my experience with dating warns me about my attraction to him. I'm conflicted because I crave companionship and affection, but I'm also scared of losing a part of myself in the bargain for love. If I fall for this guy, or any guy, I know that I may do something stupid. Mum taught by example that love can make people sacrifice everything. She would have relinquished her life for my father. I've come too far take that risk. Relationships are not reliable. But if I win a world title, it will be mine for the rest of my life. I don't want to get involved with a man right now. I want to be the champion of women's boxing.

So I make an excuse and leave the bar early.

On the tenth of January 1997, Beau and I fly through turbulence to Nashville, Tennessee. I've been called in at the last minute to replace Christy Martin in a bout on a Don King Productions Showtime card. According to Beau, "The Coalminer's Daughter" and King have had a falling out.

Topping the thirteen-bout card is heavyweight champion Henry Akinwande, followed by big-name boxers such as Felix Trinidad, Frankie Randall, Terry Norris, Nate Jones, and Fred Ladd. I've been matched up with Debra Stroman from Blackville, South Carolina, my first opponent to weigh in lighter than me. We are the only women in the lineup.

In the dressing room Beau and I discuss my possible title fight with Bonnie Canino, but not for long. I need to focus on the match that awaits me. Beau leaves me alone to get my head straight. Minutes later, he bounds back in.

"Get her out as quick as humanly possible!" he says. "I just saw her shadowbox. She couldn't spell fight if you gave her all the letters and put her on the right page of the dictionary. It's gonna look really bad if this goes past one round."

The live TV broadcast begins, and I'm summoned into the huge Nashville Arena. Colorful spotlights flash across metal trusses above the ring. Two suited men wearing headsets escort me, and a giant screen depicts my walk to the ring.

I stand in the red corner and stare at my rigid opponent, whose awkward stance and eye squint scream terror and dread. "Get her outta here," Beau reminds me. "And fast."

Right after the bell Stroman attempts to double-chop as though her arms are a pair of scissors. She hacks her right cuff on top of my head with one hand and slices her left thumb up toward my chin with the other. My punches easily cut through her unusual defense. I land several left hooks and a right uppercut that send her sliding to the canvas.

Admirably, Stroman pushes herself up. I shoot a left hook to her body and a right to her head. She stumbles so I finish her with a jab to the body and a straight right to the chin. She hits the canvas face down. As referee Steve Murff counts, a white towel floats across the ring to signal my opponent's surrender. Several minutes pass as Stroman's coach and husband presses an ice-filled towel to her jaw. She then rises to a round of applause.

After the show, Don King, sporting an elaborately spray-painted, jewel-studded denim jacket, tells me I'm the next female sensation. But instead of feeling flattered, I'm troubled. I've won my last five fights early, yet King's words uncover a latent fear of success. But he just paid me ten thousand dollars for forty-three seconds in the ring, so I should probably develop a taste for glitz and enjoy the hype.

Before I have time to get another second's practice with the glamour side of boxing, my world title bid is confirmed. Not for the original venue of Madison Square Garden, though; instead, the fight will take place in New Orleans, Louisiana, at the Lakefront Arena on March 2, 1997. My challenge in the city known as "The Big Easy" will be anything but easy. Bonnie Canino has not only had an outstanding kickboxing career, she's been the WIBF super-featherweight champion for the past two years.

My third opportunity to box for a world title will put my skills and resolve to the test. This match will prove to the world what I have learned from my losses, what I have gained from my wins, and whether I have come far enough to earn the top spot in boxing, the world championship title. The nuns at school labeled me a dreamer, and they were right. But I left my homeland and my family to train in a stinking chicken-shed gym in pursuit of my dream. I've sparred men with busted noses, men with no teeth, and a man who killed a man in the ring. I'm twenty-seven years old. I've had thirteen wins—eleven by knockout—four losses, and two draws. If I'm not ready by now, I'll never be. So I vow to myself that if I fail, my third shot will be my last. I will hang up my gloves. And I will never climb through the ropes again.

CHAPTER 23
LAST CHANCE AND FINAL ROUND

My world title fight is in seven weeks. Beau maps out a tough training schedule for me, so I have no doubt I'll be physically ready. It's my lack of self-confidence that has me worried when Mum calls from across the pond. I try not to let on that I'm mentally unprepared for my bout in March. Instead, I fake confidence as I explain the title fight is in New Orleans and that ABC will be there to film the event. But my voice wavers and must give me away, because my mother only expresses concern for my safety.

"Well," I tell her, "this is the last time you ever have to worry about me in the ring, Mum. Because if I don't win, that's it. I'm finished. I'll never fight again."

I expect elation, but my mother is silent. I thought my declaration would please her. There's a long, awkward pause before she speaks.

"I—I want to make amends, darling. For any hurt that I've caused you. I'm responsible for my behavior," she says. "And I'm sorry if I've damaged you in any way."

Her soft, crackled voice reminds me she is seventy-one years old and has struggled through a long mental breakdown that shattered her life. And she's worked hard to piece that life together again.

"Oh, okay," I mutter, stunned by her apology.

Mum updates me on my nieces and nephews and ends the conversation with a warning: "Don't fall for an exciting man," she says, "or you could become co-dependent. The boring ones are far more reliable. Always remember: *You* are the most important person in your life."

I've never heard those words before. *You are the most important person in your life.* I'm hungry to learn what inspired my mother's bizarre phone call. I want to know what shields her from the long years of fear that I'll get hurt in the ring. She used the word "co-dependent," so I rummage through my apartment for the Al-Anon book she gave me before I moved to the States. In Ireland, she encouraged me to join the organization for adult children of alcoholics and used the term co-dependent. But it made no sense for me to attend self-help meetings when my parents were the ones with problems. I don't even drink.

I search until I find the stocky little Al-Anon book stuffed in the back of a drawer. When Mum handed it to me, I liked the title *Courage to Change* on the brown marble print cover. But then I spotted "prayer" and "God" on the opening page, so I socked it away. The Loreto nuns and newsreels of bloody sectarian violence in Northern Ireland ruined organized religion for me. My reaction to mass is like that of the demonic child Damien from the movie The Omen, except mine is a secret, internal panic.

I flip through pages, scan headings, and at the back of the book I find The Twelve Steps. Sure enough, there's Mum's motivation for apology is Step 9: *Made direct amends to such people whenever possible, except when to do so would injure them or others.* In an instant, my mother's confession drags my head out of the sand. I am reminded that my painful past is not put away. It existed. My mum is dealing with it. She's not veering her car off the road. She's not jumping in the river, or taking to her bed for days and weeks. She's reclaimed her life and career by practicing dentistry at a public clinic in Dublin.

Though my mother has never spoken to me about Dad's affair, her breakdown, or the fact that she and my father abandoned me, she is showing me that it's possible to heal and move on. As with my mother, things happened that are buried in my heart and lodged in my head. Unlike my mother, I've not figured out how to keep them from slipping to the surface.

I figure the advice from *Courage to Change* is Mum's way of telling me something that's dearly important to her. Maybe there is a way for me to follow my mother's example. I continue to thumb through the pages and am heartened to find advice to deal with a lifelong problem. To discourage me from boxing, Mum often asked, "What will people think?" And it's always worried me in social situations. I'm often reluctant to mention that I am a boxer.

Unable to put down the book, I lose track of time until I notice the sun is setting. Deep orange light dapples my bedroom walls as dark purple creeps across the ceiling, so I turn on my bedside lamp. I've been reading for two hours and decide to use what's in *Courage to Change* as guidance to prepare for my championship fight.

At five-thirty the next morning, I begin Beau's seven-week training plan. I'm to run five miles a day, Monday through Friday, and then run stadium steps at the local university's football field every Saturday for six weeks. The week of the fight, I'm to do no weight training or endurance running, only sprints. I'll do light workouts and sparring, but I'll need rest to allow my body to recover from the heavy training.

Approaching the first mile of what will add up to 150 miles by the end of the next six weeks, my footsteps feel lighter as I remember Mum's apology and tap into some reservoir of energy I've never had access to before. A long-carried resentment against my mother begins to lift as I sprint through the entrance to Bendel Gardens. Newfound liberation sends me into an effortless sprint up the first hill. After five miles of running, I quickly shower and dash off to work.

After eight hours of laser engraving and sandblasting sports awards, I head straight to the gym, where I'm reminded of Beau's old-school philosophy: *If it's not a living hell, then you're not trying hard enough.* That won't be a problem, since my main sparring partner is Jason Papillion, who will fight on the same card with me for a light middleweight title. Jason is a seasoned, frequent sparring partner of the undefeated marvel Roy Jones, Jr. And Papillion emulates Jones' hands-held-low, lightning-speed, power-counterpunch style.

Into the second round of sparring, the sweat-eroded leather of Jason's black gloves mashes my lips into cracked pulp. *Ush! Ush! Ush! Ush!* he exhales with a blur of fists on a reach that seems longer than his height. An overhand right pops my skull, and my world darkens and floats away. I don't know how I'm still on my feet.

Papillion's personal trainer, Scotty, a crusty ex-convict with a greying beard and shiny, ebony bald head, cheers his protégé and underlines his loyalty to Jason by displaying a dismissive and sultry attitude toward me. He urges Jason to let go his hands and cut loose.

Of course, Beau's out of earshot when Scotty laughs out loud and snipes at my missed responses to Jason's numerous body jabs and right hands to my head. "Ah, she'll never touch Jason," says Scotty. "He's slick as owl shit."

My muscles tighten and slow down my reflexes just as Phatchit lumbers in to join the ringside criticism. Stiff with rage, I can barely breathe. Beau insists I spar with a face-saver, but the bulky headgear blinds me to Papillion's quick uppercuts that snap back my head. When Jason nails me repeatedly, Phatchit laughs and snorts. "Anytime I walk in here," he says, "somebody's beatin' the shit outta her."

I climb through the ropes humiliated, beaten, and emptied of my *Courage to Change*-inspired resolve not to let other people's behavior affect me. I do sit-ups, push-ups, squats, kneeling jumps, and duck walks until I think I'm going to keel over. I grab the sand-filled jump rope and can barely hop over the damn thing when Beau says, "You're getting an easy day. Wait till the really hard work starts. I'm gonna work you till *I* get tired."

On the Monday of my fourth week of training, my sparring partners are late, so Beau demands two extra sets of sit-ups, dumbbell reps, push-ups, and knee-splitting squats. After drumming the speedball, I punch the heavy bag until Jason Papillion, Eric Griffin, Karl Guidry, and T-Pop finally arrive. I'm grateful that today's timetable only calls for six rounds of sparring, because every move of my stiff muscles sears pain through my body.

My coach rotates my four sparring partners so I have a fresh man for every three-minute round with a thirty-second rest after each one. I spar six rounds and think I've finished sparring for the day when Beau lifts a ring rope and T-Pop climbs in.

"One more!" roars Beau. But he cannot count past "one," because after a round with T-Pop, Beau calls for Jason and on and on for six more rounds of punishment. I want to crawl out of the ring but finish my workout with twenty minutes of jumping with the sand-filled rope. I can barely keep the weighted cable turning. Worse, when I misstep, the heavy rubber slashes the swollen, tender welts across my legs and back from the previous weeks of jumping.

Every Saturday Beau meets me at Cajun Field with a dwindling number of boxers from the gym for the torturous stadium steps routine. After the fourth week, no one but Beau shows up. I understand my gym-mates' absence, because the objective is to run up and down each flight of stadium steps and finish by sprinting up and down a grass incline backward. All in the quickest time possible.

I'm fresh when I begin the lower set of steps. They are short and shallow, so I bound up and down each flight in good time. But the top section is grueling, and by the third climb, my legs scream with pain. It's like running an endless concrete hamster wheel. "Pick it up!" Beau yells, and then frowns at his stopwatch. "Five more flights to go!" My legs tremble on the disorienting descent, and I'm scared I'll fall face first down the stairs. To finish, I focus on an image of a world title belt around my waist.

By bedtime, my favorite part of the day, I'm exhausted but determined to use my only spare time to study *Courage to Change*. My favorite feature is the topic index, which lists all my preoccupations: *Worry, Doubt, Fear, Loneliness, Guilt, Belonging, Disappointment, Mistakes, Pain, Criticism, Self-Acceptance*, and on and on. It's as if this book were written just for me. I'm comforted to know I'm not the only one plagued with the same self-sabotage—so much so that the perfect words have been written on how to cope.

Tonight I revisit the advice on *Anger* and *Resentment*. But the readings don't explain how to fix or reprimand my mother for her insanity. Instead, I'm encouraged to focus only on my healing and to work on myself. This makes perfect sense, because it's clear that I could never fix Mum. Or Dad or Jean or anybody else. But I can try to fix me.

As I read more about alcoholism, I remember Dad's destructive behaviors. Was Dad really a full-blown alcoholic? I know there was wild spending, not to mention failed inventions, unpaid bills, empty kitchen cupboards, threats from bailiffs, car crashes, the affair. He left his wife and seven children for his dental nurse who shared his penchant for drink.

Against my instincts, I reluctantly see Mum's point of view. The stress and turmoil she must have endured becomes clear to me. She worked full time as a dentist, raised seven children, and was never able to balance Dad's irresponsible spending. But she tolerated it because she loved him. And then he broke her heart. Why have I never understood the difficulty of my mother's struggle until now? And why has it taken so long to accept that my beloved father is an alcoholic?

As I turn off the bedside light, my usual *Guilt* and *Loneliness* are replaced by *Forgiveness* and *Gratitude*. I no longer awaken to the bawling of my despairing mother, or have to lie in bed worried my father has died in a car crash. My childhood has passed. I don't have to live there anymore. My mother has given me the greatest gift: she has shown me it is possible *to accept the things I cannot change* and to learn how to forgive myself. I can see the power in both, and I have a lot of work to do.

Monday morning, three weeks before my fight, I'm up extra early to restudy *Conflict/disagreements*. I need to ask my boss for two days off, and I'm hoping this will help me. My title challenge is on a Sunday, but I need Friday off to promote the show in New Orleans. And I want Monday to rest after the fight.

I enter my boss's office assuming three weeks is plenty of notice for my request. But it's not. He fires me. I'm stunned, but decide I should have known better in the middle of busy season. Still, I've been here for two and a half years. After he listened to Howard Stern's praise of my Martin battle so intently, I thought I'd earned his respect, or at least his tolerance of my need for time off to fight. I mumble that I'll work the next two weeks while he finds a replacement.

When the shock of my firing wears off, I feel relieved. For the first time, I'll be able to rest properly the week before a big fight. I tell myself that the uncertainty of unemployment will just add fuel to my hunger for victory.

On Wednesday, four days before my fight, I enjoy the luxury of sleeping late. I only have to rest, sprint, and spar this week. So I sprint five sets up and down Hillside Drive in front of my apartment to keep my lungs stretched and heart rate high. Beau wants me to spar a couple more times before Sunday, so I'll be going to the gym this evening. For now, all I have to do is soak in a hot bath and read a growing collection of good luck cards from family and friends. The treasurer of Drogheda Amateur Boxing Club, Séamus McGuirk, sends me a congratulatory and encouraging letter. But my proudest and biggest card is from Dad, who inscribed, "Float like a lassie and sting like Dee."

At the gym I feel strong, not exhausted from working all day. As I spar Jason Papillion, I hold my own and box sharp. "Nice," approves Beau when I double up with a left hook to Papillion's ribs and chin. His trainer, Scotty, silently observes. In my title bid I want to throw as many body shots as possible—unleash an arsenal not volleyed in my past fights. Another body-head combination finds my slick sparring partner.

"That's it. Stop," says Beau.

He surprises me by removing my headgear.

"You boxed beautiful. You're sharp as a tack. No more sparring. You've reached your peak."

We head to New Orleans on Friday, though my fight is not until Sunday. I'm following Beau, so when we reach Metairie, a suburb of New Orleans, I chop in and out of busy lanes to keep up with him. After anxiously anticipating his Chevy's sudden twists and last-second turns, we arrive at the Landmark Hotel where all the boxing show participants will stay. The hotel is tall, round, and topped by a rotating restaurant.

The next day we board Bally's, a riverboat casino, for the weigh-in. A local TV station has sent a crew to cover the fight, which will be shown on FOX Sports. An ABC crew is also here from New York to shoot footage for a show on women's boxing.

When I step on the scale, my opponent the world champion Bonnie Canino eyes me like a hungry snake. Must be why she's nicknamed "The Cobra." With my stomach hollow and churning, I weigh 123 pounds fully clothed and easily make the WIBF Super Featherweight limit of 125. Canino strips to a black bikini and steps on the scale. She weighs a half-pound more than I do. The spectacle of her ripped body drops jaws all around the room.

"Holy shit," the promoter, Bob Walshak, whispers to Beau, "I hope Deirdre trained hard enough for this."

"Of course she has. No one trains harder than Deedra," snaps my coach. And then Beau hisses, "She'll kick Bonnie's ass."

"I'm just saying," says Walshak, "look at Canino. That's the most supremely conditioned woman I've ever seen."

"So is Deedra," insists my coach. "She's just so pale, you can't see her muscles."

Despite Beau's immovable faith, I fight against doubt. Canino is a walking billboard advertising the two gyms that she owns. Her full-time job revolves around her reputation for superb conditioning. And she has a magnificent physique of cut, long muscles that are perfect for boxing. She has plenty to back up the talk. I tell myself I have worked hard enough to beat her. Mostly I believe it.

Hours later, my stable mates and I gather in the hotel conference room to watch a live televised fight between Sugar Ray Leonard and southpaw Hector "Macho Man" Camacho. I consider it a good omen that one of my heroes is also fighting a lefty the night before my bout with southpaw Canino.

It seems one good omen leads to another as I'm seated next to Sugar Ray's former coach, the famous Angelo Dundee. I'm thrilled to learn this living legend, the man who coached fifteen world champions including Muhammad Ali, will be one of the ringside commentators for my fight tomorrow on FOX Sports.

As the boxers meet center ring, Dundee suggests the slick southpaw Camacho is a bad matchup for his former student. This is not what I wanted to hear. If a southpaw is a bad matchup for the brilliant Leonard, what does that mean for me? Maybe Dundee means it's because Sugar Ray is forty and returning from a six-year layoff. But Leonard has overcome plenty of obstacles in his career, and I expect nothing less than another dazzling performance. I'm also hoping to pick up a few new tricks to beat a lefty.

But then the fight begins, and Leonard moves slowly. He only manages anemic jabs to his opponent's body. He attempts to land looping headshots against the swift "Macho Man" but misses. I'm suddenly grateful Camacho is not considered a big puncher, because he's picking Leonard apart with ease. While Dundee shouts unheard advice to his ex-student, I anxiously wait for the real Sugar Ray Leonard to emerge.

In the fifth round, to my horror, Camacho drops Sugar Ray with a series of sharp shots. Leonard climbs to his feet but is resigned and stands like a statue. I cringe as Camacho moves in for the finish and batters the former champion on the ropes until referee Joe Cortez stops the fight. My good omen has been destroyed in five lopsided rounds.

The morning of my fight, my heavily pregnant sister arrives from Miami. Sheena has interrupted her holiday and left behind her husband and daughter to support me in my title bid. Beau takes my sister and me to the famous French Quarter. At Café Du Monde we order steamed coffee-milk and beignets. The fried pastries are hot and melt in my mouth like the powered sugar sprinkled on top. The coffee is creamy and delicious. Usually, I'm unable to eat, but this time I'm able to defy my nervous stomach and finish a pre-fight meal.

After brunch we wander around Jackson Square. In the middle is a statue of Andrew Jackson, raising his hat skyward as he straddles a rearing horse. Behind the statue sits Saint Louis Cathedral with its stucco façade, three steeples, and a round clock below the middle spire. Local artists hang colorful paintings on an ornate iron fence that surrounds the lush grounds of banana plants, azaleas, and live oak trees. A three-piece street band warms up to the clip-clop of horse-drawn carriages and the soulful whistles of steam-powered riverboats on the nearby Mississippi. The air smells like spilled beer.

Beau snaps a photo of me in front of the popular tourist attraction, and I crack a wry smile. As if sensing my anxiety, he insists I enter Saint Louis Cathedral and pray for a win. I shrug an objection, but I'm surprised when Sheena says, "Ah, let's go in—sure it will only take a minute."

I'm irritated with Beau for ordering me to revisit the smothering incensed air inside a Catholic church. Doesn't he know that my whole life, religion has either judged me or let me down? Maybe I haven't told him. I feel like the foolish little schoolgirl who pressed her knees to a wooden pew and prayed to fit in with my peers and for my brother Brian to be able to speak to me. I'm fearful that just sitting here will jinx my wish to win. So I decide not pray to the God of my youth.

Instead, I kneel in a back pew and replace the Loreto Sisters' scolding, judgmental God with a kinder, accepting Higher

Power. The God of my understanding is a combination of my boxing coaches and mentors: Pat McCormack, Jimmy Halpin, and Beau Williford. For the first time—with true conviction and without fear—I pray. I ask my Higher Power to give me strength in crisis, power over doubt, and resistance to panic as I face a win. Or a loss.

A few hours before my fight at Lake Front Arena, my sister and I follow Beau to my dressing room. My heart flutters when I discover my name on the red-corner list. My previously unsuccessful title attempts have been from the red corner. I feel silly for giving in to my old blue-corner superstition, but I'm desperate for any psychological advantage. I remind myself, from what I've been reading, *to change the things I can.*

This I can do. So I speak up and ask Beau to switch my corner. "If Dirty Dee wants the blue corner, Dirty Dee's got it!" says my coach, and he spins off to tell the promoter, who makes the switch.

Jason Papillion and I share top billing, which means our matches are the main events. It also means my fight will be second to last and Jason's will be the final bout of the night on the marathon ten-fight "Carnival of Champions" card. Sheena waits with me for hours and shifts uncomfortably in a small plastic chair. Not only is she swollen with child, she is tall, so the chair's not a good fit. We share an anxious silence, but she's quick to smile and beams when she asks, "How are you feeling? Excited?" She then stands up to remove the dry cleaner's plastic from my green-and-white satin robe.

"Yeah, excited—and scared to death," I say as I lace up my green boxing boots.

"I know. The waiting is awful."

"Waiting is the worst part of fighting," I say. "Worse than the toughest training. Worse than the hardest punches, the nastiest cuts, or the sharpest pain. Waiting is even worse than losing because at least by then you know the outcome."

"Don't even think about losing," urges Sheena. "I can't imagine anyone who deserves to be world champion more than you."

"You know, tonight I'm making the biggest purse of my career, twelve thousand five hundred dollars. But I swear,

Sheena, if someone asked me to choose between the money and the belt, I'd take the belt in a heartbeat."

"Oh, I know you would."

Beau returns to the dressing room after one of his fighters, David Rabon, wins a four-round decision. My coach wraps Bobby "The Fightin' Hillbilly" Crabtree's hands, and then he begins to wrap mine. Beau is always cheerful and optimistic about my fights. He deserves this championship, too. Despite all my setbacks, he has never faltered from the firm belief that I'm the best female fighter in the world. I don't tell Beau this is my final chance to prove to him, my staunchest supporter, that he's been right all along.

Beau's about to finish wrapping my hands when the gauze slips out of his grasp and unravels to the dressing room floor.

"Good," he says. "My guys never lose when I drop the gauze. I've tried doing it on purpose, but it never worked."

It seems even optimists have superstitions. It's the first good omen I've had all day. Beau finishes wrapping my hands and then slathers Vaseline on Bobby Crabtree's face and limbs for his bout, before mine. Crabtree is called to the ring, and everyone follows to watch his match. Before he leaves, Beau tells me to start warming up in the ninth round of Bobby's twelve-round title fight.

Finally alone, I open *Courage to Change* one last time before my bout. A random selection presents the perfect message. "*Today's reminder*: 'Though no one can go back and make a brand new start, anyone can start from now and make a brand new end.'"

It's only the third round of Bobby's match, but a monstrous roar from the crowd indicates the fight is nearing an end. So I begin to loosen up and shadowbox.

"It's over!" a Louisiana boxing commissioner shouts over the crescendo outside. "Gogarty and Canino, you're up!"

My corner crew, Beau, Keith Menard, and John McGovern, are waiting for me. Sheena lines up behind us to carry a huge Irish flag on a pole. My team escorts me to the ring to Beau's musical choice: Brian Setzer of Stray Cat's rockabilly version of "Danny Boy." Initially, I was reluctant about entering the ring to music used in the movie *The Great White Hype*, but when the melody kicks into high gear and the crowd goes wild, I'm glad I changed my mind.

The stands are packed with boxing enthusiasts, and the air of excitement ripples in the room. Several flags like mine wave as Irish fans and friends from Lafayette shout support. Familiar faces from the boxing club and even former coworkers smile and applaud and whistle. I'm touched they've traveled so far to make this the only thing close to a hometown fight I've ever had.

While I wait in my favorite blue corner, the champion struts into the ring. "The Cobra" slips between the ropes. She wears a black sports bra and shiny gold shorts with black trim. Her outfit accentuates her tanned knotted abs and wiry shoulders. Engraved Vs of muscle contract along her arms and legs as she bounces on her toes and glares at me.

Dressed in a black jacket, Canino's coach, Bert Rodriguez, is another imposing presence in her corner, with the top and sides of his head shaved and a shock of long dark braids that shoot down his back. Suddenly, I can't remember a single sentiment from *Courage to Change*. Seven weeks of self-empowerment advice evaporates.

After announcements and instructions, the ring is cleared of everyone but the world champion, the referee, and me. During a long delay as we wait for the bell, my opponent glowers at me without blinking. It's the first time I've ever been beaten in a stare-down. But then her effort to intimidate snaps me back into fight mode. Canino is trying—like so many before her—to bully me. I remember them all—from the boy who spat in my eye the first day of school to Liam who tormented and called me a boy to BBC's sports commentator Frank Bough to Phatchit on my couch. A lifetime of condescending insults revisits me in a blink, and I'm ready to fight.

And there's the bell.

In the first round I circle to my left and land jabs and left hooks over the top of my opponent's lead right hand. But Canino slings her left arm behind my neck and pulls me into a headlock. She smothers me but I dig in a few body shots. When she bulls me into the ropes, Beau shouts "Uppercut!" and I nail my foe with a nice right uppercut, which shoots back her head.

She roughs me to the ropes again, so I respond with a left hook counter that sends her backpedaling across the ring. Again, I tag her with a solid hook and she staggers. "Finish her Deedra! Finish her!" Beau screams as Canino wobbles. The bell rings.

Canino tries to stifle my attacks in the second round. She ties me up and forces a break by the referee. I welcome her wrestling tactics as an opportunity to pummel her midsection. I'm determined to deposit energy-sapping body blows into her injury bank. Then I catch her with a good right as she steps in. Her left eye swells, so I slam it with another hard right before the bell.

"The Cobra" stalks me in the third and tries to hold me in a headlock after each of her punches so I can't hit her back. She wrestles and leans, and works hard to outmuscle me. Every time I try to step around her to find room to punch, she clutches and smothers me.

She then mauls me with illegal club shots and rabbit punches to the back and side of my head. Her head bumps dangerously into my face. I should be pivoting, but if I try to step over, she'll surely push me down. The bell rings, and I fear Canino has pinched the round.

"You let her steal that round," confirms Beau. "You gotta be first."

Beginning of the fourth, Canino explodes. Her ripped muscles are driven into full gear. She ties me up and drives me back to the ropes. She bull-rushes her head into my face and traps me in a corner. My corner men scream at me to spin out. I try to escape by turning her, but she won't budge. She continues to attack me with body shots. I manage to slide off the corner pad and onto the ropes, but now the ropes slide apart as Canino shoves me out of the ring. I land with my back on the ring apron, the wind knocked out of me. I immediately roll back inside but I've lost control of the fight. Instead of retaliating against my opponent's browbeating methods, I'm falling prey to the resignation of defeat.

"You gotta give her angles," Beau advises in the corner. But Canino's pressure is suffocating and nothing seems to work. I repeat my prayer at St. Louis Cathedral to be strong, have faith, and don't panic.

In the fifth I feel my final title bid slipping away. I must take back command of the fight by using my better boxing skills. "The Cobra" is strong, but I've faced stronger. Suddenly the words flash into my mind: *Start from now and make a brand new end.* Canino coils an arm around my neck again, but referee Terry Woods stops the action and reprimands the snake for holding. When she rushes me again, I circle and counterpunch. The next time I try to sidestep, she lunges and pushes me to the ground. Back on my feet I notice a cut under her right eye. I nail her with clean right hands, and she bleeds from her nose and mouth. This time when she rushes me to the ropes, I pivot 180 degrees and trap her with an attack. The title swings back into my reach.

"How do you feel?" asks Beau as he pours water on my head.

"Good," I say.

"You came back nice, baby," says John.

A hard left to my liver stabs me early in the sixth. But solid conditioning saves me from buckling, and I'm able to keep moving my feet. I use better distance and score with a right and a left hook. Canino attempts to land bombs, but I slip away and then counter with a left hook and a right to further punish her battered face. When she launches a haymaker, I roll under the shot, turn, and catch her at an angle with a counterpunch.

I pick up momentum in the seventh, but in my impatience to attack, Canino slams me with a couple of clean left uppercuts that are more embarrassing than hurtful. Still, I'm outworking my stronger opponent and beating her at her own game of inside fighting. The body shots have proved a big payoff. I'm not boxing pretty in this ugly, foul-ridden battle, but I'm wearing down the reigning champ.

Canino is late off her stool to start the eighth, and Coach Rodriguez barks orders in her ear as she breathes through her mouth. Her left eye is swollen and she has a laceration under her right. The bridge of her nose has collapsed. She rushes me and slams her head into my face. I signal the referee to inform him it was a head butt in case of a cut. Canino's smutty tactics are pure desperation. The supreme physical specimen is supremely exhausted, and I still feel energized. I make another drop in the body bank and pound her six-pack until the bell rings.

My opponent sucks air in round nine. She is a consummate warrior, but I'm beating her to the punch. Canino's face is destroyed, and she hasn't been able to hurt me. I'm in fantastic condition and getting stronger. If I can find the right gap in her infuriating holds, I can take this fight out of the judges' hands. Just when I think the champion can no longer stand, the bell rings.

On my stride back to the corner, Beau douses my face with a handful of cold water. "Last round!" he declares. "You want the title?"

"Yes!" I say as he pours freezing water on my head. He vigorously rubs the sides of my face.

"One more for the championship, baby!" John chimes in.

"Remember all those bad decisions?" Beau says, nose pressed to mine as he looks me in the eye. "Last round, Deedra! Put a fuckin' exclamation point on it!"

Last chance and final round. The bell rings.

I immediately back Canino to the ropes near her corner. I pound her with a right-left-right to the body and go upstairs with a left hook and straight right that knocks her sideways. Canino grabs me until the ref breaks us apart. I move in and catch her with a right to the face as she steps forward. She grabs me, ties me up, and wrestles me to the ropes. The ref breaks us again.

Canino's spoiling tactics make it difficult to land clean shots. But past experience has taught me to never assume I'm ahead. She's the champion, so I must widen the point margin to take her belt. But Canino's a veteran and she continues to tie me up in order to thwart my attempts to score or knock her out.

I manage to pop off a couple of left hooks that spin her, but she steadies herself and ties up my left arm. So I bang her midsection with my right. I then slip another right over her glove and notice her hands are too far apart. She dips in and I throw a left uppercut to pick up her chin and smack her head with a right.

I continue to nail her, but she is so fatigued she falls onto me. The referee pulls us apart, and I land a flurry of thunderous shots on my wobbly rival and finish with a solid right hand to her face in the last seconds of the round. She survives until the bell rings.

I throw my hands in the air and glare at my battered opponent. Canino responds by shoving up her fists in a halfhearted pose. I stare at her until she turns her back to me, and she drags herself away. Beau, John, and Keith climb into the ring and squeeze me in a hug.

After the gloves come off, Beau hands me an Irish flag, and I wrap it around me like a cloak. My supporters wave the tricolors of Ireland and chant, "New champ! New champ! New champ!" Another group challenges with "Bon-nie! Bon-nie! Bon-nie!"

My joy is spoiled by anxiety as the referee gathers my opponent and me to stand center ring. He stands between us and holds our hands as we wait for the announcement. Time seems to slow down, and I begin to wonder if the judges have seen it my way.

Then I hear, "Ladies and gentlemen! We have a unanimous decision!"

The announcer says the first judge scored it 93 for the red corner, 97 for the blue. I look up at Beau and he's applauding beside me. The second judge scored it 94 for the red, 97 for the blue. Beau continues to clap and smile, and I raise my flag-draped left arm because the referee is still holds my right hand. The third judge scored it 94 for the red, 96 for the blue. And then it's as if all the poets of Ireland deliver the next words for how beautiful they sound in my ear:

"For the blue corner—and *new* super featherweight champion—Deir-dra Go-gar-tee!"

I jump into Beau's arms. I see nothing but flashbulbs and hear only applause. He puts me down and reaches over to hug Canino, then turns to me and says, "C'mon, Champ, go get that belt. Let Barbara belt ya!"

Barbara Buttrick enters the ring and wraps the WIBF World Title Belt around my waist. I throw my arms in the air with the Irish flag draped around me. I'm glad for the sheer beauty and weight of the belt. I need something heavy to keep me planted to the ground. My coach and I pause for a photographer, and then turn to pose for another until I see Sheena push through the crowd. Tears gush from my sister's eyes when she climbs up to the ropes. I dash over and reach across them to hug her. "You did it," she sobs. "You did it."

The press and dozens of cheering supporters crowd around me in the ring. Nobody cares that I'm covered in sweat, Vaseline, and Canino's blood. Everybody moves in close, and I gladly accept their praise and pose for more pictures.

I'm standing in the white neutral corner and shaking someone's hand when I turn and spot my coach, also pumping outstretched hands on the other side of the ring. When he sees me, Beau breaks away and rushes to meet me in the corner. He throws his arms around me in another tight embrace. He lets go just enough to peer down at my world title belt, then into my eyes. "I always knew you were the champ, Dirty Dee," says Beau. "Always knew it. Always."

EPILOGUE
THE BRIDGE OF PEACE

Ten months after my world title victory, I'm dolled up in an elegant dark-silver dress for an annual ceremony at the Westcourt Hotel in Drogheda, Ireland. Along with sixteen other athletes, I've been nominated for tonight's top award: the 1997 Sports Star of the Year.

Awards host and RTÉ TV sports presenter Des Cahill leads the way into the plush, forest-green reception room. A capacity crowd, dressed in tuxedos and gowns, applauds as we parade down the red carpet. Careful not to roll an ankle in Mum's heels, I steadily negotiate the posh, thick rug. On my insistence, with clothes hanging in her closet, my mother managed to tastefully disguise my pale arms and back with a silk, jaguar-print shawl. Except for my cautious totter to the nearest seat, this glamorous outfit could almost pass for my own. I wish Mum could be here, but she doesn't want to see Dad and Jean.

My father looks debonair in a black bowtie and tuxedo jacket as he rises from his seat beside Jean to kiss me on the cheek. At seventy, what's left of his dark hair is combed straight back, but on the side it's more unruly and threaded with silver. I notice Dad and Jean have almost polished off their first bottle of red wine.

At the end of the red carpet, a hardwood floor serves as the room's stage. The backdrop displays photographs of the Sports Star of the Year nominees: thirteen men and four women. A large video screen sits atop the photos. The picture of me smiling and holding my title belt is placed low on the exhibit.

The winner of the top prize has been voted on by the public and sent in to the local newspaper. Even though *Drogheda Independent* sports editor Hubert Murphy has documented every twist of my rollercoaster career since my pre-fight days, I don't fancy my chances for first place. I made national front-page headlines when I won the title, but I haven't lived in Ireland for years, and virtually no Irish residents have seen me in action.

Each of the seventeen nominees is displayed in their full sporting brilliance on a huge screen. Highlights of soccer, canoeing, rugby, athletics, golf, mountain biking, karate, handball, and Gaelic football shine into the ballroom. In my clip, I land a left hook that drops Monique Stroman into a sitting position against the ropes, her head jolting backward. There is a collective gasp, a chortled murmur, and loud applause.

At last, the final three awardees are called up. In third place, the Hall of Fame award goes to legendary soccer advocate Charlie Hurley. In second place, Mark McHugh, captain of the Irish rugby team, accepts the Young Sports Star of the Year award. "And in first place," announces Des Cahill, "we are honored to present the 1997 Sports Star of the Year award to Ireland's first ever female world boxing champion, Deirdre Gogarty!"

I am presented with a handsome bronze statue of the mythological Irish hero Cúchulainn, who single-handedly defended Ulster against a queen's army. "This is really, really beautiful. Thank you so much," I manage to say. I thank Joe Leonard and Séamus McGuirk with the Drogheda Amateur Boxing Club, as well as Hubert Murphy with the *Drogheda Independent* for writing about me for all these years. The audience rises in applause.

When the awards ceremony ends, everyone slowly disperses. The hotel's staff piles dirty dinnerware onto trays in the hot and stuffy room. Dad tips a weary-looking waiter who refills his and Jean's glasses. I excuse myself and grab my coat.

It's dark outside the hotel entrance on West Street. Chimney smoke rolls across the rooftops. The pavement shimmers with frost. Leftover Christmas lights sway cheerfully across the street. A giant red star flashes in front of Weavers pub, the place where I met my idol Barry McGuigan, the man who told me, "If you have a talent, Deirdre, go for it. Because without boxing, I'd've been nothin'."

It is clear to me that boxing saved my life.

Briskly, I head down West Street and turn on Georges into an arctic gust, scented by sea mud. No longer sheltered by buildings, I push across the Bridge of Peace while an east wind blasts through her steel railings. Under hazy streetlights, the River Boyne laps in a frantic chopping motion below me.

Standing in the middle of the bridge, named to symbolize peace between Catholics and Protestants, I stare down the dark throat of the river. Just around its curve rests the old Drogheda Amateur Boxing Club. The building sits empty and derelict, condemned to demolition.

I gaze into the Boyne's rushing current while reflections of my life stare back at me. Then I hear the music that unmoored me from thoughts of my watery grave at the fishmeal factory. A song floats up the Boyne as vividly as the night I sparred with Blackie. *Deir-dra! Deir-dra! Deir-dra!* It's the voices of boys who stood ringside and cheered for me to stay on my feet. I see their torn clothes, dirty faces, gapped teeth, and tangled hair.

Mist rolls across the beams of a passing car. I glance back and forth to make sure the bridge is deserted. I grab the ice-cold railing, lean over the water, and shout *Thank You!*

In two puffs of steam snatched by the wind, my voice is raised above all doubts, raised to the boys in the gym who inspired me. To the coaches, promoters, journalists, and fans of the sweet science—women and men—whose guts to defy convention granted an opportunity to answer my call to the ring.

THE END

Acknowledgements - Deirdre Gogarty

Though not mentioned in the book, many people have shown me great kindness that has touched my career and life in a special way: Tommy Ahearn, Joe Kirwan, Joe Lawlor, Glenn Armentor, Mike Shoffiett, Dr. Michael Cavanaugh, Dr. Richard Lucey, Bobby Dupre, Connie and Terry Hearen, Peggy and Bob Houlahan, and Russell Mire.

I will never forget the benevolence shown to me by friends who departed this world too soon: Jim Smith, Stephen Fagan, and Beldon E. Fox, Jr.

My special thanks to everyone involved with Ragin' Cajun Amateur Boxing Club, and to Kerry and Mickey Daigle and the entire team at keeppunching.com for their love, understanding, and encouragement while I was busy writing this book.

To Pat Meyers for her assistance with the initial outline in 2004, and to Paddy Mulhall for collecting newspaper articles on my career for fifteen years and sending them to me from Ireland.

To my friend and collaborator, Darrelyn Saloom, for her years of diligence and hard work that brought the power of my story to life.

To the love of my life, Vic Morrison; sincere thanks for your strength and support.

And to my dear friend, Dr. Phil Mayers—my deepest gratitude for showing me how to live in serenity and joy.

Although mentioned in the book, no words can express my gratitude to my family for their love, honesty, and loyalty, and to the Williford family for adopting me as a twenty-three-year-old stray.

Acknowledgements - Darrelyn Saloom

Deirdre Gogarty, thank you for putting up with me as we dug behind the curtain of your memories. I am honored that you trusted me with your story and proud to call you my friend.

Jane Friedman read part of the manuscript while publisher of Writer's Digest. She gave me an opportunity, along with tons of knowledge, to build a platform for the book. She is the first person in publishing to reach out to me, and I am forever grateful. She is also responsible for teaching me to play Canasta.

Self-described scoundrel Dave Malone is a talented writer, poet, playwright, freelance editor, and the kindest rascal I've ever known. He spent countless hours poring over the manuscript, making suggestions, and keeping me on track when the moon's light dimmed on my path.

Father-and-son team Ed and Ron Dalbec spent five years—the last years of Ed's life—reading the manuscript and providing invaluable feedback. As he lay dying, Ed learned we would publish the book. My only regret is that I didn't finish sooner, so he could hold it in his hands.

Sonny Brewer is an author I admire and first met in New Orleans at his book signing for *The Poet of Tolstoy Park*. We stayed in touch over the years. I never dreamed one of my favorite authors would not only offer to read the manuscript but would help make it better. Thank you, Sonny.

Without my youngest son, Jesse, the collaboration of this memoir would not have happened. After a near-fatal illness, Jesse started boxing and introduced me to Deirdre. He then moved to London and graduated with a master's from the London School of Economics. Thank you, Jesse, for showing me it's possible to beat the odds.

To the rest of my family: many thanks to my husband Danny for doing my chores and reminding me to eat. And to my other sons, Christopher and Zachary, who ran errands after answering my often-frantic phone calls. I also owe a lifetime of thanks to my mother, Mary Ellen, for her love, understanding, and comic relief.